8,50

BYRON'S
HEBREW MELODIES

by
THOMAS L. ASHTON

University of Texas Press, Austin

International Standard Book Number 0–292–70141–1
Library of Congress Catalog Card Number 70–165921
Printed in Great Britain by
Cox & Wyman Ltd, London, Fakenham and Reading

To
ELEANOR

CONTENTS

PREFACE ix

ABBREVIATIONS xiii

I 'THE REAL OLD UNDISPUTED HEBREW MELODIES' 1

II BYRONIC LYRICS FOR DAVID'S HARP 63

III TEXT OF THE HEBREW MELODIES 107

APPENDICES

I HISTORICAL COLLATIONS 197

II CONTENTS OF EDITIONS COLLATED 200

III CALENDAR OF MANUSCRIPTS 202

IV CALENDAR OF EDITIONS 209

SELECTIVE BIBLIOGRAPHY 227

INDEX OF TITLES AND FIRST LINES 233

PREFACE

'She Walks in Beauty' and 'The Destruction of Semnacherib' are the best known of Byron's lyrics. But very little is known about the Hebrew Melodies among which these poems are numbered. This paradoxical situation has persisted even though contemporary readers, far removed from the magnetism of the Byron myth, go first to Byron's poetry. The publication of Leslie Marchand's magnificently honest biography of Byron, and the variorum edition of *Don Juan* in 1957 marked a turning point in Byron studies. Since that time ten book-length studies of Byron's poetry have been published. But in these years of changing emphasis the Hebrew Melodies did not prosper. Of recent critical studies, only *Byron and the Ruins of Paradise* by Robert F. Gleckner is completely comprehensive in approach. Marchand surveys the poems in his *Byron's Poetry*, and M. G. Cooke analyses three of the lyrics in his *The Blind Man Traces the Circle*. The few pages these critics devote to the Hebrew Melodies, Karl Adolf Beutler's careful inaugural dissertation (*Über Lord Byrons 'Hebrew Melodies'* [Leipzig, 1912]), and Joseph Slater's important article comprise almost the entire criticism of the Hebrew Melodies. If Byron is to be Byron the poet, his lyric talent needs to be valued equally with his satiric genius. His most important collection of lyrics, the Hebrew Melodies, merits our greatest attention. But as the editors of the variorum *Don Juan* discovered, critical examination required a definitive text, and such a text required a history of its own. In the case of the Hebrew Melodies, one more question needed to be answered: Just what are Byron's Hebrew Melodies?

Byron's Hebrew Melodies are not melodies. Byron wrote poems. The composer Isaac Nathan set those poems to 'ancient' melodies that he had arranged for contemporary performance. Poems and music were first published in a volume entitled, *A Selection of Hebrew Melodies Ancient and Modern with appropriate Symphonies & Accompaniments by* I: Braham and I: Nathan *the Poetry written expressly for the work by the Right Honble. Lord Byron.* Aside from the facts that not all the melodies were ancient, that not all the poems had been written 'expressly' for the work, and that some of the poems have nothing to do with the Jews, this title is an accurate label of the volume's contents. But even this limited accuracy was to suffer. Shortly after the publication of *A*

Selection, an edition of Byron's poems without their musical accompaniments was published, and this edition was misleadingly entitled *Hebrew Melodies*. It should have been called 'Poems from the Hebrew Melodies'. The mistaken title has come to be generally accepted today, causing confusion in some minds and many libraries. The titles of individual poems employed throughout this work are those of *Hebrew Melodies*. Six titles used in that work differ from those employed in *A Selection of Hebrew Melodies*. The titles of *Hebrew Melodies* are found in Lady Byron's fair copies. The differing titles of *A Selection* are first-line titles employed when no title was authorized. The titles of the six Hebrew Melodies not published in *Hebrew Melodies* are those of the respective poems' first publication. The spelling of words used in the titles is that of the original; so, Byron's 'Semnacherib' is not silently amended as in subsequent editions. The capitalization of titles and of first-line titles taken from less than the full line follows standard usage. Capitals have been reduced on first lines used as titles. An index of titles and first lines is given at the conclusion of this work.

ACKNOWLEDGMENTS

I want here to record my indebtedness to the many individuals who have enabled me to complete this work. Chief among them are the Earl of Lytton and the late Sir John Murray. To Lord Lytton I am indebted for making the Hebrew Melodies manuscripts in the Lovelace Papers available to me and for permission to quote from them, and from *Astarte*, the copyright of which he holds as the heir of the 2nd Earl of Lovelace. Mr Malcolm Elwin, Lord Lytton's literary advisor, courteously came to my aid as well. To Mr Kenneth H. Callow and Miss M. V. Stokes of Messrs Coutts & Co., the trustees of the Earl of Lovelace's will, I am indebted for co-operation in the task of assembling and examining the manuscripts. I have also quoted material from two works based on documents in the Lovelace Papers: Malcolm Elwin's *Lord Byron's Wife* (by permission of Harcourt, Brace & World, Inc.) and Ethel Colburn Mayne's *Life of Lady Byron* (by permission of Charles Scribner's Sons). To Sir John Murray I am indebted for allowing me to examine the Hebrew Melodies manuscripts in his collection, and for permission to quote from them, from works in which the firm of John Murray holds the copyright, particularly *Lord Byron's Correspondence* (1922), and, with Charles Scribner's Sons and Octagon Books, Inc., from E. H. Coleridge's annotations in Vol. III of *The Works of Lord Byron, Poetry* (1900). I am also indebted to him for his courtesy and for his recitation from memory of 'The Destruction of Semnacherib'. To Mr John Grey Murray I am indebted for his answers to my questions, and for making my visits to Albemarle Street pleasant. To the following institutions and individuals I am indebted for permission to quote from manuscripts or to make references to unpublished material: the Miriam Lutcher Stark Library of the University of Texas, particularly the Manuscript Committee, and the Librarian, June Moll; the British Museum; the Bodleian Library; the Beinecke Rare Book and Manuscript Library of Yale University, particularly Mr Herman Liebert and Marjorie G. Wynne; the Henry E. Huntington Library; the Henry W. and Albert A. Berg Collection of the New York Public Library, particularly its curator, the late John D. Gordan; the Houghton Library of Harvard University; the Folger Shakespeare Library; and the Carl H. Pforzheimer Library. For their

xi

help I am also indebted to the staff of the Pierpont Morgan Library, and to Mr Eugene P. Sheehy and the Inter-Library Loan Service of Columbia University Library. Apart from those debts to Byron scholars, critics, and editors which have been acknowledged in the notes, I must record special thanks to Leslie A. Marchand, who early encouraged my work, answered my questions, made available material from his own researches, and read the typescript of this work; to David Erdman for making information from his own notes available; to Mr G. S. Manners; to Miss Susan Shannon; to the late David Bonnell Green; and to Jerome Meckier, John Clubbe, and Donald Reiman. To Professors T. G. Steffan, W. W. Pratt, and E. J. Lovell Jun., I am indebted for scholarship and hospitality. To Professors Carl Woodring and Elizabeth S. Donno of Columbia University I am deeply grateful for their meticulous reading of my work, for comments and corrections, for patience often tried, and for warm-hearted understanding. To the trustees of the Henry E. Huntington Library I am indebted for a research fellowship that contributed to this work.

ABBREVIATIONS

ASHM   *A Selection of Hebrew Melodies Ancient and Modern* with *Appropriate Symphonies & Accompaniments by I: Braham & I: Nathan the Poetry Written Expressly for the Work by the Right Honble. Lord Byron.* 2 Nos. London: Isaac Nathan, 1815–16.

Beutler   Karl Adolf Beutler. *Über Lord Byrons 'Hebrew Melodies'.* Inaugural Dissertation. Leipzig: August Hoffman, 1912.

BNYPL   Bulletin of the New York Public Library.

Elwin   Malcolm Elwin. *Lord Byron's Wife.* London: Macdonald, 1962.

FP   Isaac Nathan. *Fugitive Pieces and Reminiscences of Lord Byron.* . . . London: Printed for Whittaker, Treacher & Co., 1829.

Hebrew Melodies   Generic title of thirty poems written by Byron.

HM   George Gordon Byron, 6th Baron. *Hebrew Melodies.* London: John Murray, 1815.

K–SJ   *Keats–Shelley Journal.*

L & J   George Gordon Byron, 6th Baron. *The Works of Lord Byron. Letters and Journals.* Edited by Rowland E. Prothero. 6 vols. London: John Murray, 1898–1901.

LBC   ———. *Lord Byron's Correspondence.* Edited by John Murray, 2 vols. New York: Charles Scribner's Sons, 1922.

Marchand   Leslie A. Marchand. *Byron: A Biography.* 3 vols. New York: Alfred A. Knopf, Inc., 1957.

Poetry   George Gordon Byron, 6th Baron. *The Works of Lord Byron. Poetry.* Edited by Ernest Hartley Coleridge. 7 vols. London: John Murray, 1898–1904.

Slater   Joseph Slater. 'Byron's Hebrew Melodies'. *Studies in Philology,* 1952, XLIX, 75–94.

Works   George Gordon Byron, 6th Baron. *The Works of Lord Byron*. 17 vols. London: John Murray, 1832–3.

Abbreviations used in the Bibliography of the Modern Language Association of America have been employed for references to periodicals.

For Sigla Employed in the *Apparatus Criticus* (Chapter III) see p. 119; for Sigla employed in the Historical Collations (Appendix I) see p. 195.

The luckless Israelites, when taken
By some inhuman tyrant's order,
Were ask'd to sing, by joy forsaken,
On Babylonian river's border.

Oh! had they sung in notes like these
Inspir'd by stratagem or fear,
They might have set their hearts at ease,
The devil a soul had stay'd to hear.
'Granta'. 1806.

I
'THE REAL OLD
UNDISPUTED HEBREW MELODIES'

The First Number of *A Selection of Hebrew Melodies*, bringing together the poetry of Byron and the musical accompaniments of Isaac Nathan, was published in 1815. The first printed edition of *Beowulf*, the work of G. J. Thorkelin, was published in the same year. That these two works, so different in age and content, should have shared a mutual debut was no mere coincidence. The romantic movement in England was to be 'distinguished for research into poetical antiquities', as Walter Scott remarked in his preface to the poems of Patrick Carey. The romantic sense of distance lured antiquarians back to older days and primitive civilizations where *sublime* works that would inspire a fallen present might be found. The principle of national self-determination that had emerged from the ideals of human rights at work in the revolutions of the late eighteenth century, found an outlet when sentiment for the past joined hands with a subdued nationalism as men's minds dwelt upon ancestral freedoms.

The past was to provide another kind of literary inspiration as well. No longer were the language and style of other days considered indecorous or vulgar. Robert Lowth, in his *Lectures on the Sacred Poetry of the Hebrews* (1753), had demonstrated that the style of the Bible, reflecting the more 'vehement emotions of the mind', was one of mankind's highest accomplishments. Hebrew poetry, what Wordsworth called 'Jewish Song', had no peer when it came to sublimity. In the *Excursion* it becomes a fount 'of ancient inspiration serving me'. By composing poetry to ancient or biblical melodies, a modern poet might elevate his work, making it a worthy successor to that of older bards. If Sternhold and Hopkins, whose metrical psalms had made their authors household words, had lost their appeal, new men might succeed. If the taste for the ancient, the national, and the sublime yielded contemporary volumes in which the poetry of Byron, Moore, and Scott was joined to accompaniments by Haydn, Stevenson, and Beethoven, no one looked too closely. This was the best that an Age of Bronze attempting to echo an Age of Gold could do.

Throughout the eighteenth century antiquarians and poets, Scotsmen in the main, had been collecting the traditional music and literature of their countries. A sophisticated imperialism found this expression of the aspirations sparked by offended nationality tolerable, so long as sentimental longing did not give way to militant pride and prices kept the collections from the wrong hands. The Scots music publisher, George Thomson, initiated the national-melodies vogue with his *Select Collection of Original Scottish Airs* (1793). This work joins the words of Burns and the accompaniments of Ignace Pleyel; the second edition (1804) includes music by Haydn and Leopold Kozeluch. Thomson's success was the result of his anti-national joining of native lyrics and Continental embellishments. His predecessors, concerned with the purity of musical tradition, had not sufficiently gauged the rococo Regency musical taste. Thomson, wishing to please his public, sent his melodies abroad where they were graced by the incongruous accompaniments of German composers. In later editions rude traditional verses were supplanted by those of modern authors; it was not the past, but rather its imitation that pleased a less concerned public.

In London, Thomas Preston published Thomson's subsequent collections. In Dublin, James Power (who later set up shop in the Strand) became the chief rival of Thomson and Preston. Power published the First Number of *A Selection of Irish Melodies* in 1808, beginning a ten-part series with supplements that stretched out to 1834. He recruited Sir John Stevenson for the music to which was joined the poetry of Tom Moore. (Moore looked into Edward Bunting's *General Collection of Ancient Irish Music* [1796] and Lady Morgan's [Sydney Owenson's] *The Lay of an Irish Harp* [1807] before starting to work.) Power challenged his rival with *A Selection of Scottish Melodies* in 1812. Henry Bishop, who replaced Stevenson for the later numbers of the *Irish Melodies*, provided the accompaniments. The verses were by Horace Twiss, who sent off a copy of the work to Byron.[1] Thomson took up the challenge with his *Select Collection of Original Irish Airs* (1814). Thomson had tried and failed to obtain Byron's services for this volume. The competition forced Power to other fields. In 1816 he published the First Number of Moore's *Sacred Songs*; the Second Number appeared in 1824. A slip acknowledging William Gardiner's *Sacred Melodies* (1812–15) as the source of several of the accompaniments was inserted in the First Number. In 1818 Power brought out the First Number of Moore's *National Airs* which ran to six parts by 1827. Included in this work were Austrian,

---

[1] Byron to Lady Melbourne, 16 May 1814: 'Horace Twiss has sent me his melodies, which I perceive are inscribed to you . . .' *LBC*, I, 258.

Icelandic, Italian, and, as the author noted, many 'Moore-ish' melodies.

By 1813 a multitude of national melodies collections had been published.[2] No reader familiar with the numerous collections by Thomson and Power would have been greatly shocked by the announcement of musical interest which appeared in the *Gentleman's Magazine* for May of that year:

> J. Nathan is about to publish 'Hebrew Melodies,' all of them upwards of 1000 years old and some of them performed by the Antient Hebrews before the destruction of the Temple.

J. Nathan and Isaac Nathan were one and the same. This advertisement is the first mention of the idea that was to bear fruit in 1815. A young, enterprising musician, recognizing the taste for the ancient, the patriotic, and the biblical, had embarked on a path that ultimately would lead to collaboration with Byron.

Isaac Nathan was born in Canterbury in 1790 and died in Sydney, Australia, in 1864.[3] His father, Menehem Mona (d. 1823), was a Jewish scholar and 'almost certainly' the Cantor of the Jewish community in Canterbury by the time of Nathan's birth. Of his origins, of the mother of Isaac Nathan, and of the source of the name Nathan nothing is known.[4] Isaac Nathan was intended for the rabbinate. Though little is known of his upbringing, he tells us that he was sent to Cambridge in 1805, having attended the first Anglo-Jewish boarding school, which was established by the Rev. Solomon Lyon, a scholar who is known to have taught Hebrew to the Duke of Wellington. Byron was at Cambridge intermittently between October 1805 (at the age of seventeen) and December 1807. He

[2] Cecil Hopkinson and C. B. Oldman in 'Thomson's Collections of National Song', *Edinburgh Bibliographical Society Transactions*, 1940, II:i, 1–64, and 1954, III:ii, give a total of thirty editions and issues varying from one to six volumes in length by Thomson alone. Percy Muir in 'Thomas Moore's Irish Melodies, 1808–1834', *Colophon*, 1933, XV, discusses editions and issues of those poems.

[3] There are two brief biographies of Isaac Nathan: Olga Somech Phillips, *Isaac Nathan, Friend of Byron* (London: Minerva, 1940), and Catherine Mackerras, *The Hebrew Melodist, A Life of Isaac Nathan* (Sydney: Currawong, 1963). Mrs Mackerras's work is more particularly concerned with Nathan's Australian career. See Edward R. Dibdin, 'Isaac Nathan', in *Music and Letters* (January 1941), a review of Mrs Phillips's biography.

[4] Mona is buried under the name of 'Menehem, son of the scholar, Rabbi Judah the Polack' in London's Jewish Cemetery (Mackerras, p. 13).

returned briefly in the summer of 1808 for his degree. But Nathan and Byron did not meet during this period, as Nathan's second letter to Byron makes clear. Byron's interest in music began and ended with John Edleston, the young Cambridge chorister with whom he was in love and whose voice made a lasting impression on him. While Byron's new image of idealized youth sang, Nathan studied Latin, Hebrew, and mathematics. But he soon abandoned all for music and was shortly thereafter packed off to London to be apprenticed to a music master.

Domenico Corri (1746–1825), Nathan's new teacher, was then one of the most distinguished foreign musicians in London.[5] In 1771 Corri had been invited to conduct the concerts of the Musical Society of Edinburgh, and it was at one of these concerts that, listening to Corri's wife, George Thomson conceived of his musical mission:

> At the St. Cecilia concerts I heard Scottish songs sung in a style of excellence far surpassing any idea which I had previously had of their beauty, and that too, from Italians, Signor Tenducci the one, and Signora Domenica Corri the other. . . . It was in consequence of my hearing him and Signora Corri sing a number of our songs so charmingly that I conceived the idea of collecting all our best melodies and songs, and of obtaining accompaniments to them worthy of their merit.[6]

Corri established himself as a singing-master and concert promoter, but the failure of his theatrical speculations forced him into music publishing. Even before Thomson had started, Corri brought out *A Select Collection of Forty Scotch Songs* (1780), a work designed to capitalize on the popular taste. Sometime before 1790 Corri moved his large musical family to London. More important, in 1802 Corri wrote several songs for T. J. Dibdin's *The Cabinet*, the first important operatic farce that John Braham performed after returning from his Continental tour. By 1804 Corri was arranging songs directly for Braham. His son Montague wrote the music for *The Devil's Bridge* (produced in 1812), another of Braham's vocal successes. Corri's daughter Fanny, who became a world famous mezzo-soprano, studied with John Braham as well as with the renowned Angela

[5] J. A. Fuller-Maitland, 'Domenico Corri', in *Grove's Dictionary of Music and Musicians*, 5th ed. (London, 1954); by the same author, 'Domenico Corri', in the *Dictionary of National Biography*.

[6] Quoted in J. Cuthbert Hadden, *George Thomson, The Friend of Burns* (London: Nimmo, 1898), p. 20.

Catalani. In coming to the Corri establishment, Isaac Nathan was joining a family involved in the publishing of national melodies and connected with the greatest tenor of the age, John Braham. Later Braham's name appeared alongside Nathan's on the title page of the First Number of *A Selection of Hebrew Melodies*.

Isaac Nathan was fond of naming his children after the famous people with whom he had become associated. The composer's firstborn, his son Charles Braham Nathan, commemorates his association with the Regency tenor John Braham. (Among Nathan's large family, a son, Walter Byron, takes his name from two of the literary giants of the age, and a daughter, Louisa Caroline, is named after her godmother, Lady Caroline Lamb.) Braham was 'justly admitted on all hands to be the greatest tenor England had ever reared', as one of his musical contemporaries noted.[7] 'He was gifted with the most extraordinary genius and aptitude for the exercise of his profession that was ever implanted in a human being,' another claimed.[8] Charles Lamb enjoyed Braham's singing most of all. Elia's essay on 'Imperfect Sympathies' compliments the tenor on his abilities, and, in his letters, Lamb gives vent to stronger praise:

> Do you like Braham's singing? The little Jew has bewitched me.
> I follow him like as the boys followed Tom the Piper. He
> cured me of melancholy, as David cured Saul; but I don't throw
> stones at him, as Saul did at David in payment. I was
> insensible to music till he gave me a new sense. . . . Braham's
> singing, when it is impassioned, is finer than Mrs. Siddon's or
> Mr. Kemble's acting; and when it is not impassioned, it is as
> good as hearing a person of fine sense talking. The brave little
> Jew![9]

Characteristically, Leigh Hunt, in his *Autobiography*, was less lavish in his praise and more discerning in his sensibility:

> He [Braham] had wonderful execution as well as force . . . This
> renowned vocalist never did himself justice except in the

[7] Rev. William Coxe, *Musical Recollections of the Last Half-Century*, 2 vols (London: Tinsley Bros., 1872), I, 45. See H. F. Chorley, *Thirty Years' Musical Recollections*, 2 vols (London: Hurst & Blackett, 1862); and 'Mr. Braham', in *The Quarterly Musical Magazine and Review*, 1818, I, 86–95 (Coxe [I, 26] identifies the editor as Richard Mackenzie Bacon). There is no full-length study of Braham.

[8] Earl of Mount Edgcumbe, *Musical Reminiscences*, 4th ed. (London: John Andrews, 1834), p. 247.

[9] Lamb to Manning, 26 February 1808, *The Works of Charles and Mary Lamb*, ed. by E. V. Lucas, 7 vols (London: Methuen, 1905), VI, 383.

compositions of Handel. When he stood in the concert-room or the oratorio, and opened his mouth with plain, heroic utterance in the mighty strains of 'Deeper and deeper still,' or 'Sound an alarm,' or 'Comfort ye my people,' you felt indeed that you had a great singer before you. His voice which too often sounded like a horn vulgar, in the catchpenny lyrics of Tom Dibdin, now became a veritable trumphet of grandeur and exaltation . . .[10]

Michael Kelly, the musical director of Drury Lane, was a good friend of the Corri family, and Braham probably met Domenico Corri at Drury Lane. No doubt Nathan's association with Corri brought him from the periphery of the musical world near to its centre and ultimately to Braham. Nathan himself explains how Braham's name came to be entered on the title page of *A Selection of Hebrew Melodies*. Originally intending to publish his work by subscription, Nathan met Braham, who wished to put his name down for several pounds.[11] Nathan then offered the tenor half share in the profits if he would agree to introduce the work to the public. Braham assented; what could be more natural for the man who had made Handel's *Israel in Egypt* his signature?

By 1810 Nathan was chief assistant at Corri's musical finishing school and had begun to compose songs. His good looks, humble position, and romantic origins made him an ideal mate for a Lydia Languish, should one come along. In 1812 Elizabeth Rosetta Worthington did. She eloped with Nathan at the age of seventeen, having put aside a novel of Mrs Radcliffe for her own *Elvington*, written the year before.[12] By 1813, as we have seen, Nathan had hit upon the idea of publishing a collection of Hebrew melodies. The work was intended, we can suppose, to mark his debut as a major

[10] Ed. by Roger Ingpen, 2 vols (London: Constable, 1903), I, 139–40.

[11] *FP*, p. vii. In Washington Irving's *Analectic Magazine* (1815, V, 87) an advance notice shows the plans which Nathan had made before he interested Braham and Byron in his project:

Mr. I. Nathan has announced by subscription, a selection of Hebrew Melodies, twelve of which are arranged as songs, and others harmonized for two or more voices. Each melody will have notes descriptive of the days on which they are sung; and, in addition to the poetry that will be expressly written for this work by an approved modern author, the ancient Hebrew characters, with the English translation, will be given.

[12] Her two novels à la Radcliffe are: *Elvington* (London: Stockdale, 1819), and *Langreath* (London: Whittaker, 1822). The chapters of the latter work are, in the main, headed with quotations from Byron's works.

music publisher. National melodies were still returning excellent dividends. Nathan's own master had published a volume of them and was still publishing others. Success beckoned, but taste demanded that a well-known poet provide the verses. Nathan aimed for the best; he wrote to Scott. Scott declined. Then Nathan sent Byron a musical setting he had struck off:

> 7 Poland Street,
> Oxford Street
> June 13th, 1814

My Lord,

 With the greatest deference and respect I have ventured to enclose you a copy of 'This rose to calm my brother's cares' [Bride of Abydos, 1.287] which I hope your Lordship will do me the honour to accept. It has been composed some time ago, but fearful the music did not do ample justice to the inimitable beauty of the words, I was diffident of presenting it to your Lordship, till encouraged by the flattering reception I have since met with.

> I have the honour to remain my Lord,
> Your Lordship's
> Most humble, obedient
> I. Nathan[13]

Words were what Nathan wanted, but Byron seems to have been shy of providing them – inimitable or not. No answer to this letter has survived. Two weeks passed before Nathan tried again on 30 June:

My Lord,

 The high character your Lordship bears for liberality of feeling could alone induce me to trespass thus on your attention, but having endeavoured in vain to obtain an introduction, and not being fortunate enough to succeed, will I trust, plead my apology for the unwarrantable liberty I now take in thus addressing you.

 I have with great trouble selected a considerable number of very beautiful Hebrew melodies of undoubted antiquity, some of which are proved to have been sung by the Hebrews before the destruction of the Temple of Jerusalem. Having been honoured with the immediate patronage of Her Royal Highness the Princess Charlotte of Wales, the Duchess of York and most

---

[13] Quoted in Phillips, p. 38.

of the names of the Royal Family together with those of a great number of distinguished personages, I am most anxious that the Poetry for them should be written by the first Poet of the present age, and though I feel and know I am taking a great liberty with your Lordship in even hinting that one or two songs written by you would give the work great celebrity, yet, I trust your Lordship will pardon and attribute it to what is really the case, the sincere admiration I feel for your extraordinary talents. It would have been my most sanguine wish from the first to have applied to your Lordship had I not been prevented by a knowledge that you wrote only for amusement and the fame you so justly acquired. I therefore wrote to Walter Scott offering him a share in the publication if he would undertake to write for me, which he declined, not thinking himself adequate to the task, the distance likewise being too great between us, I could not wait on him owing to my professional engagements in London.

I have since been persuaded by several Ladies of literary fame and known genius, to apply to your Lordship even at the risk of seeming impertinence on my part, rather than lose the smallest shadow of success from your Lordship acceding to my humble entreaties. If your Lordship would permit me to wait on you with the Melodies and allow me to play them over to you, I feel certain from their great beauty, you would become interested in them, indeed, I am convinced no one but my Lord Byron could do them justice.

If I should have, through too great an anxiety to obtain this, my most sanguine hope, in any way invaded on the respect so justly your due, I trust your Lordship will pardon and place it to the real cause, my ardent wish of having that publication in any way countenanced by your Lordship.

I have the honour to be

My Lord

Your Lordship's

humble and devoted servant,

I. Nathan[14]

No. 7, Poland Street,
Oxford Street
June 30th 1814

[14] Quoted in Phillips, pp. 39–40.

Byron's answer, if answer he made to this grovelling missive, has gone unrecorded. Yet within less than a year's time he had presented Nathan not with 'one or two songs', but with twenty-nine!

Isaac Nathan had not been the first to send Byron letters seeking words for music. His request for songs had been anticipated as early as 1812, by the Scots music publisher, George Thomson. Declaring his admiration of the lyrics in *Childe Harold* Thomson had written to Byron on 10 July 1812 requesting 'congenial verses' for several melodies then in his portfolio:

> I am filled with apprehension that your Lordship may think
> me too bold in making my request. Indeed, my courage has
> repeatedly failed when I sat down with the intention of writing
> to you, but the solicitude I feel to obtain songs every way
> worthy of the music has at last overcome my scruples, and I
> venture to throw myself on your Lordship's liberality and
> goodness. I might perhaps have been able to procure a friendly
> recommendation to your Lordship, but I really thought, if you
> should not be inclined to write for the Muse's sake you would
> not care to write at all; and much as I should regret it,
> I would rather that you rejected my suit than that you were
> obliged to reject that of a friend.

In the tone and phrasing of this letter, the psychology of Nathan's letter is at work. But the cagier Thomson failed to recognize that anticipating a negative reply was no way to get on with Byron. Thomson's greatest error was his seeming rejection of the idea of a friendly third-party suit, for it was just such a suit that led to Nathan's success. Despite his mistakes, Thomson seems to have received some encouragement. On 22 September he sent Byron five Irish airs anticipating 'great pleasure from singing ... your Lordship's verses'.[15] Disappointment was his reward. In September, Thomson wrote to Byron's publisher, John Murray:

> On receipt of your [Murray's] very obliging letter in April, I
> ventured to address Lord Byron again, but having waited thus

[15] Quoted in Hadden, pp. 188, 189.

long not honoured with any reply, I fear that it will be in vain
for me any longer to cherish the hope of his writing the songs
for me . . . I find beautiful verses in the *Hours of Idleness*. From
that work and from *Childe Harold* I have selected three songs
which I should be happy to set to music. I mean 'Lochnagarr,'
particularly the first three stanzas (for as a *song* I think it were
best to close with the line 'They dwell in the tempests of dark
Lochnagarr'); 'Oh, had my fate been joined with thine'; and
'The kiss, dear maid, thy lip has left.' May I presume to
request the favour of your asking whether his Lordship will
have the goodness to permit me to unite these songs with
characteristic music, which I am sure will delight every hearer.[16]

So wrote one Scots publisher to another. Murray, who had rallied to
Thomson's cause, did raise the issue with Byron once more. This
time Byron wrote directly to Thomson:

Septr. 10th. 1813

Sir,

Mr. Murray informs me that you have again addressed him
on y[e]. subject of some songs which I ought long ago to have
contributed. – The fact is – I have repeatedly tried since you
favoured me with your first letter (and y[e]. valuable musical
present which accompanied it) without being able to satisfy
myself – judge then if I should be able to gratify you – or
others – A bad song would only disgrace beautiful music – I
know that I could rhyme for you – but not produce anything
worthy of your publication. – It is not a species of writing
which I undervalue – on the contrary Burns in your country –
& my friend Moore in this – have shewn that even their
splendid talents may acquire additional reputation from this
exercise of their powers. – You will not wonder that I decline
writing after men whom it were difficult to imitate – &
impossible to equal. – I wish you every success – & I have only
declined complying with your request – because I would not
impede your popularity. – Believe me your well wisher & very
obed[t]. Sev[t].,

Biron

P.S.   You will not suspect me of caprice nor want of

[16] Thomson to Murray, 2 September 1813, quoted *ibid.*, pp. 190–1. 'The kiss,
dear maid . . .' (first published with *Childe Harold*) was published with music in
Thomson's collection of *Irish Airs*, 1816, II, 89; 'Oh, had my fate . . .' in his
Scottish Airs, 1818, V, 214.

inclination – it is true you may say I have already made
attempts apparently as hazardous – but believe me I have again
& again endeavoured to fulfill my promise without success –
nothing but my most decided conviction that both you & I
would regret it – would have prevented me from long ago
contributing to your volume. –[17]

Byron had already entered the literary doldrums which he describes
in the dedicatory letter to Tom Moore prefaced to the *Corsair*. He
felt that his recently published *Bride of Abydos* had captured an
audience rightly belonging to Moore's unfinished *Lalla Rookh*, and he
had no wish to tread again on his friend's toes by writing Irish
Melodies for Thomson. Nor did he relish the thought of what
seemed like production on order. Doubtless he recalled the problems
that the preceding year's Drury Lane address written at Lord Holland's
request had created. Much to Thomson's disappointment, the
answer was 'no'. Three months later Byron summed up his feelings
in his journal: 'A Mr. Thomson has sent a song, which I must
applaud. I hate annoying them with censure or silence; – and yet I
hate *lettering*.'[18]

Byron's correspondence with Thomson suggests that Isaac Nathan
would not succeed with his plans. Song-writing was the least of the
poet's preoccupations during these years of fame. Byron did have a
brief affair with an Italian soprano while at Cheltenham in the
autumn of 1812, he did find music books convenient for passing
notes to Lady Frances Wedderburn Webster, and he did enjoy
hearing Moore's melodies sung at gatherings of the *haut monde*. Aside
from these activities, his musical concerns were nil. Whether
Nathan's letter of 30 June met with 'censure or silence' is not known,
but it is likely, as Thomson's experience suggests, that Byron
declined the proposal. During the summer and early autumn of 1814
he makes no mention of Hebrew Melodies in his correspondence.
Writing to Annabella Milbanke from Six Mile Bottom on 25
August, he replied to an earlier question about his activities:
'You ask me what "my occupations" are? The "dolce far niente" –
nothing. What my "projects" are? I have none.'[19]

*   *   *   *   *

[17] T. G. Steffan, 'Some 1813 Byron Letters', *K-SJ*, 1967, XVI, 15.
[18] Journal, 6 December 1813, *L & J*, II, 367. Subsequent references to this
edition of Byron's letters are identified in the text by volume and page number.
[19] Quoted in Ethel Colburn Mayne, *The Life and Letters of Anne Isabella Lady
Noel Byron* (London, 1929), p. 106.

Byron returned to London on 23 September. He took a new 'project' with him, for in the closing days of a sojourn at Newstead he agreed to write the Hebrew Melodies. After little more than a month's stay in town, he departed, taking a circuitous route that would bring him to the Milbankes' residence at Seaham. But during this month in London he set to work on the Hebrew Melodies in earnest: Isaac Nathan had succeeded! Byron's first and most detailed reference to the poems is to be found in a postscript to a letter written to Annabella on 20 October 1814:

> Oh, I must tell you of one of my present avocations. Kinnaird (a friend of mine, brother to Lord Kd.) applied to me to write words for a musical composer who is going to publish the *real old undisputed Hebrew melodies*, which are beautiful & to which David & the prophets actually sang the 'songs of Zion' — & I have done nine or ten on the sacred model — partly from Job &c. & partly my own imagination; but I hope a little better than Sternhold & Hopkins. It is odd enough that this should fall to my lot, who have been abused as 'an infidel.' Augusta says 'they will call me a Jew next.'[20]

Here Byron explains Nathan's success. Sometime during the late summer of 1814 Nathan had been able to secure the aid of Douglas Kinnaird, a banker involved in the management of Drury Lane Theatre. Kinnaird was a Cambridge associate of Byron's closest friend, John Cam Hobhouse, and so a friend of Byron's as well. On 15 September, Kinnaird applied to Byron to gain the poet's collaboration for Nathan:

> Dear Byron,
>   Your grim white woman [Byron's housemaid Mrs Mule] gives me no hope of finding you in Town for some time, I am reduc'd therefore to the necessity of recording a piece of indiscretion which I am only anxious you should not consider as quite unpardonable. — It is no less than to endeavour to put your poetical talent in requisition for the benefit of a composer of Music, whose very singular merits, both as a composer and a man, have interested me in his behalf. — He is about to publish some *Hebrew Melodies* as they are call'd. — They are the very identical religious airs sung by the Jews, 'ere our blessed

---

[20] Quoted in Mayne, *Lady Byron*, p. 469. Cf. Milton, *Paradise Regained*, IV:347, 'Zion's songs, to all true tastes excelling.'

Lord & Saviour came into the world to be the cause of the persecution of these bearded men. − He very properly concludes that, if you would give him a few lines (if only for one air) the sale of his work would be Secur'd & his pocket enrich'd −

The music is beautiful certainly − and I shall be greatly gratified if your determination shall be in favor of the Petitioner. He already set to a very beautiful piece of composition those six lines in *Lara* beginning with 'Night Wanes' − The music is in Handel's style, & I am much mistaken if all the musical world do not 'ere long mouth your lines after their usual fashions. −[21]

Byron's 'determination' was indeed in Nathan's favour. The motives underlying his acquiescence are complex; before they can be considered, it is first necessary to study the more immediate question of Kinnaird's relationship with Nathan.

In 1829, Nathan denied that Kinnaird had introduced him to Byron. By that time, Kinnaird had called Nathan a 'toadeater', and Nathan had responded with 'brainless blockhead'. Nathan's remarks upon Kinnaird must be treated with caution; his denial is hardly acceptable in the light of the correspondence of Byron and Kinnaird. The subsequent history of Nathan's relationship with Kinnaird makes it doubtful that the latter would have volunteered his aid. Nor has evidence linking the two men in advance of the Hebrew Melodies scheme been found. However, Kinnaird's reference to the musical world's mouthing Byron's lines suggests the source of his 'indiscretion'. The 'singular merits' that 'interested' Kinnaird in Nathan's 'behalf' were likely to have belonged to John Braham. Braham, a performer whose presence assured the success of a musical production, was associated with Kinnaird at Drury Lane.[22] As we have seen, Braham had met Nathan through Corri, and Braham's financial stake in the Hebrew Melodies probably prompted him to take an interest in Nathan's attempt to recruit Byron's talents. Perhaps Kinnaird advanced Nathan's suit as a favour to Braham. On the other side, Byron certainly was acquainted with Braham, though no record of their meeting has survived. Writing in his journal, Byron used one of Braham's popular *bons mots* to describe his feelings

[21] Murray MSS.

[22] Braham wrote to Kinnaird on 8 August 1813, inquiring about his Drury Lane salary. British Museum, Add. MS. 38071, f. 72. Nathan himself may have been connected with Drury Lane in a musical capacity.

for Walter Scott: 'I like the man – and admire his work to what Mr. Braham calls Entusymusy.'[23] In any case it was not Nathan's letter which was the means of securing Byron's services, as Byron made clear:

Braham is to assist – or hath assisted – but will do no more good than a second physician. I merely interfered to oblige a whim of Kinnaird's, and all I have got by it was a 'speech' and a receipt for stewed oysters.[24]

Byron's interference was positive and immediate. Though his letter answering Kinnaird's request has not survived, it is clear that he agreed to Nathan's proposal and sent Kinnaird several poems. On 19 September, only four days after making his request, Kinnaird wrote to thank Byron for his willingness to participate and for the poems he had sent:

My dear Byron,
  You desire me to acknowledge the safe arrival of your letters at your Rooms in Albany; but I am too impatient to thank you, not to give myself a chance of saying to you what I feel, before you leave Newstead. . . .
  The benefit conferr'd on my protegé is really an important one; & that thought makes me still more thankful to you. – It is a great satisfaction to me to be able to assure you, that your kindness & Poetry will be conferr'd on both worth & talent. – And, that he has met with misfortune in his career, will I am sure be no ill recommendation to your notice. –
  Be assur'd that your lines shall be made use of with discretion. – The lines beginning 'Sun of the Sleepless!' are beautiful. – If you hereafter give him leave to set them to music, well & good. – But I would not for the world that he separated

[23] 17 November 1813, *L & J*, II, 322. Relating some 'Anecdotes of Braham' in his *Southern Euphrosyne* (pp. 150–1), Nathan explains 'entusymusy'. Braham, rehearsing *The Cabinet*, stumbled over the word reciting, 'They followed me to the field with *enthusiasm*'; on his third attempt 'he could not recall the *jaw-breaker* to his memory, and vexed at his own seeming dullness, he vociferated with "towzy mowzy." This anecdote was communicated to us by Edmund Kean, in the presence of Thomas Moore, Cam Hobhouse, and the honourable Douglas Kinnaird, which afforded us so much mirth that henceforth *towzy mowzy* became the cant term in our circle of *enthusiasm*.'

[24] Byron to Moore, 22 February 1815, *L & J*, III, 180. 'Hath assisted' is correct for Braham's assistance, as Nathan's account shows. Kinnaird never fully explained his 'whim' to Byron.

the lines from *Lara*, from the music he has added to them. – I am delighted at your proposal to hear the airs play'd & chaunted to you. – You shall then hear the lines from *Lara* sung. – You will be *delighted*. – For I can almost venture to say the music is worthy the lines. – I have heard nothing so good, that is not in Handel. – I have no doubt that, as the *Oratorios*, when it will be produc'd, it will create a great sensation. –

The lines beginning, *Oh! weep for those that wept by Babel's stream*, are I think, very well suited to the style of some of the Hebrew Melodies – & are beautiful. – None of the verses not to be set to music shall pass out of my hands; but shall be return'd uncopied to you. –[25]

From Kinnaird's letter we may infer that Byron had not hesitated to provide a selection of short lyrics. These were the poems that Byron had been at work on at various times in the summer and autumn of 1814. Perhaps he enclosed a selection of poems, instructing Kinnaird to have what he deemed suitable copied for Nathan's use. Of the poems Kinnaird refers to directly, 'Sun of the Sleepless!' had been composed early in September, in advance of Kinnaird's request, but Byron thought it suitable for the Hebrew Melodies. 'Oh! Weep for Those' was probably composed, as its simple construction suggests, in the interval following Byron's receipt of Kinnaird's request. Having so provided Nathan with words for more than 'one air', Byron probably conceived of his involvement as terminated. But he did listen to Nathan recite his airs, and as the year progressed he found himself attracted to Nathan and more deeply involved in the Hebrew Melodies.

Byron allowed Kinnaird to draw him into Nathan's project. As a letter written to Moore on 8 March shows, however, he was not an unwilling accomplice: 'Have I not told you it was all Kinnaird's doing, and my own exquisite facility of temper?' (III, 184). In part Byron's response was shaped by a desire to please his future bride. As we have seen, he was careful to point out to Annabella: 'It is odd enough that this should fall to my lot, who have been abused as "an infidel".' If Hebrew Melodies would improve his reputation, as seen both by the world and his reforming angel, Byron would be happy to acquiesce.

Byron was sensitive enough to recognize the incipient nationalism in the public's taste for national melodies, and this nationalism also

[25] Kinnaird to Byron, 19 September 1814, Murray MSS.

sat well with his sentiments. These were the sentiments that would yield some of the finest poems in the work, as one reviewer noticed:

> The present state of the Jewish people – expatriated – dispersed – trodden down – contemned, – afforded the noble poet a very fine subject; and . . . he has not neglected to avail himself of it.[26]

But his sympathies for the downtrodden were not the deepest feeling to be tapped by the writing of national melodies. He had listened to enough of Moore's *Irish Melodies* to realize that the lamentation for lost freedom that is their mainstay might serve as a means for the expression of his personal melancholic sense of lost innocence and his nostalgia for what had been. These feelings were closely linked to his idealization of youthful beauty and were the source of much of his early poetry, particularly the Thyrza poems that celebrate his love for John Edleston, who had died in 1811. Edleston's voice had made a particularly lasting impression on Byron. Hearing Nathan rehearse his sacred songs perhaps awakened feelings in Byron that helped to make collaboration with the musician possible. In 1812 he had heard the Hon. Mrs George Lamb sing a selection of sacred tunes and been stirred by similar emotions that came to the attention of one observer:

> He admires her [Caroline Lamb] very much, but is supposed by some to admire our Caroline (the Hon. Mrs. George Lamb) more; he says she is like Thyrza, and her singing is enchantment to him.[27]

Later in the same year, her singing prompted Byron's 'Hear my Prayer!':

> The sacred song that on mine ear
> Yet vibrates from that voice of thine,
> I heard before from one so dear,
> Tis strange it still appears divine.

Earlier, at the close of 1811, he had sent a copy of another poem on the Thyrza theme, 'Away, away ye notes of woe!', to his friend Francis Hodgson. 'I wrote it a day or two ago,' Byron remarked, 'on

[26] *Christian Observer*, 1815, XIV, 545.
[27] Elizabeth Duchess of Devonshire to Augustus Foster, 4 May 1812, *Poetry*, III, 31n.

hearing a song of former days.'[28] Nathan's voice, limited in power but exquisitely trained, perhaps recalled Edleston's to Byron's mind. The Hebrew Melodies would be, in part, another memorial to that young man.

Whatever the reason, Byron continued to write Hebrew Melodies between 23 September, when he returned to London, and 20 October, when he mentioned the poems to Annabella. His trip to Seaham interrupted the composition of the poems, but this visit to his fiancée, begun on 29 October, ended inconclusively. By 24 November, Byron had returned to London and had resumed work on the lyrics. One month later he again departed for Seaham — this time to marry. During his honeymoon at Halnaby and his later stay at Seaham, Byron continued to work on the poems. Finally, he and his bride began their journey to London on 9 March, leaving Seaham behind and the Hebrew Melodies seemingly completed. The majority of the poems were written in two broad periods of approximately two months each: October and December 1814 (in London); and January (Halnaby) and February (Seaham) 1815. (Generally, the poems composed during the first period were those published in the First Number of Nathan's *Selection*, and those of the second period appeared in the Second Number.) Not all the Hebrew Melodies were composed during the winter of 1814–15. In June of 1815, after Nathan's First Number had been published, Byron presented the composer with one new poem, the lines beginning 'Bright be the place of thy soul'. This was the last composition he gave to Nathan. But at the very start of his collaboration, Byron had provided several lyrics composed in the spring and summer of 1814. These poems, written before Byron had ever heard about Hebrew Melodies, are the first that need to be accounted for.

As early as November of 1813, Byron was trying to write songs. The repeated requests of Thomson had opened his mind to the idea

[28] 8 December 1811, *L & J*, II, 82. There is another reference to Edleston's voice in the 'Stanzas to Jessy': 'I would not hear a Seraph Choir,/Unless that voice could join the rest.' Professor Marchand has theorized that Byron's 'There be none of Beauty's daughters' with its reference to 'thy sweet voice' was 'written to Edleston, perhaps while he was still alive' (Marchand, I, 313n). The poem is commonly believed to have been addressed to Claire Clairmont because it was first published in 1816, not long after Byron met her. Coleridge gives as the date of the MS.: 'March 28 [1816].' At that time Nathan had taken to visiting the poet in order to ease his sorrow by performing Hebrew Melodies on Byron's piano. Perhaps Nathan's singing again called Edleston to mind and so prompted the composition.

of composition for music. On the 17th Byron wrote in his journal: 'I have begun, or had begun, a song, and flung it into the fire' (II, 324). Still, he kept on working and did succeed with several short lyrics that *might* easily be set to music. The poems found their way into the second edition of the *Corsair* (1814) and the seventh edition of *Childe Harold* (1814). Those lyrics that could serve as scenic set pieces became additions to the texts of his Turkish tales, whose length increased with every edition. In the spring of 1814, he wrote to Murray: 'I think you told me that you wanted some smaller poems for the small Edition you intended some time or other to print . . . if I can find, or create, any more, you shall have them.'[29]

[29] 22 April 1814, *L & J*, III, 73–4. One lyric written in the spring of 1814 has never been published. On 18 April 1814, Byron set down the following lines:

Magdalen

The hour is come – of darkness and of Dread –
That makes Earth shudder to receive the dead –
When the first Martyr to his offered creed –
The man of heaven – the Son of God must bleed!
The hour is come of Salem's giant Sin –
The doom is fixed – the bloody rites begin –

There be loud cries on Sion's lofty place –
And struggling crowds of Israel's swarthy race –
Stamped on each brow an idiot hatred stood –
In every eye an eagerness of blood –
Each scornful lip betrayed its wayward thirst
Of ill – & cursing him became accurst –

Wroth without cause – revenged without a wrong –
Tribes of self sentence! ye shall suffer long –
Through dark Millenniums of exiled grief –
The outcast slaves of sightless unbelief! –
Stung by all torture – buffeted & sold
Racked by an idle lust of useless gold –

Scourged – scorned – unloved – a name for every race
To spit upon – the chosen of disgrace –
A people nationless – whom every land –
Receives to punish – & preserves to brand –
Yet still enduring all – & all in vain –
The doomed inheritors of scorn & pain –
Untaught by sufferance – unreclaimed from ill –
Hating & hated – stubborn Israel still!

Good Friday (8 April) and Napoleon's abdication (11 April) came one after the other in 1814, and their concurrence perhaps occasioned these lines. Byron makes no reference to the poem in his published correspondence, but the manuscript survives in the Lovelace Papers. It may be that he erred in setting down the date, intending 1815 for 1814. If he did slip, the poem would mark the finish of the

We should not be surprised then if one or two of these ready-made lyrics found their way into the Hebrew Melodies. Such was the case with the lines beginning 'I speak not, I trace not, I breathe not thy name'. This dramatic statement of his feelings for Augusta was sent to Moore in May of 1814:

> Dear Tom,—Thou hast asked me for a song, and I enclose you an experiment, which has cost me something more than trouble, and is, therefore, less likely to be worth your taking any in your proposed setting. Now, if it be so, throw it into the fire without phrase.[30]

Though Moore got the song that Thomson had wanted, Nathan was the first to publish it. He did so in 1829 in a new edition of the Hebrew Melodies. Subsequently Moore published the poem without music in his edition of Byron's Letters and Journals (1830). There he acknowledged Nathan's earlier publication: 'The above verses have lately found their way into print, but through a channel not very likely to bring them into circulation.'[31] Byron had given the poem to Nathan and later asked the composer to suppress it or to assign the 1814 date to the poem. Nathan kept back the poem until Byron's death.

'She Walks in Beauty', the most enjoyed of all the Hebrew Melodies, was similarly composed before Byron's collaboration with Nathan. The poem was written in 1814 during the 'summer of the sovereigns'. Established in his new chambers at the Albany, Byron had sampled London society and then tired of it. On 11 June, he wrote to his friend, James Wedderburn Webster (III, 92):

> Your Lady Sitwell has sent me a card for to night, but I shan't go. I have had enough of parties – for this summer at least.

But Byron did attend this party, as Webster tells us in a note he scribbled at the foot of the letter:

[30] 4 May 1814, L & J, III, 80. On the date of this letter see p. 129, below.
[31] I, 554-5. E. H. Coleridge gets the sequence correct (though he misses an intermediate edition of Nathan's Selection) in his preface to the Hebrew Melodies (Poetry, III, 377), but he then turns round and assigns the first publication of 'I Speak Not – I Trace Not – I Breathe Not' to Moore's Letters and Journals beneath the text of the poem (Poetry, III, 417).

major work on the Hebrew Melodies and Byron's increasing dissatisfaction with Nathan. Nathan does not mention the poem. It seems unlikely, considering the content of the lines, that Byron would ever have mentioned the work to him.

I did take him to Lady Sitwell's Party in Seymour road. He there for the first time saw his cousin, the beautiful Mrs. Wilmot [who had appeared in mourning with numerous spangles on her dress]. When we returned to his rooms in the Albany, he said little, but desired Fletcher to give him a tumbler of Brandy, which he drank at once to Mrs. Wilmot's health, then retired to rest, and was, I heard afterwards, in a sad state all night. The next day he wrote those charming lines upon her – 'She walks in Beauty like the Night. . . .'

Anne Horton, the Derbyshire heiress, had married Robert Wilmot, Byron's first cousin. She was a woman of great beauty and talent, and the lines that Byron had written upon her were to open *A Selection of Hebrew Melodies*.

On 8 September 1814 Byron set down another embryonic Hebrew Melody. Apparently only eight lines in the centre of the lengthy verse fragment entitled 'Harmodia' he composed that day pleased him, for, recognizing their lyric potential, he scrapped the remainder of the fragment and rewrote the lines. Just when he conceived of 'Sun of the Sleepless!' as an individual poem is not known. But it is clear that he had done so before Kinnaird referred to the poem in his letter of 19 September. On the 24th John Murray wrote to his wife: 'He [Byron] says he has written some small poems which his friends think beautiful, particularly one of eight lines, his very best – all of which, I am to have. . . .'[32] From this we may infer that by the time of his return to London on 23 September Byron had finished another lyric which Nathan was 'to have' ultimately.

'I Speak Not – I Trace Not – I Breathe Not', 'She Walks in Beauty', and 'Sun of the Sleepless!' can definitely be assigned to the months immediately preceding Byron's work on the Hebrew Melodies. Perhaps Byron's 'I Saw Thee Weep', also belongs to this period. That brief but beautiful love lyric seems to be addressed to Lady Frances Wedderburn Webster whom Byron 'spared' in October 1813. The fair copy of the poem that has survived is on paper bearing the watermark 'J GREEN 1814'. Both Byron's letter to James Perry of 7 [6] October 1814 and the holograph of 'The harp the monarch minstrel swept' are on similar paper of the same date. This suggests

[32] Quoted in Samuel Smiles, *A Publisher and His Friends, Memoir and Correspondence of the late John Murray*, 2 vols (London, 1891), I, 252.

that 'I Saw Thee Weep' was either composed, or copied from an earlier draft, during the initial period of Byron's work on the Hebrew Melodies. The lack of even a vague reference to a Jewish theme supports the latter inference.

As we have seen, on 20 October Byron told Annabella that he had completed 'nine or ten' Hebrew Melodies. While it is relatively easy to separate the poems composed in 1814 from those composed in 1815, it is difficult, in the absence of manuscripts, to determine the order of the poems composed in 1814. Kinnaird refers to 'Oh! Weep for Those', in his letter of 19 September, indicating that poem as perhaps the first that Byron composed with the Hebrew Melodies in mind. Byron's reference to a poem modelled on Job suggests that the lines beginning 'A spirit passed before me', which he entitled simply 'From Job', were composed in October as well. On the back of the holograph of that poem, Byron set down his 'On Jordan's Banks', and this suggests that it too was composed at this time. On the evidence of watermark 'The harp the monarch minstrel swept' belongs to this early period as well. 'Thy Days are Done' belongs to 1814, but only perhaps to October of that year. The poem may be an alternative to the lines 'On the Death of Sir Peter Parker' (which Byron sent to Perry on 6 October), an alternative that Byron thought fitting to use in the Hebrew Melodies.[33]

Two more poems composed in the early period are 'Oh! snatched away in beauty's bloom' and 'If that High World'. Annabella inscribed the first of these lyrics: 'Given me at Seaham before my Marriage', indicating that Byron presented the poem to her during his first visit (November). She also refers to having received 'If that High World' before her wedding. That Charles Hanson made a copy of 'Oh! snatched away in beauty's bloom' on 8 February 1815, the same day that he copied 'The harp the monarch minstrel swept', adds to the evidence for early composition.

Byron's journey to Seaham delayed work on the Hebrew Melodies. But hesitancy and financial problems intervened to terminate a visit that should have ended in marriage. On 24 November he returned to London. (One month later he again departed for Seaham – this time to marry.) While in town Byron resumed his work on the Hebrew Melodies; he spent his leisure time dining with Kinnaird and attending performances at Drury Lane. Hobhouse's diary preserves an excellent record of Byron's activities during

[33] See T. L. Ashton, 'Peter Parker in Perry's Paper: Two Unpublished Byron Letters', *K-SJ*, 1969, XVIII, 49–59.

this period. Under the date 'Saturday Nov. 26 [1814]' Hobhouse wrote:

> Went to London in to the Orchestra at Drury Lane and saw Kean in Macbeth. . . . Supped with Kinnaird & his piece & a Mr. Nathan a music master a Jew for whom Ld. Byron has written words to Jewish melodies Ld. B was at supper – we had a scene – which is a good lesson against keeping—poor B was taken to task for making Mr. N impudent by shaking hands with him.[34]

Byron when genuinely attached to someone was less given to snobbishness than were some of his friends. He seems to have genuinely enjoyed Nathan's company. Hobhouse and Kinnaird had their doubts, and it was probably on this evening that Kinnaird insultingly remarked: 'Mr. Nathan I expect a–a–that–a–you bring out these Melodies in good style–a–a–and bear in mind that–a–a–his Lordship's name does not suffer from scantiness in their publication.'[35] Despite the 'speeches' the dinners continued. On Wednesday, 30 November, Hobhouse again visited Kinnaird: 'Went up to London and dined at the Royal Society Anniversary. . . . From the society I went to Kinnaird's and passed the evening with Byron & Nathan.'[36] Nor was Byron shy about inviting Nathan to his chambers in the Albany (III, 167):

Albany, Saturday Morn^g.

My dear Nathan, – You must dine with me to-day at Seven o'clock. I take no refusal.

Yours truly,
Byron

Clearly a good many of the Hebrew Melodies were written during

[34] John Cam Hobhouse, holograph Diary, 1 July 1814–29 March 1815. British Museum, Add. MS. 47232, f. 39^v.

[35] *FP*, p. 93. Earlier, on 2 November, Kinnaird wrote to Byron: 'I inclose a copy of Nathan's proposals – I hope you will approve the manner in which your name is introduc'd – His pupil proceeds with great success – Two Professional Judges are to hear her next Sunday – Nathan made us laugh exceedingly the other evening by a trait of simplicity – He was speaking of a female lodger in his house, who had contriv'd to swindle him out of monies; & on one occasion he ventur'd to tell her he thought she equivocated – to which the lady replied, her arms akimbo, "You lie" – "Then you know", said Nathan, "I began to see thro' her"–.' (Murray MSS) As Byron warmed to Nathan, Kinnaird's humour changed to resentment.

[36] Hobhouse Diary, 1 July 1814–29 March 1815, f. 40.

this period and set to music in Byron's presence. By the time of Byron's second departure for Seaham the following additional poems had probably been composed at the Albany, at Kinnaird's, and in the Green Room of Drury Lane Theatre: 'The Wild Gazelle', 'My Soul is Dark', and 'Jephtha's Daughter'.[37] Probably 'They say that Hope is happiness' was composed at this time as well. In his *Fugitive Pieces*, the single source of the poem, Nathan implies that Kinnaird's adverse remarks on the poem prompted Byron's destruction of the lines in Nathan's presence. This indicates that the poem was probably an early one, written during the period of close collaboration before Kinnaird's falling out with Nathan.

Following their wedding on 2 January 1815, Byron and his bride departed for Halnaby where they were to honeymoon for several weeks. There Byron resumed work on the Hebrew Melodies. 'Herod's Lament for Mariamne' was completed and inscribed 'Halnaby, January 13, 1815'. Annabella, dutiful wife that she was, prepared fair copies for the printer. While writing to Augusta one day, she decided to enclose the poem she had been copying in her letter. 'He objected', she writes of Byron, 'when I wished to send her his gloomy compositions, one of which was "O Mariamne."'[38] Two poems modelled on Psalm 137 were also written at Halnaby. Byron had already referred to the psalm in 'Oh! Weep for Those'. He returned to it in 'By the Rivers of Babylon', inscribed 'Jan. 15, 1815 Halnaby', and in 'In the Valley of Waters', inscribed 'Halnaby, 1815'. Byron thought of the poems as variations upon a theme, and on Lady Byron's fair copy of 'By the Rivers' (beneath a large '2'), he pencilled a note:

Dear Kinnaird —
Take only *one* of these marked ['sic' has been deleted in the

---

[37] Kinnaird may have suggested the topic of 'Jephtha's Daughter': in a letter of 2 November to Byron he writes: 'I sent you . . . the manuscript poem of my friend Smedley – Pray read it & return it with any remarks you may be kind enough to make on it – I think there is a large proportion of beautiful lines – Smedley intends correcting, as it is printed; for he is forc'd to print it – After the erasure of a few couplets which here & there appear redundant; & the insertion of a few lines, to prepare the mind for the entire omission of all mention of the Sacrifice, I think it will be very good – His reason, for making no mention of the said sacrifice is, that it is a disputed point whether the worthy gentleman's vow meant to shed her blood or condemn her to perpetual virginity.' (Murray MSS) Nathan debated the same point in his note to 'Jephtha's Daughter' in the second edition of *ASHM*. The Rev. Edward Smedley won the Seatonian Prize for a poem on an *announced* biblical subject with his *Saul* (1814) and *Jephtha* (1815).

[38] Quoted in Elwin, p. 264.

25

original] *1 & 2* – as both are but different versions of the *same thought* – leave the choice to any competent person you like.

Yours

B——[39]

'In the Valley of Waters' was not selected and remained unpublished until 1829 when Nathan published it – even though Byron earmarked it 'the *best* of the two' in a note to Kinnaird. The last of the poems composed at Halnaby was 'On the Day of the Destruction of Jerusalem by Titus', which Byron inscribed, 'Halnaby, Jan. 18, 1815'.

Byron and Annabella cut short their stay at Halnaby in order to celebrate Byron's birthday, 22 January, at Seaham. There he and Annabella passed the time together making bouts – rimés in the drawing-room.[40] Byron got out the Milbanke family Bible, what he called in a note to the manuscript of the 'Song of Saul' a 'translation of the Scriptures – Edition 1608', to foster the writing of Hebrew Melodies that he then resumed. Probably the first of the poems to be completed at Seaham was Byron's 'Saul'. The manuscript is inscribed 'Seaham Feb. 1815', but the watermark is that common to the paper he used at Halnaby, suggesting that the poem was begun there and completed at Seaham. Byron's 'To Belshazzar' is dated 'Feb. 12, 1815'. The poem was not published until 1831, and it has never been grouped with the Hebrew Melodies. But it is another version of Byron's 'Vision of Belshazzar', and (as with 'In the Valley of Waters')

---

[39] *Poetry*, III, 402n, corrected from MS.

[40] In a letter to the author of 20 August 1965 the late Sir John Murray, speaking of the Hebrew Melodies MSS in his collection, noted: 'There are eleven in Lady Byron's handwriting and I imagine that they never were in Byron's own handwriting.' Following Byron's marriage Lady Byron provided fair copies for Murray (who had a clerk copy some of the poems composed during the earlier period); the holographs she worked from remained at Seaham. In the margin of her copy of Medwin's *Conversations of Byron*, next to a passage containing Byron's remarks on her penchant for inaccurate character sketches, Lady Byron has written: '*During the whole time from the Marriage to the Sep*ⁿ. Lady Byron shewed but one thing she had written, beginning "Stranger on earth" – which she was anxious to add to the Hebrew Melodies, – but she declined.' (Thomas Medwin, *Conversations of Lord Byron*, ed. by Ernest J. Lovell, Jr [Princeton: Princeton University Press, 1966], p. 47n). This (as is frequently the case) does not agree with Byron's feelings as represented by Medwin: 'Lady Byron had good ideas, but could never express them; wrote poetry too, but it was only good by accident' (Medwin, p. 48). Finally, an analysis of the manuscripts does not support the hypothesis that Lady Byron composed any of the Hebrew Melodies. Manuscripts in Byron's hand of ten of the eleven fair copies Murray refers to are extant.

26

was rejected in favour of that poem. Seemingly 'Vision of Belshazzar', its companion piece, was composed at Seaham as well. The 'Song of Saul Before His Last Battle', inscribed 'Seaham 1815', was composed at this time, along with: 'The Destruction of Semnacherib' (inscribed 'Seaham Feb. 19, 1815'), 'Were my bosom as false as thou deem'st it to be' (inscribed 'Seaham 1815'), and 'When coldness wraps this suffering clay' (inscribed 'Seaham Feb. 1815'). Probably the last of the poems to be composed at Seaham is Byron's '"All is Vanity, saith the Preacher"'. Byron inscribed the holograph 'Seaham 1815'. The lyric beginning 'There's not a joy the world can give like that it takes away', composed near the end of the Byrons' stay at Seaham, was written on paper of the same watermark.

It seems best to disregard chronology momentarily at this point in order to discuss the composition of the three remaining Hebrew Melodies: 'It is the Hour', 'Francisca', and 'Bright be the place of thy soul'. 'It is the Hour' was first published in the First Number of Nathan's *Selection*, and 'Francisca' in the Second Number. No manuscript of the poems survives, and if nothing further had developed, the poems might be conjecturally assigned to one of the earlier periods of composition. But something else did happen: the publication of Byron's *Parisina* (jointly with the *Siege of Corinth*) on 7 February 1816. It must have surprised readers who had found 'It is the Hour' the most beautiful of the Hebrew Melodies to find that lyric (without revision) serving as the opening stanza of *Parisina*. Appending a note to the last line of the first stanza of *Parisina*, Byron explained: 'The lines contained in Section I were printed as set to music some time since: but belonged to the poem where they now appear'. He also altered his unpublished poem 'Francisca' – changing the heroine's name, revising three lines, and adding two – and turned this Hebrew Melody into the second stanza of *Parisina*.[41] Nathan makes no mention of *Parisina*, and it is likely that he was unaware of the source of these two scenic pieces. Though 'It is the

---

[41] *The Siege of Corinth. A Poem. Parisina. A Poem* (London: John Murray, 1816), p. 91. Slater (p. 87) argued that the Second Number of Nathan's *Selection* 'appeared probably, late in 1815'. He assumed that Byron's note to *Parisina* referred to *both* that poem's first and second stanzas. If 'Francisca' had been 'printed as set to music some time since' in Nathan's Second Number, that Number would have preceded *Parisina* in publication. But that is not the case, and Byron's note is not 'to lines 15–28 of *Parisina*' (Slater, p. 87n). The note refers to 'Section I' – lines 1–14. Slater relies on E. H. Coleridge's note to line 14 which reads 'contained in this section' (*Poetry*, III, 507); the note in the first edition reads 'contained in Section I'. Coleridge gives no reason for the change.

Hour' and 'Francisca' may be spoken of as fragments of *Parisina*, their claim to inclusion among the Hebrew Melodies is genuine.[42] If both poems have little to do with the Bible or the Hebrews – the same may also be said of many of their companion pieces. Byron certainly had given Nathan 'It is the Hour' before the publication of *Parisina*, and it is likely that 'Francisca' was given to Nathan at the same time. When or for what occasion the verses were composed is a matter for conjecture, but Byron did give them to Nathan, seemingly with the knowledge that the poems would first appear among the Hebrew Melodies.[43]

---

[42] 'It is the Hour' was excluded from Murray's collected edition of 1819 and has not been reprinted in subsequent editions. 'Francisca' never appeared in an edition published by Murray; the poem was included in the Galignani collected edition of 1831.

[43] In Byron's note to the first stanza of *Parisina*, he also speaks of the genesis of that tale, 'the greater part of which was composed prior to *Lara* [1814], and other compositions since published'. In a letter to Leigh Hunt, referring to *The Siege* and *Parisina* Byron remarked, 'the most part of both of them and of one in particular, *written* before *others* of my composing, which have preceded them in *publication*' (26 February 1816, *L & J*, III, 266). Gleckner (pp. 164–6, 177, 183) has summarized the new evidence for dating both poems and thinks that *The Siege* was begun as early as 1813 and *Parisina* in 1814. If Gleckner is right, the two 'fragments' must have been written before Nathan's collaboration with Byron. At first it seems unlikely that, having given Nathan many more than the 'one or two' poems he had requested, Byron would mine *Parisina* for new lyrics. But at that point what Byron was dealing with were probably only early scraps of the manuscript that was to become *Parisina*, or it may be that he was not dealing with *Parisina* at all. While at Seaham in January 1815, Byron was working on *The Siege of Corinth*, for Lady Byron remembered having copied part of the poem at that time (Elwin, p. 271). If Byron were reworking an abortive start on the poem, the lyrics he gave to Nathan may derive from *The Siege*. Francisca may be Francesca of *The Siege*. Byron was fond of the name. Another Francesca became Medora, as the manuscript of *The Corsair* reveals (*Poetry*, III, 239). R. C. Dallas asserts: 'In the original manuscript of the *Corsair*, the chief female character was called Francesca, in whose person he meant to delineate one of his acquaintance; but, before the poem went to the press, he changed the name to *Medora*' (*Recollections*, p. 184). (That Bianca of *Parisina* was also originally Medora suggests just how early *Parisina* may have been started [*Poetry*, III, 511].) Francesca or Francisca is ultimately Dante's, and as such had always been a literary favourite of Byron's. Perhaps *Parisina* may have originally been conceived of as the story of Paolo and Francesca. Leigh Hunt's *Story of Rimini*, which Byron knew of in advance of publication, might have put him from the subject until Teresa Guiccioli successfully urged him to revert to it in 1819.

It should be kept in mind that Byron's note to *Parisina* may be nothing more than a device to put scandal-seeking readers of that poem off the track, and that he was in the habit of lengthening his tales by the addition of short scenic set

'Bright be the place of thy soul' is the last of the poems Byron gave
to Nathan. It was composed, Nathan tells us, during a morning visit
to Byron and recited by Byron the same evening to the comedian
William Dowton in the Green Room of Drury Lane.[44] This event
probably took place after the publication of the First Number of *A
Selection* but before Byron's departure for the Continent. Nathan had
kept up his visits in order to rehearse the settings of the poems
published in the Second Number. Perhaps the poem was thought of as
a candidate for inclusion in that number. But Byron did not restrict
his giving. If a poem long since given to Moore could be given to
Nathan, a poem given to Nathan could be given to Leigh Hunt as
well. Hunt and Byron had begun to see one another, following the
former's release from prison in February 1815, and Hunt was the
first to publish 'Bright be the place of thy soul'. The poem appeared
in the *Examiner* on Sunday, 11 June 1815.[45] Two days earlier, Byron
had copied the first stanza of the poem and inscribed the date 'June 9,
1815' on the calling card of Lady Louisa Katherine Forester. John
Murray included 'Bright be the place of thy soul' in *Poems* (1816),
the volume devoted to Byron's 'Poems of the Separation'. But before
that volume appeared the poem had been pirated by Rodwell and
Martin.[46] Nathan reacted to Hunt's publication by issuing the poem
as a separate song sheet, probably in 1815.[47] Since he did not publish 'Bright be the place of thy soul' in the Second Number of 1816,
its publication in *Poems* (1816) may have prevented his numbering
the work among the Hebrew Melodies. But of the twenty of Byron's

[44] *FP*, p. 114.

[45] No. 389, p. 381. Not 4 June as Coleridge would have it (*Poetry*, III, 427).

[46] *Fare Thee Well – A Sketch from Private Life – With Other Poems* (London,
1816). The poem is also found in *Poems on His Domestic Circumstances*, Second
Edition (Bristol: Printed for Wm. Sheppard, 1816). Rodwell and Martin printed
from the *Examiner*; Sheppard's edition derives from Murray's. Dugdale did not
include the poem in his numerous piracies of the 'Poems of the Separation'. See
Davidson Cook, 'Byron's "Fare Thee Well" Unrecorded Editions', in *TLS*, 18
September 1937, p. 677.

[47] Discussing 'Bright be the place of thy soul', Graham Pollard noted that the
poem 'had appeared in the same paper [the *Examiner*] on 4 June 1815 [Coleridge's
incorrect date]; this may derive from the undated song sheet with music by Isaac
Nathan for whom Byron had originally written the poem. But in any case the

pieces. He may simply have composed the lyrics after having met Nathan, perhaps
with an unspecified tale in mind, given the poems to his composer, and finally
found them suitable for *Parisina*. In the absence of the holograph manuscript of
that work, little can be ascertained. Lady Byron's fair copy, the Murray proofs,
and the Huntington proofs do not bear on the question.

lyrics that Nathan set to music (without Byron's collaboration) and issued as individual song sheets, only this poem is included along with the Hebrew Melodies in *Fugitive Pieces*.[48] The fact that Nathan's song sheet is independent both of Hunt's and Murray's versions of the poem indicates that Byron intended the poem for Nathan. Though it had been published before 1829, its inclusion in Nathan's *Fugitive Pieces* may be accepted as extending the canon of Hebrew Melodies to thirty poems in that year.[49]

*   *   *   *   *

[48] Nathan placed the poem among the additional reminiscences that had not been printed as notes to the revised edition of *A Selection*. It may be that he was planning on a Third Number to contain 'Bright be the place of thy soul' and the four Hebrew Melodies he had not published in the first two numbers and published the song sheet after the *Examiner* had made the poem public.

[49] 'Bright be the place of thy soul' has been the source of much confusion in modern editions of Byron's works. In John Wright's edition of the *Works* in seventeen volumes (1832–3), the poem will be found printed correctly as two stanzas in Vol. X (312). However, the same poem is also found printed as four quatrains dated '1808' in Vol. VII (211) of Wright's work. The two versions have plagued those modern editions that either reprint Wright's work or essentially derive from it. In Page's Oxford edition of Byron's *Works* the poem has been tabled twice and printed twice, as in Wright's edition. E. H. Coleridge ignored the four-stanza version without comment in his edition. Paul Elmer More gives only the four-stanza version dated '1808' in his edition.

The source of the version dated '1808' in Wright's edition is unknown. Wright may have seen an earlier manuscript, but there are good grounds for accounting for that version of the poem on the basis of an error in imposition. In *Poems* (1816) 'Bright be the place of thy soul' precedes 'Farewell! if ever fondest prayer'. As both poems are untitled and separated only by a rule, the date given for the latter poem, '1808', may have been thought to apply to 'Bright be the place of thy soul' when this order was reversed in Vol. VII of Wright's work. As the first stanza of the version in four stanzas is on the recto and the remaining stanzas are on the verso, an error in imposition resulting from the division into two formes may account for the difference in the number of stanzas. A similar error, involving 'To Thyrza', was made in the collected edition of 1815, see p. 112, below.

song sheet is the real first edition; and this has not been noted before' ('Pirated Collections of Byron', *TLS*, 16 October 1937, p. 764). Nathan's song sheet is watermarked '1815', though an advertisement for the 'Just Published' Second Number of 1816 is given on its front cover. But the collation shows that the *Examiner* version could not have had its source in the song sheet (see p. 191, below). Nathan saw an independent manuscript, and because his song sheet (and the *Examiner* as well) includes the revisions made in the latest extant manuscript, Nathan's copy was set down later. Probably Hunt and Nathan received fair copies with slight changes. The poem's final form is that of *Poems* (1816). Byron revised the poem in the proofs of that work, and the final version differs from that given in the song sheet and the *Examiner*.

The thirty Hebrew Melodies are far from the 'one or two' poems
Isaac Nathan originally requested. Byron was lavish in his gifts. We
shall see, however, that his unrestricted giving cut two ways. While
at Seaham Byron received a request for poetical contributions from
Richard Alfred Davenport, the editor of the *Poetical Register*. Davenport
had learned of Byron's promise to provide James Hogg, the Ettrick
Shepherd, with several poems to be used in Hogg's *Poetic Mirror*
(1816); he therefore hoped that Byron would provide him with
poems for the ninth volume of the *Poetical Register* to be published
during the coming spring, or for a tenth volume then in the
planning stage. Addressing his letter from 'Seaham – Stockton on
Tees', Byron answered Davenport on 7 February 1815:

> I am not at this moment in possession of any thing worth
> insertion or perusal unless some short things meant to be songs
> (written for a set of Hebrew Melodies) should be thought
> better of than they deserve. – To three or four of these – yet
> unpublished – you shall be very welcome – but if they
> disappoint yourself and your readers – recollect that I hinted
> as much before hand – and do not hesitate to omit any one or
> all that may appear faulty or unsuitable.[50]

But Byron did not send any poems for Davenport's readers. His
work does not appear in the first eight volumes of the *Poetical
Register* (1802–14). The ninth and tenth volumes were never published.

Having promised to send some poems to Davenport, on 2 March
1815 Byron sent one to Moore instead (III, 181):

> I feel merry enough to send you a sad song. You once asked
> me for some words which you would set. Now you may set or
> not, as you like. . . .

[50] T. L. Ashton, 'Hogg to Byron to Davenport: An Unpublished Byron
Letter', in *BNYPL*, 1967, LXXI, 40–1. Davenport tried again in 1816, and Byron
wrote to him on 6 March 1816: 'I feel truly sorry for any disappointment or delay
that may have been occassioned [*sic*] by the circumstances you mention – & only
fear that you overrate the importance of any communication [*sic*] I could have
made or can make. – When you wrote to me last year – the unpublished songs of
the H. Melodies – were much at your service – had your work been sent forth at
that time – but in the interim the Musical publishers printed the words – & M^r.
Murray inserted them in his collection – & I could only regret that they had not
first appeared in your volumes. –' Bound in Huntington Library AC 90327,
Vol. I.

His next letter to Moore, written on 8 March, explained (III, 183):

> An event — the death of poor Dorset — and the recollection of
> what I once felt, and ought to have felt now, but could not —
> set me pondering, and finally into the train of thought which
> you have in your hands. I am very glad you like them, for I
> flatter myself they will pass as an imitation of your style. I
> wrote them with a view to your setting them, and as a present to
> Power, if he would accept the words, and you did not think your-
> self degraded, for once in a way, by marrying them to music.

But why, one asks, had he not sent the very beautiful 'There's not a
joy the world can give like that it takes away' to Isaac Nathan?

While separated from Nathan at Seaham, Byron allowed his
disapproving friends to come temporarily between poet and composer. Tom Moore had been particularly irritated by Byron's
collaboration with Nathan and feared Byron's entry into the world of
song. The poem on Dorset's death had been a gift designed to quell
Moore's resentment. Moore tells us that he had 'taken the liberty of
laughing a little at the manner in which some of his Hebrew Melodies
had been set to music'.[51] On 22 February Byron attempted to shrug
off this criticism with a remark: 'Curse the Melodies and the Tribes to
boot' (III, 180). On March 8 he wrote again: 'Sun-burn Nathan! —
why do you always twit me with his vile Ebrew nasalities?' (III,
184). Unless Moore actually had the opportunity to see Nathan's
unpublished settings, he could not have criticized the composer's
work at this early date. He had been disturbed by Byron's *Bride of
Abydos* (1814) appearing in advance of the *Lalla Rookh* (1817) he had
conceived of in 1813; now Byron was spoiling the market for
another of Moore's unfinished products — the *Sacred Songs* he had first
thought of in 1812. 'I should be very glad to undertake with
Stevenson', he wrote to Power in that year, 'a series of *Sacred Songs*.'[52]
The work was to be dedicated to his friend, Edward Dalton, to whom
he wrote on 25 January 1814: 'My appearance as a "sweet singer of
Israel" is near at hand. ...'[53] Moore learned of the Hebrew Melodies
late in 1814; coming to London at that time, he was admitted into
Kinnaird's dinner circle. On 12 November 1814 (while Byron was
completing his first visit to Seaham), Moore wrote to Power: 'My

---

[51] *Works*, III, 150n.

[52] June 1812. Thomas Moore, *Letters*, ed. by Wilfred S. Dowden, 2 vols
(Oxford: Clarendon Press, 1964), I, 201.

[53] *Ibid.*, I, 297. Cf. II Samuel 23:1.

decided wish is to be let off all tasks but the Sacred Melodies.' In January of 1815, he again wrote to Power: 'I intend to . . . send you another Sacred Melody. I think I can promise to make up twelve for you before the end of March. . . . You may depend upon my dispatching them as quick as possible.'[54] But it was not until June 1816, one year after the publication of Byron's *Hebrew Melodies*, that Moore's *Sacred Songs* appeared.

Among Byron's circle Moore was not alone in resenting Isaac Nathan. Byron's publisher, John Murray, had hoped 'to have' and to publish the small poems that Byron was writing in 1814. The poems were to help fill the fourth volume of Murray's projected edition of Byron's *Collected Works*. In an undated letter to Byron, Murray explained that this volume would contain all of the poet's shorter lyrics: 'I am advancing in the Fourth volume of the Works, which will consist of: "Ode to Buonaparte," "Poems at end of Childe Harold," "Poems at end of Corsair," "Death of Sir P. Parker," and anything unpublished.'[55] Murray's letter must have been written after 6 October, and 'anything unpublished' must include a reference to the Hebrew Melodies. Soon Murray made a specific request for the poems. Byron answered from Halnaby on 6 January 1815: 'Mr. Kinnaird will, I dare say, have the goodness to furnish copies of the Melodies, if you state my wish upon the subject. You may have them, if you think them worth inserting' (III, 165–6). Having granted his approval, Byron wrote to secure Nathan's:

January, 1815

Dear Nathan, – Murray being about to publish a complete edition of my *poetical effusions* has a wish to include the stanzas of the *Hebrew Melodies*. Will you allow him that privilege without considering it an infringement on your copyright? I certainly wish to oblige the gentleman; but you know, Nathan, it is against all good fashion to give and take back. I therefore cannot grant what is not at my disposal: let me hear from you on the subject.

Dear Nathan, yours truly,
Byron.[56]

[54] *Ibid.*, I, 339, 350. Byron may have been aware of Moore's forthcoming work. He had met the Daltons in July of 1813.

[55] Smiles, I, 232.

[56] *L & J*, III, 167–8. It should be noted that Nathan's *Fugitive Pieces* (p. 145) is the source of this letter.

Byron, thinking that there would be no trouble in securing Nathan's approval, had granted Murray permission to copy the poems. But Nathan balked. On 26 January Byron wrote to Hobhouse: '"The Melodies," – damn the melodies, I have other tunes – or rather tones – to think of; but Murray *can't* have them, or *shan't*, or I shall have Kin^d. and Braham upon me.'[57] It is possible that Nathan viewed the idea as a plan to offer up Byron's words to music publishers who would pirate them before he had completed his own settings. Though Nathan set about using his influence with Braham and Kinnaird, Murray, who had Hobhouse on his side, won the day. He was allowed to copy the poems and to publish them, both as a part of Byron's *Collected Works* and in a separate edition. Four clerk's copies survive today, two of which are endorsed: 'Copied from Manuscript 8 Feb. 1815 Ch[arles] H[anson].' Murray's ledger, in which copyright charges are regularly recorded, makes no mention of any payments to Nathan. Probably Murray's 'wish' was granted without charge. The fight did not leave Murray and Nathan the best of friends, and the publisher did not hide his feelings from Byron when he wrote on 17 February:

> I am delaying the publication of our edition in four volumes only until you find a leisure moment to strike off the dedication to your friend Mr. Hobhouse, who still thinks that it is not precisely the same thing to have music made to one's poems, and to write poetry for music; and I advise you most con- scientiously to abide by the determination of Mr. Hobhouse's good sense.[58]

Byron, however, did not prevent Nathan from going ahead with his publication, though Moore, Murray, and Hobhouse would have been pleased had he done so.

As we have seen, Byron finished the last of the poems while at Seaham. With that work behind him, he and Annabella departed for London on 9 March. By May the affair was one of the past, as Kinnaird noticed in a letter to Hobhouse:

> I write this to anticipate your gratulatory epistle on my

---

[57] Hobhouse proofs (proof sheets of an edition of Byron's letters by Lady Dorchester set up in type but never published). British Museum, c.131.k, f. 51.
[58] Smiles, I, 351.

elevation into the Committee of Management of a *real play-house*. . . . What will you say to me for drawing our friend Byron into the same situation? Scarcely out of his Hebrew scraps e're I get well into this – well Sir, the Lord is delighted with his office, & will, I think, fill it nobly. . . . Lady Byron is in the family way.[59]

While Byron and Kinnaird occupied themselves with meetings of the Sub-Committee of Management of Drury Lane, the Hebrew Melodies were left to the charge of Isaac Nathan.

Having completed the arrangements of twelve poems, Nathan proceeded with the publication of the First Number of *A Selection of Hebrew Melodies*. The architect Edward Blore (1787–1879) was commissioned to design an ornamental title page and an elaborately ornamented dedication to the Princess Charlotte. Blore was making drawings for John Britton's English Cathedrals series and in 1816 was commissioned by Scott to rebuild Abbotsford as a Gothic house. Blore's designs for Nathan were engraved by William Lowry. Next Nathan interested his friend Robert Harding Evans of *The Times* in the work. Evans prepared a long and learned 'Preliminary Discourse' that surveys the references to music in the Bible and asserts the sublimity of biblical music. Quoting from the works of Bishop Lowth, Dr Burney, Quintilian, and Lady Mary Wortley Montagu, he assured the antiquity-minded public of the authenticity of Nathan's melodies:

That considerable doubts may be at first entertained with respect to their [Nathan's melodies'] origin, seems very possible . . . It is true, that a great many ages have passed away since the dispersion of the Jews. . . . But Dr. Burney relates a very remarkable fact, which proves, that the real character of the ancient Hebrew music is preserved in the East to this day. . . . The Persians have derived their manner of singing 'from the ancient Oriental Jews,' and if such manner accords with that of the Germans, the latter must possess the true harmony of their ancestors; and hence it will follow that if you have selected your Melodies, as I understand is the fact, from a variety of chaunts which were sung to you by German

[59] 15 May 1815. British Museum, Add. MS. 47224, f. 3.

Jews, those Melodies are justly entitled to the originality they claim. . . .[60]

Evans' work was not, however, to serve as a preface to the First Number of *A Selection of Hebrew Melodies*. Probably it had Byron's approval, but Nathan's claim that his melodies antedated the destruction of the temple did not sit well with Douglas Kinnaird.[61] Nor had Nathan's finished products been the musical triumphs they were meant to be; difficulty in arranging the tunes had lent a forced quality to the settings. Kinnaird, whose supervisory eye had remained on the project, insisted that a brief preface of his own composition replace Evans' work. That preface acknowledges a corrupt musical tradition that accounts for the difficulty in arranging the songs and assures that credit shall go where credit is due: 'Of the Poetry it is necessary to speak, in order thus publicly to acknowledge the kindness with which Lord Byron has condescended to furnish the most valuable part of the Work.'

Kinnaird's preface, signed by Braham and Nathan, is dated, 'April, 1815'. In that month the First Number of *A Selection of Hebrew Melodies* was issued from the press of 'C. Richards, Printer, 18, Warwick Street, Golden Square'. The work was advertised for the first time in the *Morning Chronicle* of 6 April 1815,[62] and on Sunday, 23 April, Leigh Hunt printed 'Oh! snatched away in beauty's bloom' in the *Examiner*, using Nathan's edition as copy. In the same month 'It is the Hour', 'The Wild Gazelle', and 'Oh! snatched away in beauty's bloom' were reprinted in the *Theatrical Inquisitor* (1815, VI, 299–300). Nathan entered the volume at Stationers' Hall on 15 May 1815.[63]

---

[60] Robert Harding Evans, *An Essay on the Music of the Hebrews, Originally Intended as a Preliminary Discourse to the Hebrew Melodies, Published by Messrs. Braham and Nathan* (London: John Booth, 1816), pp. 42–6. A bibliographical description is given below, p. 222. Evans' songs arranged and published as song sheets by Nathan are 'The Invitation', 'O, Come, Maria', and 'The Sorrows of Absence'.

[61] Kinnaird seems to have sensed the sceptical remarks Nathan's claims generated. A reviewer in the *Gentleman's Magazine* quoted Leopold Kalkbrenner's *Histoire de la Musique* (I, 34): 'Les Juifs Espagnols lisent et chantent leur Pseaumes bien différement que les Juifs Hollandais; les Juifs Romaines autrement que les Juifs de la Prusse et de la Hesse, et tous croient chanter comme on chantait dans le temple de Jerusalem' (1815, LXXXV:i, 539).

[62] Nathan also advertised the volume in the *Courier* of 27 May 1815 and 8 June 1815. C. Richards, in 1817, was to print Keats's first volume of *Poems*.

[63] Stationers' Register, 22 September 1813–15 January 1816, f. 296.

The large folio contains, as readers who were willing to pay a guinea for the work discovered, the following twelve poems:

> She Walks in Beauty
> The harp the monarch minstrel swept
> If that High World
> The Wild Gazelle
> Oh! Weep for Those
> On Jordan's Banks
> Jephtha's Daughter
> Oh! snatched away in beauty's bloom
> My Soul is Dark
> I Saw Thee Weep
> Thy Days are Done
> It is the Hour

Because Nathan's volume had been made to resemble Thomson's work, these poems were printed as set to music and individually as well. (Nathan took the wording of his title from Power's volumes.) The music in the First Number was printed from engraved plates, and Byron's lyrics were engraved on the plates. In addition to this engraved text, a letterpress text of the poems was provided on individual leaves inserted immediately after the respective accompaniments. (The folio is made up of single disjunct leaves.) These two texts do not agree on substantives in two instances and differ widely with respect to accidentals. In no copies of the First Number have the variant readings been corrected by altering either text, and no manuscript evidence bears on this point. But a study of the Second Number, where manuscript evidence is abundant, supports the authority of the letterpress text. It seems likely that the engraver for the First Number worked from the letterpress text, which he punctuated haphazardly, shunning the use of the apostrophe. Furthermore, the fact that the closing stanzas of the longer lyrics were not set to music suggests priority of the letterpress text. Probably the variation in the texts is the result of the engraver's indifference. In later editions of Nathan's *Selection*, engraver worked from engraved copy and compositor from letterpress copy, maintaining the discrepancies in punctuation and readings and adding new errors.

In May, approximately a month after the publication of the First

Number of *A Selection of Hebrew Melodies*, John Murray published a demi-octavo volume bearing the misleading title:

Hebrew Melodies[64]

Kinnaird had granted his wish; 'the most valuable part' of Nathan's volume, the 'songs from the Hebrew Melodies', was now published separately at the greatly reduced price of 4s. 6d. *Hebrew Melodies* was printed by Thomas Davison of Lombard Street. Davison was regularly employed by Murray and had printed Murray's editions of Byron's earlier works.[65] A small advertisement following the title page makes clear the order of publication and Byron's involvement in such a project:

> The subsequent poems were written at the request of the author's friend, the Hon. D. Kinnaird, for a Selection of Hebrew Melodies, and have been published, with the music, arranged, by Mr. Braham and Mr. Nathan.

By 23 May 1815, advance copies of Murray's newly bound edition had been delivered to the Byrons. On that day Lady Byron inscribed several copies to her friends and advisers. Dr J. R. Fenwick, the Durham physician who had seen Annabella through an attack of scarlet fever in 1797 and had since become one of her most trusted advisers and a close friend of the Milbankes, received a copy inscribed: 'Dr. Fenwick – With Lord & Lady Byron's kindest regards – May 23, 1815.'[66] On the same day Annabella inscribed a copy to Mr William Hoar of Durham.[67] Hoar, Sir Ralph Milbanke's financial adviser, had drawn up Annabella's marriage settlement. To the famous actress Sarah Kemble Siddons, another acquaintance, went a copy inscribed: 'Lady Byron requests Mrs. Siddons' accept-

---

[64] After describing this edition in his *Bibliography of the Writings in Verse and Prose of George Gordon Noel, Baron Byron* (2 vols [London: Printed for private circulation, 1933]), Thomas J. Wise remarks: 'In the same year the *Hebrew Melodies* were republished with music by Isaac Nathan.' This is incorrect and was first pointed out to be so by John Carter in his review of Wise's work ('Notes on the Bibliography of Byron', *TLS*, 27 April 1933 and 4 May 1933). The error remains in Dawson's reprint of Wise's *Bibliography* published in 1963.

[65] Davison probably took an interest in the Hebrew Melodies. Timperley notes of Davison: 'In company, the musical sweetness of a voice rarely equalled for compass and expression, imparted a charm to his companionship and made him everywhere welcome' (*A Dictionary of Printers and Printing* [London, 1839], p. 919).

[66] This copy is now in the Henry E. Huntington Library. Acc. No. 90129.

[67] The inscribed title page is in the Pforzheimer Library.

ance of the "Hebrew Melodies" with her own very sincere & affectionate remembrance. May. 28. 1815,' and it was probably at this time that Annabella mustered the sentiments necessary to inscribe a copy of the work 'To Mrs. Clermont – With the grateful remembrance of her affectionate friend – A[nnabella] N[oel] Byron'.[68] After the Byrons had received their advance copies, Murray entered the work at Stationers' Hall on 9 June.[69]

Murray's *Hebrew Melodies* contains twenty-five poems published without music. The first twelve are those of Nathan's First Number and the order of their appearance in that work is preserved. To these twelve poems Murray added another twelve Hebrew Melodies published for the first time:

> Song of Saul before his Last Battle
> Saul
> 'All is Vanity, Saith the Preacher'
> When coldness wraps this suffering clay
> Vision of Belshazzar
> Sun of the Sleepless!
> Were my bosom as false as thou deem'st it to be
> Herod's Lament for Mariamne
> On the Day of the Destruction of Jerusalem by Titus
> By the Rivers of Babylon We Sat Down and Wept
> The Destruction of Semnacherib
> From Job

The twenty-fifth and final poem published in the volume is Byron's 'On the Death of Sir Peter Parker', which is distinguished from the Hebrew Melodies by a rule in the table of contents and a double rule in the text.

The fact that the order of the first twelve poems in *Hebrew Melodies* repeats that of Nathan's First Number, the earliest edition for twelve of the poems, would seem to indicate that the First Number was used as copy for Murray's edition. In only one instance do the letterpress text of the First Number and the text for the first twelve poems in *Hebrew Melodies* disagree on a substantive matter, and this variant (see this edition, p. 148) reading probably represents a change in the

[68] Houghton Library, EC8. Sil 35. Zz814t and British Museum, Ashley 5454*. The Milbankes were authorized to use the name of Noel on 20 May 1815, following the death of Lord Wentworth on 17 April.

[69] Stationers' Register, 22 September 1813–15 January 1816, f. 336; Murray Ledger, Vol. B, f. 127.

proofs of *Hebrew Melodies* made by Byron himself.[70] The accidentals used in the First Number and in *Hebrew Melodies* rarely agree, but this difference results from Murray's compositor having followed house style in providing alternatives for the dashes that Byron used as a universal punctuation mark, and which were followed in the First Number. With the exception of the single variant and the difference in accidentals, the letterpress text of the First Number and the text of the first twelve poems in *Hebrew Melodies* agree, and this agreement is the strongest argument for the thesis that the First Number served as copy for the first twelve poems of *Hebrew Melodies*. It seems doubtful that any two compositors working from Byron's scrawled holographs could have produced such agreement.

Murray used Lady Byron's fair copies, corrected by Byron, to print the second twelve poems in *Hebrew Melodies*, and his edition is thus the first edition of *those* poems. Unless we postulate that Lady Byron also made fair copies (which have since disappeared) of the first twelve poems and that these were then given to Murray,[71] the simplest way to account for the copy of Murray's *Hebrew Melodies* is that the letterpress text of Nathan's First Number served as copy for the first twelve poems while the manuscripts in Lady Byron's hand served as copy for the remainder. As we have seen, Nathan's edition was the earliest to appear; as we shall see, Nathan, in turn, used the text of eleven of the second twelve poems in Murray's edition as the copy for his Second Number, an edition published after Murray's *Hebrew Melodies*. In this way two editions of twenty-four poems were published, one in two volumes called numbers (Nathan's) and the other in one volume (Murray's). Both the First Number of Nathan's *Selection* and the second part of Murray's *Hebrew Melodies* are first editions.

In June 1815 the first London edition of Byron's *Collected Works* was published. In the fourth volume devoted to Byron's miscel-

---

[70] That Byron worked on the proofs of *Hebrew Melodies* seems clear, for the text of the second twelve poems printed therein differs at points from the fair copies that it was set from. Byron's revision is discussed below, p. 110.

[71] As no copies in Lady Byron's hand of the poems in the First Number are extant, it appears unlikely that such copies were ever made. Had they been prepared it seems likely that Murray would have retained them, for he did retain Lady Byron's fair copies of the second twelve poems in *Hebrew Melodies*. We know that Charles Hanson made copies for Murray of two of the poems in the First Number, but those copies are so poor that they could not have been used. Nathan's resentment of Murray's edition makes his co-operation with Murray doubtful and Murray's reliance on the First Number for copy more likely.

laneous poems, *Hebrew Melodies* was reprinted. A reviewer in the British *Critic* advised the public on the order of appearance:

> These poems were written . . . for a selection of Hebrew Melodies, which were published accordingly, with the music arranged to them by Messrs Braham and Nathan. In this form they first appeared, and they have been subsequently published both separately and at the conclusion of the last collective edition of the noble Lord's works.[72]

Murray had wanted the poems for his four-volume, small-octavo collected edition from the start, but that edition was not the only collected edition published by Murray in 1815. He had also brought out subsequent editions of Byron's early poems (*Childe Harold*, *The Corsair*, etc.) in uniform size, the same size as that of his edition of *Hebrew Melodies*, and he took occasion to append four leaves to *Hebrew Melodies*, listing titles and half-titles. As a result, a purchaser could have the previously published works and *Hebrew Melodies* in uniform size bound together as the *Collected Works* in two volumes, 1815. Thus *Hebrew Melodies* included in the two-volume collected edition is a new issue, not a new edition.[73] It is identical in text with *Hebrew Melodies*, and *Hebrew Melodies* was also the source of text for the four-volume collected edition. These early collected editions were followed, in Byron's lifetime, by at least twenty collected editions.[74]

[72] 1815, 2nd ser., III, 603.

[73] Unfortunately T. J. Wise has used the term 'issue' to distinguish copies of *Hebrew Melodies* in which the advertisement on E4 has been altered while the work was in the press. There are two issues of *Hebrew Melodies*, but these should not be confused with the two states which characterize one issue. Discussing the vexing term issue in his *Principles of Bibliographical Description*, Bowers does not refer to a situation which parallels that considered here. But if we adhere to the principle that alterations to produce 'ideal copy' constitute state, *Hebrew Melodies* in the two-volume collected edition must be considered an issue, particularly because the leaves of titles are a proper part of the text and because the general titles were after a time altered to indicate a specific order of contents (see p. 213, below).

[74] Only the collected editions issued by Murray in 1815 have been described in the Calendar. However, every collected edition issued by Murray from 1815 to 1832 has been collated. The following conservative list of collected editions published in Byron's lifetime is based on *CBEL*; *Poetry*, VII; and Elkin Mathews, *Byron & Byroniana: A Catalogue of Books* (London, 1930): 2vi815; 4vi815 (5vi817, 6vi818, 7vi819, 8vi820); 3vN.Y.1815; 3vPhila.1816; 1vN.Y.1817 (Phila., Bost., Balt.); 6vParis1818; 6vZwickau1818–19; 13vLeipzic1818–22; 3vi819; 6vParis1819; 7vBrussels1819; 4vN.Y.1820; 5vi821; 5vParis1821; 16vParis1822–24; 4vi823 (5,6,7vi824–25); 12vParis1822–24 (with the added notices of the life by Sir Cosmo Gordon).

On 20 June 1815, Byron received a visit from George Ticknor, a young American lawyer with literary inclinations, who was to become the first influential professor of modern literary studies at Harvard. Ticknor presented Byron with a two-volume edition of his *Poetical Works* published by Moses Thomas at Philadelphia in 1813. That publication attests to Byron's popularity in America, and in the year of Ticknor's visit, editions of the Hebrew Melodies were published in New York by T. and J. Swords, and by Longworth; in Boston by the firm of Thomas Wells and John Eliot; and in Philadelphia by James Parke. These unauthorized editions reprint Murray's *Hebrew Melodies*, with the exception of Longworth's, which was in fact reprinted from the first New York edition. Nathan's *A Selection of Hebrew Melodies* also crossed the Atlantic, for song sheets reprinting individual melodies from Nathan's work were soon on sale in New York.[75]

The publication of pirated editions of the Hebrew Melodies in England was limited. *Don Juan* and *The Vision of Judgment*, the bane of respectable publishers, were pearls cast to the radicals. Byron's pious poems were not. Of London's radical publishers, only William Dugdale seems to have published editions of the Hebrew Melodies. Between 1822 and 1825 Dugdale published no fewer than fifteen editions of various poems by Byron. Among these works were two editions of *Hebrew Melodies*, the first published in 1823, the second (reprinted from the first) in 1825. Murray's collected edition of 1821, collation indicates, was the source of Dugdale's edition of 1823.

Turning back to 1816, we need now to discuss the Second Number of Nathan's *A Selection of Hebrew Melodies*, which completes Nathan's two-number edition of twenty-four poems. Having completed the settings of the remaining melodies, Nathan offered his Second Number to the public in April 1816. An advertisement in the *Courier* of 18 April tells us that the work was 'published this day', and it was promptly reviewed in the April issue of the *Critical Review* (5th ser., III, 357–66). On 4 November, Nathan entered the work at Stationers' Hall.[76] The Second Number is similar in appearance to the First, though its title page bears a vignette depicting the monarch minstrel at his harp receiving inspiration from a cherub floating

---

[75] A song sheet of 'Jephtha's Daughter from the Hebrew Melodies by Braham & Nathan' was published by Firth and Hall of New York (Library of Congress, M 1. A 13, f. B).

[76] Stationers' Register, 15 January 1816–27 June 1817, f. 278.

about his crown. The layout was designed to facilitate binding up with the First Number, and the paging is continuous.[77]

Nathan's Second Number, as stated above, contains twelve Hebrew Melodies. The contents are as follows:

> Song of Saul Before His Last Battle
> By the Rivers of Babylon We Sat Down and Wept
> Vision of Belshazzar
> Herod's Lament for Mariamne
> Were my bosom as false as thou deem'st it to be
> The Destruction of Semnacherib
> Saul
> When coldness wraps this suffering clay
> 'All is Vanity, saith the Preacher'
> On the Day of the Destruction of Jerusalem by Titus
> Francisca
> Sun of the Sleepless!

The poems are not given in the same order as those in *Hebrew Melodies*, and more important, Nathan has not included 'From Job'. Instead, he includes 'Francisca', which had not been published in 1815. Why he did not include the last poem in *Hebrew Melodies* in his Second Number and why he added 'Francisca' are not known. It may be that Nathan had difficulty in setting 'From Job' to music, or it may be that he wished to retain a clearly biblical lyric for a projected Third Number. Whatever the reason, by including 'Francisca' in his Second Number, Nathan extended the canon of Hebrew Melodies to twenty-five in 1816.

Despite the omission of 'From Job', the text of the Second Number appears to derive from *Hebrew Melodies*. The work of the same printing house, Nathan's First Number and Second Number differ in their choice of accidentals, but the Second Number duplicates the pointing of *Hebrew Melodies*. Further evidence is to be found in the titles of the poems. With two exceptions, the titles of the poems published in the Second Number have their source in the respective poems' first lines. On the five occasions that this results in a title which differs

[77] Nathan's Second Number did not appear alone. It was published jointly with a reprint of his First Number. The First Number of 1816 is a page-for-page reprint of the First Number of 1815; the engraved text is actually the text of 1815, for the plates used to print the music of the earlier number were used again. However, the pointing of the letterpress text of the reprint has been altered (by reducing the use of the dash) to bring the text into conformity with the Second Number.

from that employed in *Hebrew Melodies*, the title used in *Hebrew Melodies* is given immediately beneath the first-line title in the Second Number. Finally, except for several misprints, the letterpress text of the Second Number agrees with that of *Hebrew Melodies*.[78] But if *Hebrew Melodies* is the source of eleven poems for Nathan's Second Number, we must remember that *Hebrew Melodies* was derived in part from Nathan's First Number. Following the publication of Nathan's First Number, divided authority prevailed.

Eight days after the publication of Nathan's Second Number, Byron left England for good. He had nothing more to do with the Hebrew Melodies. Those poems had passed from his hands; now literary critics and the public took them up. 'Here certainly his lordship has failed,' wrote Josiah Conder in the *Eclectic Review*. The failure was one of faith:

> One is at a loss to imagine how an admirer of the poetical beauties only, of the Old Testament writings, could sit down to execute such a travestie of their genuine character. . . . In order to sweep the harp of David, a man needs be not only preëminently a poet, but emphatically a Christian. . . . It ought to excite no surprise that the hand of Genius itself should become withered by an unhallowed attempt to touch the Ark.[79]

The *Christian Observer* also took up the cudgel against the infidel, calling the volume 'a slight work' that 'might rather seem the fruit of a single day of leisure'.[80] The most hostile Defenders of the Faith were 'Rivington's Reviewing Parsons' of the *British Critic*. In an

---

[78] The engraved text of the Second Number differs from the letterpress text of the Second Number in thirteen instances. Five of these differences are clearly errors; the remaining eight are variants. In five of these eight variants, the letterpress text agrees with the extant manuscripts. In two instances, the engraved text agrees with the manuscripts, and for one of these an erratum given below the index of the Second Number corrects the letterpress text. Carelessness accounts for most of the variance in the engraved text and for the occasional misprint in the letterpress text. It is likely that the letterpress text was the source of the engraved text as appears to have been the case with the First Number (see p. 37, above).

[79] 1815, 2nd ser., IV, 94–6. Portions of this review were published in the *Analectic Magazine*, 1815, VI, 292–4.

[80] 1815, XIV, 542–9.

offensive sermon peppered with anti-Semitism they took Byron to task for aligning himself with the Jews:

> Lord Byron has accepted the proffered chaplet of his Jewish brethren, and may now be considered as poet laureate to the synagogue. . . . Let not a peer of the realm, who is *ex professo*, at least, a Christian, enter into so close a literary union with these worthy gentlemen [Braham and Nathan] as to expose himself to the unpleasant dilemma of being supposed either to entertain an attachment to the Jewish cause, which in him would at best be ridiculous, or to feign that affection towards a sacred object, to which his heart is in reality a stranger. . . . Let the noble Lord maintain his station upon Turkish ground, the hill of Zion alone is forbidden ground![81]

Palestine belonged to Reginald Heber (later Bishop Heber), whose Oxford Prize Poem of that name had been published in 1807. Those critics who spared the Jews reserved their scorn for these 'wretched specimens' of Byron's muse. 'The name of Byron is deservedly high in public estimation,' wrote a reviewer in the *Theatrical Inquisitor*. 'We cannot lightly forgive him when he writes to disgrace it.'[82] The *Gentleman's Magazine*, however, remained staunch in its support: 'To say that these "Melodies" are Lord Byron's is to pronounce them elegant.'[83] The *Ladies' Monthly Museum* advised readers of the gentle sex that 'the volume may be opened', for 'a softer and more amiable feeling [than that displayed in the Turkish tales], for the most part, pervades the work'.[84] The poems no doubt revealed the influence of Byron's marriage. Annabella had reformed the infidel, and the Hebrew Melodies were what E. H. Coleridge styled 'the first-fruits of a seemlier muse'.[85] The work gained the favour of Francis Jeffrey as well. In the *Edinburgh Review*, Jeffrey wrote that though 'obviously inferior' to *Childe Harold*, 'the Hebrew Melodies especially display a skill in versification, and a mastery in diction, which would have

---

[81] 1815, 2nd ser., III, 602–11.

[82] 1815, VI, 377–8; and 1816, VIII, 442–4.

[83] 1815, LXXXV:ii, 141. 'I Saw Thee Weep' was reprinted in 1815, LXXXV:i, 450.

[84] 1815, 3rd ser., II, 169–72. Other reviews not cited are to be found in *Augustine Review*, 1815, I, 209–15; *European Magazine & London Review*, 1815, LXVIII, 37; *New Universal Magazine*, 1815, III, 37–8; *Critical Review*, 1815, 5th ser., II, 166–71, and 1816, 5th ser., III, 357–66; *British Review*, 1815, VI, 200–8, by W. Roberts; *British Lady's Magazine*, 1815, I, 358–60.

[85] *Poetry*, III, p. 375.

raised an inferior artist to the very summit of distinction.'[86] To Moore, Jeffrey wrote:

> I have just got a set of Lord Byron's works, and read his Hebrew Melodies for the first time. There is rather a monotony in the subjects, but a sweetness of versification to which I know but one parallel, and a depth and force of feeling which, though indicated only by short sobs and glances, is here as marked and peculiar as in his greater pieces.[87]

Moore reported Jeffrey's sentiments to Byron, who wrote in reply on 4 November 1815: 'It is very kind in Jeffrey to like the Hebrew Melodies. Some of the fellows here preferred Sternhold and Hopkins, and said so; – "the fiend receive their souls therefor!"' (III, 244–5).

Whatever the opinions of reviewers, Byron's friends were dead set against the work. The unkindest cut of all came from Francis Hodgson, one of the poet's Cambridge associates. Shocked by the scepticism of the second canto of Childe Harold, Hodgson had tried to convert Byron in 1811. Now, writing in the Monthly Review, Hodgson expressed his dismay at finding that 'the greater number' of the Hebrew Melodies had 'no connection' with religion. Those few that did were not up to the standard propounded by Bishop Lowth:

> In fact, those specimens in this little volume which, on account of scriptural subjects or allusions, seem to possess a Hebrew character, are tame and uninteresting, because we insensibly compare them with originals of transcendent sublimity . . . while those which are on miscellaneous subjects disappoint us by their generality.[88]

Hodgson concluded that 'the publication is not calculated to advance his Lordship's high poetic fame'. Caroline Lamb was happy to coincide in this conclusion. The Hebrew Melodies were not at all to her taste:

> 'She walks in beauty like the night' for example – if Mr. Twiss had written it how we should have laughed! Now we can only weep to see how little just judgment there is on earth, for I

[86] 1816, XXVII, 291.

[87] 11 June 1815, L & J, III, 294–5n. This shows how early copies of the Collected Works were available.

[88] 1815, LXXVIII, 41–7. The British Critic echoed Hodgson's sentiments: 'There is nothing beyond the titles and the occasional introduction of a name, to support the designation of Hebrew.' Hodgson expanded upon his views in a critique written a year later published in James T. Hodgson's Memoir of the Rev. Francis Hodgson (London: Macmillan, 1878), II, 1–6.

make no doubt the name of Byron will give even these lines a grace. I who read his loftier lay with transport will not admire his flaws and nonsense. You will say it is only a song, yet a song should have sense.[89]

Lady Caroline's 'just judgment' was mostly pique. Caroline was not the 'she' of Byron's 'She Walks in Beauty', and it was probably this 'sense' that she objected to in Byron's lyric.

The most vicious remarks on the Hebrew Melodies came from another of Byron's friends, Tom Moore. Jeffrey had hinted that the poems had reminded him of Moore's work, and the British Critic made the source of Moore's antagonism explicit: 'These songs . . . stand a fair chance of rivalling in popularity the compositions of his friend Moore, of which indeed they often remind us.' Moore expressed his resentment in a series of letters to his music publisher, James Power. 'It is very amusing to think of Byron becoming a "sweet singer of Israel",' wrote Moore, ironically using the words he had once applied to himself, 'but you will find but little of the poetry actually his.'[90] To Moore most of the words seemed very like his own. Therefore Nathan was the real villain:

How Lord Byron must curse that fellow Nathan, who is puffing off his Jewish wares in all sorts of quackish ways. He had a Puff about them the other night directly under the Lottery Squibs, in the small type part of the Courier. Talking of the Jew − I have the second verse of 'Fall'n is thy throne O Israel!' to send you. . . . I flatter myself it is both words and music, a very tolerable hit. Was there ever any thing so bad as the Hebrew Melodies? Some of the words are of course good, tho' not so good as might have been expected − but the Music! 'Oh Lord God of Israel!' what stuff it is! and the price! If the Angel in the title page had four Crowns instead of one and the odd shilling tucked under his wing, it would be four times more emblematical than it is.[91]

[89] Caroline Lamb to Murray, indicated in the Murray MS. as received 19 August 1814 [15?], quoted in Peter Quennell and George Paston [E. M. Symonds] (eds), *To Lord Byron* (London: Murray, 1939), p. 66. Byron had received a copy of Horace Twiss's *Scotch Melodies*, see p. 4, above.

[90] *Notes from the Letters of Thomas Moore to His Music Publisher, James Power*, ed. by Thomas Crofton Croker (New York: J. S. Redfield, 1853), p. 46.

[91] *Ibid.*, pp. 42–3. Nathan's work was priced at £1.1s. hence the pun. The *Irish Melodies* cost the public only 15s. a number, but Power sold Moore's *Sacred Songs* at Nathan's price.

Nathan had won a portion of Byron's patronage, and Moore resented Byron's gifts. Moore's unfinished *Sacred Songs* would no longer take the public by surprise. Byron, writing on 7 July 1815, refused to take his Irish friend's anger seriously: 'La! Moore – how you blasphemes about "Parnassus" and "Moses!"' (III, 209).

Moore was not the sole member of the national-melodies establishment to disapprove of the Hebrew Melodies. His sentiments were echoed by George Thomson:

> My daughter has played and sung all the Hebrew melodies to
> me more than once. I think very little of the music. With the
> exception of one or two melodies they do not appear to me at
> all worthy of Byron's verses. To some of the melodies, indeed,
> it is scarcely practicable to sing the words with any effect
> whatever. The latter do not seem to have the least affinity with
> the former, and their union confounds measure, rhythm, sense,
> and everything belonging to a good song. In short, Jew and
> Christian could not possibly agree worse.[92]

Thomson had been the man with melodies worthy of Byron's verses, but Byron had rejected all his offers. To the veteran publisher the poet's choice of a Jewish amateur rankled. His carping about the music did not prevent his dashing off a new letter to 'the most renowned living poet whom England can boast of':

> I would not, perhaps, have mustered courage enough to take
> the liberty of addressing your Lordship again on the subject of
> song, but for the recent proofs you have given to the world
> how pre-eminently you succeed in that species of poetry, the
> Hebrew songs being diamonds of the first water, of which I
> have not words to express my admiration. Let me earnestly
> beseech your Lordship to think of a few stanzas for the three
> Welsh melodies which I venture to enclose . . .[93]

Thomson was not destined to gain Byron's collaboration. It was, as he knew, a collaboration bound to be successful with the public. Despite adverse criticism and the complaints of Byron's circle, Nathan's work proved a huge success. Ten thousand copies of *A Selection of Hebrew Melodies* were sold, it has been said, for a profit exceeding five thousand pounds.[94] Murray's edition of the *Hebrew*

---

[92] To William Smyth, 30 May 1815, Hadden, pp. 192–3n.

[93] 24 August 1815, Hadden, pp. 192–3.

[94] Phillips, p. 78. No source is given for these figures.

Melodies without the music yielded a profit of £836. 5s, on the sale of six thousand copies.[95] Nathan's music, Braham's concert-room introduction, and Byron's ability to versify the Bible had not gone for naught.

By May of 1815, as we have seen, the Hebrew Melodies had passed from Byron's attention. On 10 December Ada was born; by 15 January 1816 wife and daughter had left London. During this period Byron and his composer remained on amicable terms. Visiting Byron in the spring of 1816, Leigh Hunt met Nathan at Piccadilly Terrace:

> I was present one day ... when that gentleman [Nathan] came to give Lord Byron a specimen of his Hebrew Melodies. The noble Bard, who was then in the middle of that unpleasant business about his wife, asked him for the one respecting Herod and Mariamne, which he listened to with an air of romantic regret. ... Mr. Nathan had a fine head; and made the grand pianoforte shake like a nut shell under the vehemence of his inspiration.[96]

This suggests that Nathan was working out the settings of the Hebrew Melodies to be published in his Second Number in Byron's presence. 'Herod's Lament for Mariamne' had not yet been published as set to music, and Nathan no doubt presented this and other settings for Byron's comment. In his *Fugitive Pieces*, Nathan tells us that he was with the poet 'at his house in Piccadilly, the best part of the three last days before he left London, to quit England'.[97] When the time of their final parting arrived, Byron gave the composer a fifty-pound note. It was Passover, and, remembering Byron's fondness for biscuits, Nathan returned the favour with a gift of matzos (III, 283n):

> I cannot deny myself the pleasure of sending your Lordship some holy biscuits, commonly called unleavened bread, denominated by the Nazarenes *Motsas*, better known in this enlightened age by the epithet passover cakes; and as a certain

[95] Murray Ledger, Vol. B, f. 127. In 1817 the price of this edition was raised from 4s. 6d. to 5s. 6d.

[96] Leigh Hunt, *Lord Byron and Some of His Contemporaries*, 2 vols (London: Henry Colburn, 1828), I, 187–8.

[97] P. 87. Hobhouse, who resided with Byron at this time, makes no mention of Nathan in his diary for this period.

angel at a certain hour, by his presence, ensured the safety of
a whole nation, may the same guardian spirit pass with your
Lordship to that land where the fates may have decreed you to
sojourn for a while!

At Piccadilly Terrace the atmosphere was one of hurry, and defiance.
Byron thanked his composer with a short note (III, 283):

> Piccadilly, Tuesday Evening
>
> My Dear Nathan —
>
> I have to acknowledge the receipt of your very seasonable
> bequest, which I duly appreciate; the unleavened bread shall
> certainly accompany me in my pilgrimage; and, with a full
> reliance on their efficacy, the *Motsas* shall be to me a charm
> against the destroying Angel wherever I may sojourn; his
> serene highness, however, will, I hope, be polite enough to keep
> at a desirable distance from my person, without the necessity
> of besmearing my *door posts* or *upper lintels* with the blood of any
> animal. With many thanks for your kind attention, believe me
> my dear Nathan,
>
> Yours very truly,
>
> Byron

Besmearing Byron's reputation was the work of the press. The
appearance of 'Fare Thee Well!' and 'A Sketch from Private Life' (a
nasty satire directed at Mrs Clermont) in John Scott's *Champion* of
14 April had provoked a host of anti-Byron sentiment. The news-
papers, according to their political leanings, condemned or supported
the poet. The *Courier*, a prominent evening paper, took a moderate
stand, but it sided enough with Lady Byron to poke fun at the
Hebrew Melodies and to criticize Byron in doing so. On Saturday,
13 April, one day before the publication of 'Fare Thee Well!' in the
Champion, the *Courier* published the first of a series of 'English
Melodies', remarking:

> It has been a subject of national reproach that the *English* have
> no national songs. Everybody knows that the Irish and the
> Scotch have, by their National Melodies, just published, added
> to their reputation and to our humiliation, and even the Jews
> have of late found a *David* in Lord Byron, who has endeavoured
> to place them in the same scale (of the *gamut* at least) with
> their Christian neighbours.
>
> A *patriotic* society of English individuals have determined, as

far as in them lies, to retrieve our national character; and to enter the lists with the Irish, Scotch, and Hebrew melodists.

The 'English Melodies' were a series of parodies of well-known National Melodies. Moore's 'Oh! the days are gone when beauty bright' was treated first. On 16 April, Byron's 'The Destruction of Semnacherib' was parodied in the 'Debate on the Navy Estimates':

Oh! Tierney came down like the wolf on the fold,
And his phalanx of voters was boasting and bold;
And the noise of their cheering resembled the roar,
As you shoot London Bridge, when the tide is half o'er.

Like the rose-bush of summer, all budding and green,
Their hopes, while the question was putting, were seen;
But, in two hours contest, so blighted and shorn,
The bud was all gone; there remain'd but the thorn.

For the breath of the Ocean came strong on the blast;
And bung'd up the eyes of old George as it pass'd;
And the hopes of his Party began to grow chill,
And their hearts gushed with sorrow, their voices were still.

And there lay black Broom with his nostrils all wide,
But though they there curl'd, it was not with pride;
And the froth of grey Bennet lay light on the turf,
And the mouth-piece of Wynne foam'd with anger & surf.

And there, Lambton lay, more than commonly pale;
And there ugly Bob, with a face like a tail;
Harry Martin awoke, even Newport was dumb;
And Baring look'd almost as frightful as B[rougha]m.

And the waiters at Brook's are loud in their wail;
And mute is the Holland-House-Temple of Baal;
And the might of the Party, in spite of big words,
Hath melted like snow, both in Commons and Lords.

On 18 April the Courier published 'Fare Thee Well!' with its companion parody, 'The Lost Leader', the fourth of the 'English Melodies'. Shortly after, Peter Pindar protested that the English character was at its best in nursery rhymes. A series of satiric 'Infantile Lyrics' deposed the 'English Melodies', but not before Byron's 'Sun of the Sleepless!' had appeared above

To —— ——
Son of the faithless! melancholy rat!
Whose circling sleeve still polishes thy hat,
Offering at once thyself and it to sell;
How like are thou to him remembered well,
The apostate Lord, the rat of other days,
Enrich'd but never warm'd by Royal rays!
The rising Sun still watching to behold,
Clever but callous, shrewd but tame and cold.[98]

Byron was not able to appreciate this parody published on 25 April. On 24 April 1816 he had left London, Isaac Nathan, and the Hebrew Melodies behind.

Twenty-four years were to pass between Byron's flight and Nathan's equally abrupt journey to Australia in December 1840. During these years the musician divided his energies among three activities: publishing, writing for the theatre, and teaching. Nathan's association with Byron had brought Sir Walter Scott on a visit to his studio in 1815 to hear the Hebrew Melodies recited by their composer. Later that autumn Nathan wrote to the Ariosto of the North, to call a new national-melodies project to his attention:

> When you did me the honour of a visit, you very politely offerr'd to assist me in my professional labours. Encouraged by your kindness I take the liberty to mention that I have recently obtained from a friend a few Polish Songs, which I propose to Melodize and accompany with *original English Poetry* in six Numbers 12 songs in each on the same plan as the Hebrew Melodies, and I should esteem myself fortunate indeed if you could find leisure to write for the work.[99]

[98] 'English Melodies' not noticed in the text are I, 'Oh! the time is past when Quarter-day'; III, 'Believe me when all those ridiculous airs' published on 17 April with Moore's 'Believe me when all those endearing young charms'; V, a single, untitled satire attacking Sydney Smith published on 19 April (on that day Sir Ralph Noel's letter to James Perry and a parody of Byron's 'Lines to a Lady Weeping' in which Ada becomes Princess Charlotte were published in this paper); VI, a satire attacking Brougham entitled 'The Black Broom' published by itself on 20 April (on that day were published Perry's reply and 'A Sketch', and 'Fare Thee Well!' was reprinted; on the 22nd a paragraph of advice to Byron and 'Oh! Forget Me', a poem answering 'Fare Thee Well!' were published).
[99] 22 November 1815, quoted in Slater, p. 88n.

Nothing came of this Polish venture; Scott declined the offer just as he had declined to write the words for Nathan's Hebrew airs. However, Caroline Lamb did not decline to provide verses for Nathan's musical publications. The composer wrote and published music for six 'Byronic' lyrics that appeared in Caroline's *Ada Reis* (1823). But Lady Caroline Lamb's were not poems to make a music publisher's fortune; that task had required and still required a Scott or a Byron.

Though Byron was no longer about or willing to write verses for Nathan, there were numerous songs among the poet's works that an enterprising musician might arrange and publish. In his first letter to Byron, Nathan had enclosed a setting of 'This rose to calm my brother's cares' from the *Bride of Abydos* (I, 287). By the time of the publication of the First Number of *A Selection of Hebrew Melodies* (as an advertisement published in that work advises) he had set four others of Byron's lyrics to music: 'Thou art not false, but thou art fickle' (*Childe Harold*, 7th edition), 'The Fair Haidee' ('I enter the garden of roses', *Childe Harold*, 1812), 'My Life I Love You' ('Maid of Athens', *Childe Harold*, 1812), and 'Night Wanes' (*Lara* II, 1). While the work was at press, Nathan added another song to the list: 'The kiss, dear maid! thy lip has left' (*Childe Harold*, 1812). By the time of the publication of the Second Number of *A Selection of Hebrew Melodies* in 1816, he had added five additional songs to his *Catalogue*: 'Ah were I sever'd from thy side' (*Bride of Abydos* I, 319), 'The sun's last rays are on the hill' (*Giaour* l. 537), 'Think not thou art what thou appearest!' (*Bride of Abydos* I, 383), 'Love Indeed is Light from Heaven' (*Giaour* l. 1131), and 'Bound where thou wilt my barb!' (*Bride of Abydos* II, 396). By 1824 'When we two parted' (*Poems*, 1816) and 'Ada' (*Childe Harold* III: i) had been published as songs. By 1829 Nathan had added four new songs: 'Well! Thou art Happy' (*Hours of Idleness*), 'Tambourgi, Tambourgi' (*Childe Harold* II, ff. lxxii), 'As o'er the cold sepulchral stone' ('Lines written in an Album, at Malta', *Childe Harold*, 1812), and 'This Votive Pledge' ('Stanzas to a Lady with the Poems of Camoëns', *Hours of Idleness*). Three additional songs fill out Nathan's *Catalogue*: 'The castled crag of Drachenfels' (*Childe Harold* III, ff. lv), 'When friendship or love' ('The Tear', *Hours of Idleness*), and 'When I rov'd a young highlander' (*Hours of Idleness*). Byron's poetry had provided Nathan with twenty additional songs to publish.[100]

*   *   *   *   *

[100] Sources: various catalogues of *Music Composed by Mr. Nathan*; a song book

Though occupied with publishing other songs by Byron and songs of other poets, Nathan did not forget about his stock-in-trade, the Hebrew Melodies. In 1824, he felt that the time was ripe for a new edition of *A Selection of Hebrew Melodies*, and he wrote to John Braham, seeking a partner in the new venture.[101] 'I must decline', replied Braham, but Nathan went ahead with his plan, probably spurred on by the effect of Byron's death in the same year. The projected edition was to consist of four numbers. Each number would cost the public fifteen shillings; in this way Nathan would be able to raise the price of his *Selection* from two guineas to three pounds and so help out his failing finances. But the public was not likely to pay more for more of the same. In the new edition, Nathan promised to include notes to each of the poems illustrating the nature of his collaboration with Byron. By the close of the year, the First and Second Numbers of the 'newly arranged harmonized corrected and revised' edition had been printed by Thomas Davison.[102] The numbers were 'published for the proprietor' by the music publisher J. Fentum. But events conspired to delay the remaining numbers of the new edition. In the winter of 1824, Nathan's wife died in childbirth. This tragedy was followed by the British financial crisis of 1825–6. But even before the business decline, Nathan had assigned the copyright of the Hebrew Melodies to his sister Rachael, probably to protect it from creditors.[103] In

[101] 6 April 1824, *ASHM*, rev. ed., reprinted 1827, I, preface.

[102] An advance notice was printed on the cover of Nathan's song sheet of Byron's 'Well! Thou art Happy': 'An entire new edition of the Hebrew Melodies will shortly be published.' The sheet is watermarked '1823' (New York Public Library, Drexel 5535).

[103] 'Memorandum of Assignment of the Copyright of the Hebrew Melodies together with the Poetry written for them by Lord Byron assigned to Miss Rachael Nathan by Isaac Nathan the composer of the music Dec. 4th 1824', British Museum, Add. MS. 28721, f. M. Phillips (p. 76), asserts incorrectly that Nathan's affidavit (which she had not examined) refers to an original assignment dated 20 April 1814, that is prior to Nathan's earliest letter to Byron. Mackerras

probably belonging to one of Nathan's students containing the First and Second Numbers of *A Selection of Hebrew Melodies* and all of the first thirteen songs of Byron plus other works by Nathan published before the date on the cover stamped: 'Miss Percy 1824' (Beinecke Library, In. B996/+G815 copy 1); J. P. Anderson, 'Bibliography', in Roden Noel, *Life and Writings of Lord Byron* (London: Walter Scott Publishing Co., 1890), listing seven settings by Nathan. Nathan's music was frequently advertised, and on 2 October 1833 he wrote to George & Munby of 85 Fleet Street, 'Good gentlemen have the kindness to "remember not to forget" – that it is my wish to have my music regularly advertised in the quarterly Westminster Review – every quarter until further orders' (Huntington Library, HM6520).

1826, Nathan married his sister-in-law Henrietta Buckley, and by 1828 (with work on the second edition resumed), Nathan was conducting a new music-selling and publishing enterprise with his brother, Baruch Nathan, at the 'Mount House Assembly Rooms, opposite the Asylum, Westminster'.[104] It was not until 1827 that work began again on the new edition. In that year, the First and Second Numbers of the revised edition were reprinted by the firm of J. & C. Adlard and published for Rachael Nathan by J. Fentum.[105] (The plates used to print the engraved text of 1824 were used again.) In these reprinted numbers, Nathan added to the notes appended to each poem. The Third Number of the new edition was published in 1828 by Mary Ann Fentum, who carried on her husband's business following his death. The Fourth Number followed in 1829 and was published by the music-seller H. Faulkner. Faulkner had sold some copies of the first edition of the First Number of Nathan's *Selection*, and he later acquired the plates of all four numbers of the revised edition and reissued the entire work in 1830.

With additions, Nathan's four-number revised edition of *A Selection of Hebrew Melodies* derives directly from his two-number edition printed in 1816. (That edition, it may be recalled, consists of the reprint of the First Number of 1815 and the first edition of the Second Number.) In preparing the revised edition, the compositor worked from the letterpress text of the earlier edition and the engraver from the engraved text. Thus the discrepancy between those texts was preserved in the revised edition. But both compositor and engraver added errors of their own to the previous errors, and the discrepancy between the two texts was widened. Even the erratum printed in the Second Number of 1816 was ignored.

Though the text of the revised edition underwent some changes owing to errors, the contents of the early numbers added nothing new. The First Number and the Second Number of the revised edition consist of twelve poems, six each, the twelve poems printed in the First Number of the first edition. Nathan, however, has provided nineteen settings to accompany the poems. At the foot of

[104] Given at the foot of the cover of a song sheet of 'If that High World' watermarked '1828' and printed from the plates used to print the First Number of the second edition of *ASHM* (New York Public Library, Drexel 4733).

[105] The reprinted numbers of the second edition were registered at Stationers' Hall on 24 January 1827. Stationers' Register, 26 October 1826–30 April 1828, f. 65.

wisely avoids the question of 'the complicated quarrel over the copyright of [the] Hebrew Melodies which the best efforts of Nathan's earnest biographer, Olga Somech Phillips have failed to disentangle' (p. 34).

the joint index to the First and Second Numbers he reported: 'Numbers III & IV are in the Press.' When the last appeared, it fulfilled the promise also given beneath the index to the First and Second Numbers: 'This Edition will contain (in addition to those formerly published) some new Melodies, with original MS. Poetry, by Lord Byron.' Nathan had made good on his promise to provide new melodies in the First and Second Numbers. In the Third Number, he printed eight poems from the Second Number of the first edition, and beneath the index to that Number, he noted: 'No. 4, Which is preparing for press, will complete the Hebrew Melodies.' The first three numbers of the revised edition thus account for twenty of the twenty-four poems published in the two-number first edition; the Fourth Number reprints the remaining four poems of the first edition. In addition, it prints four Hebrew Melodies not found in the first edition: 'From Job', 'I Speak Not – I Trace Not – I Breathe Not', 'In the Valley of Waters', and 'They say that Hope is happiness'. The first of these poems is not 'new' (though its melody would be new to owners of Nathan's first edition) for it had appeared in Hebrew Melodies. The remaining three poems were published for the first time. Nathan had suppressed the lines to Augusta, 'I Speak Not – I Trace Not – I Breathe Not', at Byron's wish. Now, with Byron dead, he gave them to the public. 'In the Valley of Waters' is the version of Psalm 123 rejected in favour of 'By the Rivers of Babylon'. 'They say that Hope is happiness' had been destroyed by Byron at Kinnaird's instigation, but Nathan had preserved a copy of the lines. The three poems were genuine and 'new' Hebrew Melodies. The canon of Hebrew Melodies, extended to twenty-five poems by 1816 (where it remained during Byron's lifetime), was now extended to twenty-eight poems.

By 1829, the Recollections-of-Byron industry was at its peak. Nathan realized this, and in May of that year he brought out a work designed to capitalize on the trend, as the title he chose indicates:

Fugitive Pieces and Reminiscences of Lord Byron containing an entire new edition of the Hebrew Melodies with the addition of several never before published; the whole illustrated with critical, historical, theatrical, political, and theological remarks, notes, anecdotes, interesting conversations, and observations, made by that illustrious poet: together with His Lordship's autograph; also some original poetry, letters, and recollections of Lady Caroline Lamb by I. Nathan.[106]

[106] London: Printed for Whittaker, Treacher and Co., 1829. The work was

In a single volume, which excluded music, Nathan brought together the poetry and accompanying notes of his revised four-number edition of *A Selection of Hebrew Melodies* with additional notes, new reminiscences of his days with Byron, a strongly worded reply to Douglas Kinnaird's strictures upon the Byroniana that had appeared in the revised edition, two facsimiles of Byron's handwriting, and some poems and letters of Caroline Lamb. The rather disjointed work that resulted is the memorial of Nathan's friendship with Byron and Lady Caroline Lamb. In addition, it is the last of the authoritative editions of the Hebrew Melodies.

In *Fugitive Pieces*, Nathan added a twenty-ninth poem to the twenty-eight Hebrew Melodies of the revised four-number edition. That poem is Byron's 'Bright be the place of thy soul'. Though it was not numbered among the Hebrew Melodies until 1829, 'Bright be the place of thy soul', the last of the Hebrew Melodies in order of composition, was not last in publication. The thirtieth and last to be published of the Hebrew Melodies appeared in 1831. In that year Murray included Byron's 'To Belshazzar', the alternative to the 'Vision of Belshazzar', in an edition of Byron's *Collected Works*.[107] Fair copies of both poems reached Murray's, but in 'To Belshazzar' Byron spared neither divine right nor the Regent in retelling the story of the handwriting on the wall. His cautious publisher, perhaps at Kinnaird's request, withheld the poem for sixteen years. Ironically, Murray did not number the poem among the Hebrew Melodies.

Music publishing failed to keep the bailiffs from Nathan's door. To help out his finances, he turned to the stage, for which his voice was not suited, and earned Hazlitt's adverse criticism with his appearance at Covent Garden as Henry Bartram in *Guy Mannering*.[108] The success of his operatic farces, however, made up for the failure of his voice. Mme Vestris' rendition made Nathan's 'Why are you wandering

---

[107] VI, 427. 'I Speak Not – I Trace Not – I Breathe Not' became one of the 'collected works' in the same edition (VI, 401). The first four volumes of this edition are identical with the four-volume edition of 1830.

[108] William Hazlitt, *Complete Works*, ed. by P. P. Howe (London, 1933), XVIII, 289.

---

briefly noticed in the *Court Journal*, 23 May 1829; the *Sun*, 29 May 1829; the *Dorset County Chronicle*, 28 May 1829, and 11 June 1829; *Atlas*, 7 June 1829; and *John Bull*, 14 June 1829.

here I pray?', from his operetta, *Sweethearts and Wives* (1823, libretto by James Kenney), one of the song hits of the age. The Polish songs he had mentioned to Scott found a home in the moderately successful *Alcaid* (1824, libretto by James Kenney). Nathan supplemented these theatrical activities by writing a biography of Mme Malibran de Beriot, one of the most famous singers of the nineteenth century and the daughter of the great singing-master, Manuel Garcia.[109] Nathan himself was a singing-master of some repute. Charles I. M. Dibdin, then the manager of Sadlers Wells, employed several of Nathan's pupils and duly noted this fact in his *Memoirs*.[110] But the most successful of Nathan's pupils, the young Robert Browning, earned his fame elsewhere.[111] Nathan's scholarly reputation rested on *An Essay on the History and Theory of Music and on the Qualities, Capabilities, and Management of the Human Voice* (1823).[112] This important work demonstrates his understanding of his art with a thoroughness later generations found useful. But even these activities failed to support the Nathan *ménage*. By 1831 Nathan was applying to the Literary Fund for aid, and wrote to William Jerdan, editor of the *Literary Gazette*, to add to his application.[113] Finally Nathan's financial difficulties drove him to Australia in December 1840.

[109] *Memoirs of Madame Malibran de Beriot* (London: Joseph Thomas, 1826). In this work (p. 51), Nathan tells us that he sent a presentation copy of *A Selection* to Mme Malibran, and that she liked 'Jephtha's Daughter' best.

[110] Charles I. M. Dibdin, *Professional and Literary Memoirs*, ed. by George Speaight (London: The Society for Theatre Research, 1956), pp. 149, 151.

[111] See Herbert E. Greene, 'Browning's Knowledge of Music', *PMLA*, 1947, LXII, 1098; and *Astarte* (1905), p. 19n.

[112] *Musurgia Vocalis* is an enlarged second edition published in 1833. It adds the reminiscences of *FP* to *An Essay*.

[113] Nathan's letter has been overlooked by his biographers:

> 19 Holland Street North Brixton
> late 34 Clapham Road Place
> Feb. 9th 1831

Dear Sir

I have used every exertion to procure a copy of my History & Theory of Music without success, I hope this will not interfere with my object since the work has had the good fortune to meet with your public approbation.

Since my application to the Literary Fund Society I have had additional affliction in my family – my mother is seriously ill – my sister dying – and a child three years of age in an alarming state of health and who is attended by Mr. Hilleaid of Stockwell whose attentions I can never forget, Mr. Smith, 38 Clapham Road Place has also for some time attended my wife & child –

I herewith enclose you a few witnesses of my distressed situation which I have sent you in a small box and which you will have the kindness to keep

Nathan arrived in New South Wales, then a colony, in 1841. He was the first professional musician to establish himself in Sydney, and by the time of his death in 1864 had earned the title of 'Father of Australian Music'. He presented concerts at which the Hebrew Melodies, sung by his daughter Jessy Rosetta, were a prominent feature; wrote patriotic Australian songs; and served as a singing-master. The Southern Euphrosyne (1849) is the major work of Nathan's Australian period. Its title is characteristic of his predilection for length and of his interest in ancient national music:

The Southern Euphrosyne and Australian Miscellany, containing oriental Moral Tales, original anecdotes, poetry and music. An Historical Sketch with examples of the Native Aboriginal Melodies, put into modern rhythm and harmonised as solos, quartettes, etc., together with several other original vocal pieces arranged to a Piano Forte accompaniment by the Editor and sole proprietor, I. Nathan, author of the Hebrew Melodies, the Musurgia Vocalis, the successful music in 'Sweethearts and Wives', 'The Illustrious Stranger', 'The King's Fool', etc.[114]

This portmanteau volume should probably be thought of as the First Number of the 'Australian Melodies'. A carriage bearing Byron's crest was sent out to Australia nearly half a century after the poet's death.[115] Had Byron survived to make the journey, and Nathan remained alive, who knows what would have resulted?

With Byron dead and Nathan in Australia, the Hebrew Melodies did not go unaffected by heavenly influences. In 1856 a poem purporting to be a new Hebrew Melody was published by an astrologer. In the fifth edition of Raphael's Witch!!! or the Oracle of the Future, an astrological boudoir book, the table of contents includes: 'An Hebrew Melody, by Lord Byron, "Yes, He hath said the Day shall come," with Four pages of Music, (page 207) expressly for this work, by J. Blewitt, Esq.'[116] In the first edition of this work, published twenty-five years

[114] 'Published by Whittaker, & Co., Ave Maria Lane, London; and, at the Editor's Residence, 105, Hunter-Street, Sydney.'
[115] K. T. Borrow and Dorothy Hewlett, 'Byron: A Link with Australia', KSMB, 1963, XIV, 17–20.
[116] London: William Charlton Wright, 1856, p. 4. The poem is found on p. 152.

for me in your own possession until I do myself the honour of waiting upon you.

Dear Sir
I am yours very Respectfully
I. Nathan

Bodleian Library, MS. d. 114, f. 104.

earlier in 1831, no mention is made of the poem's being by Byron. There one learns, however, that 'The above Melody had been much admired in my annual Work, "The Prophetic Messenger" for 1830.' The *Prophetic Messenger* is an astrological almanac and weather guide in which poems and verse fragments are used extensively to justify Raphael's forecasts. Part of the December weather prediction, 'Yes, He hath said the Day shall come' assures us that 'drizzling rain or sleet' will yield to spring. Here too no mention of the poem's being by Byron is made. The original Raphael was the Oxford mathematician, Robert C. Smith. On Smith's death in 1832, John Palmer assumed the title, but Palmer died in 1837. The successor who fraudulently attributed the poem to Byron is unknown.[117] 'Yes, He hath said the Day shall come' is not Byron's and does not confirm spiritual communication as neat editorial practice:

> Thine heart is sad, thine heart is sad!
> And thoughts of sorrow vex thy soul;
> But Judah's God can make thee glad,
> And burst the clouds that round thee roll.
> Thy broken spirit shall be whole,
> And light and joy arise on thee,
> To end thy dark captivity!

> For all things own his wondrous sway,
> In heaven, or earth, or ocean wide;
> And sun and shower, and night and day,
> Praise him as their Almighty guide!
> Even the cold grave in vain would hide
> Our sins and sorrows from his sight,
> Whose arm is power, whose eye is light.

> The sun blight, and the sickening moon,
> And hurtful demons he shall chase;

---

[117] Palmer's accession is noted in the *Prophetic Messenger* for 1833. In the twentieth century, Robert Cross (d. 1923) revived the name. Mr G. S. Manners has written to *The Times Literary Supplement* to report another posthumous printing ('Byron on Job', *TLS*, 2 October 1969, p. 1132). Byron's 'From Job' was included in the *Poetical Remains* of Henry Savile Shepherd, selected and arranged by Rev. Joseph Garton, Devonport, 1835 (p. 53). A corrigendum (p. 210) explains: 'The poem on Job, page 53, by a distinguished Author, was inadvertently sent to the press by the Editor.' Variants have been included in the Historical Collations.

I am indebted to Ronald Hall, Librarian of the John Rylands Library, Manchester, for first calling the poem to my attention.

Then *fear not*, since the Lord shall soon
 Awake thy tongue to gladsome lays,
 Tuning thine heart unto his praise!
And from his treasured blessings shed
A double portion on thy head!

Soon shall the wintry storms be o'er,
 And all the floods and rains be past;
The vines shall blush with grapes once more,
 And flowers upon the earth be cast.
 And, for the sad and howling blast,
Our land shall hear the turtle's voice,
And the glad time when birds rejoice.

Yes! He hath said the day shall come
 When Zion shall in glory reign;
When shouting to their beauteous home,
 Her scattered tribes shall march again;
 When from the mountain to the plain
Shall Salem's banners be unfurl'd,
And David's sceptre rule the world!

With these lines, neither real, nor old, nor undisputed, the history of the Hebrew Melodies is at an end.

II
BYRONIC
LYRICS FOR DAVID'S HARP

'How the devil should I write about *Jerusalem*, never having yet been there?' quipped Byron in 1816.[1] He found no irony in his having written about Jerusalem only the year before in the Hebrew Melodies. Childe Harold had not journeyed to the Temple; nor had Byron embraced the religion of the Jews. The Hebrew Melodies are not a collection of hymns or psalms brimming with the faith of the Old Testament. They are merely thirty poems Byron wrote at various times during 1814 and 1815 and then gave to Isaac Nathan (or intended to do so), who in turn set them to music. But it is just this fact that binds the poems together, for they share in the essential unity of Byron's lyric corpus. In their own peculiar way, they almost seem to be a later edition of Byron's *Hours of Idleness*, his best-known collection of lyrics. The seemingly biblical poems are *Byronic*. We can best perceive their unity by comparing the poems with the entire body of lyric poetry Byron wrote before 1816. The themes and postures of the Hebrew Melodies at first seem nothing more than varying restatements of thoughts expressed in many of Byron's earlier lyrics (and in the first two cantos of *Childe Harold*). But the comparison reveals differences as well. The Hebrew Melodies share to some extent a community of biblical subject; they have been influenced by the conventions of the national-melodies genre; and they are in the main dramatic lyrics. As we shall see, because of these differences, in the Hebrew Melodies, more so than in the earlier lyrics, we are made to experience and to understand the romantic myth of sympathy that the Byron of 1815 wished to articulate. With this in mind, we can say that generally the Hebrew Melodies differ in kind, because they differ in degree. Their variety is the variety of Byron's early collections and of the lyrics published with his longer poems. Anyone attempting to classify the poems must recognize

[1] To John Murray, 9 December 1816, *L & J*, IV, 22. Murray had inquired about the spurious 'Lord Byron's Pilgrimage to the Holy Land', offered for sale by the Cheapside printer James Johnston. Cf. Hobhouse to John Hanson, 8 June 1811: 'I have received a letter from Lord Byron of the date of last February in which he mentions his intention of going to Jerusalem. . . . His Lordship talks of extending his tour into Egypt.' Nils Erik Enkvist, 'British and American Literary Letters in Scandinavian Public Collections', *Acta Academiae Aboensis, Humaniora*, 1964, XXVII. iii, 91.

these facts. Joseph Slater (p. 86) finds that 'nine of the poems are Biblical in subject but Byronic in treatment; two are love songs; five are reflective lyrics, neither Jewish nor Christian; and five are expressions of what might be called proto-Zionism' (nine are unaccounted for). We should not be surprised, for Byron's *Poems on Various Occasions* were not much different.

The alternation in subject reflects the circumstances of the Hebrew Melodies' composition. First Byron gave Nathan the secular love lyrics he had written in the spring and summer of 1814. Then, warming to the composer, he provided some vaguely Jewish poems. Finally, after marriage to his reforming angel, he sent Nathan poems dealing directly with Old Testament subjects. Can we criticize Nathan for failing to reject any of this mixed but valuable gift? The pious who hoped to find sacred poetry by Lord Byron in the Hebrew Melodies found instead a collection resembling the twenty-nine lyrics published in 1814 with the seventh edition of *Childe Harold*. They should have known better. Only a year before the publication of *A Selection of Hebrew Melodies*, Byron had elaborated on his themes in a letter to Annabella: 'I do not believe that there be 50 lines of mine in all touching upon religion.'[2] The Hebrew Melodies added little to this figure.

Byron's supposedly pious poems could not be orthodox in their sentiments. 'Of Religion I know nothing, at least in its *favour*', wrote Byron to Edward Long in 1807. Four years later his rebellious mood had not mellowed, and he turned to shocking his conservative friend Francis Hodgson: 'I do not believe in any revealed religion, because no religion is revealed: and if it pleases the Church to damn me for not allowing a *nonentity*, I throw myself on the mercy of the *"Great First Cause, least understood"*. . . . Let us make the most of life, and leave dreams to Emanuel Swedenborg.'[3] Hodgson's attempt to purge *Childe Harold* II was unsuccessful. William Gifford, Murray's editor, was more able. To Gifford, Byron wrote in 1813: 'To your advice on Religious topics, I shall equally attend. Perhaps the best way will be by avoiding them altogether.'[4] Byron did avoid religious topics, as his remarks to Annabella show, and in the Hebrew Melodies he

---

[2] 15 March 1814, quoted in Mayne, *Lady Byron*, p. 92.

[3] 16 April 1807, *L & J*, II, 19n; 13 September 1811, *L & J*, II, 35–6. See *L & J*, II, 18 for another statement of Byron's position.

[4] 18 June 1813, *L & J*, II, 221.

avoided orthodox religious piety. But those poems are not at all free from one kind of peculiarly Byronic religious sentiment. In the same letter, Byron told Gifford that he had attended 'a Calvinistic Scotch school where I was cudgelled to Church for the first ten years of my life'. What he learned there he did not forget. Annabella believed that his 'early Calvinistic impressions, and later Oriental observations, had tended to infix in his mind' what she called a 'dark predestinarianism'.[5] Her phrase suggests the attitude Byron made explicit in one of his conversations with James Kennedy, the evangelical army physician he met in Cephalonia in 1823:

> ... if there is, as we all admit, a Supreme Ruler of the universe, and if, as you say, he has the actions of the devils, as well as of his own angels, completely at his command, then those influences, or those arrangements of circumstance, which lead us to do things against our will, or with ill-will, must be also under his direction.[6]

Byron's Supreme Ruler is very much like the God of the Old Testament, and the Old Testament strain of Byron's Hebrew Melodies is bound up with his variegated Calvinistic fatalism. Byron could never accept the full import of Calvinism.[7] But he does not spare us the plangent sorrow of the Old Testament wailing complaints. It is no wonder that Annabella called the Hebrew Melodies 'his gloomy compositions'.[8]

If Byron rejected the faiths of Calvinists and Jews as a theme, he did not reject the Bible per se. 'Of the Scriptures themselves I have ever been a reader & admirer as compositions, particularly the Arab-Job – and parts of Isaiah – and the song of Deborah,' he wrote to Annabella.[9] The selection is significant: 'Arab' Job for the infidel

[5] Statement L, 1816, quoted in Elwin, p. 270.

[6] Quoted in James Kennedy, M.D., *Conversations on Religion with Lord Byron* (London: John Murray, 1830), p. 189.

[7] From the opposite perspective, Jerome McGann writes: '[Byron] was a benevolist but preserved a strong element of skepticism in his makeup which prevented him from ever fully accepting the progressive meliorism of Lady Byron and Priestley' (*Fiery Dust: Byron's Poetic Development* [Chicago, 1968], p. 251). In the preface to 'Julian and Maddalo', Shelley provides the best commentary on Byron's religion: 'What Maddalo [Byron] thinks on these matters is not exactly known.'

[8] Narrative Q, 1816, quoted in Elwin, p. 264.

[9] 15 February 1814, quoted in Mayne, *Lady Byron*, p. 87. His frequently quoted

Calvinist, Isaiah for its nationalism, and Deborah for its defiance and archaic expression. These were just the strains to be interwoven in the Hebrew Melodies, where the sacred would be sacrificed to the political and the political to the romantic. Before this can be shown to be so, it is necessary to define the extent of the Old Testament influence on the Hebrew Melodies. Twelve of those thirty lyrics have nothing whatsoever to do with the Bible. The remaining poems vary in their connections with that work. A very few of them are modelled directly on Old Testament passages. 'From Job' is Byron's version of Job 4:13–21; 'By the Rivers of Babylon' and 'In the Valley of Waters' are attempts at Psalm 137; 'Oh! Weep for Those' refers to the same psalm and borrows a line from Psalm 55. On the other hand some poems are connected with the Old Testament by geography alone. Only references to 'Jordan', 'Judah', 'Galilee', 'Jerusalem', and 'Sion' tell us that 'On Jordan's Banks', 'The Wild Gazelle', 'Were my bosom as false as thou deem'st it to be', and 'On the Day of the Destruction of Jerusalem by Titus' have to do with the Jews. In the majority of cases, however, what Byron has done in the Hebrew Melodies is to use a story from the Bible or an incident from Jewish history as the basis of a dramatic lyric. As we shall see, in 'Jephtha's Daughter', in 'Herod's Lament for Mariamne', in 'To Belshazzar', and in 'My Soul is Dark', Byron has exploited Old Testament personae with romantic intent.[10]

Where Byron was outright in his rejection of piety, he did not entirely eschew the conventions of the national-melodies genre. Tom Moore helped to create the national-melodies style, and Byron learned that style and its meaning from him. In the preface to the *Corsair*, Byron told Moore: 'Ireland ranks you among the firmest of her patriots.' The poetic redress of 'the wrongs of your own country' was Moore's task.[11] The *Irish Melodies* were national melodies and not trifling lyrics. The suppressed preface to the Second Number of the *Irish Melodies* explains the political logic of those lyrics:

[10] Patricia Ball's strictures on the reading of romantic lyrics are well suited to the Hebrew Melodies. We must avoid 'reading them in that over-simplified fashion which takes their use of the word "I" at its face value and also ignores their dramatic bias . . .' (*The Central Self* [London, 1968], p. 65).

[11] *Poetry*, III, 223. Byron's remarks frightened Murray, and another preface was prepared. But Moore, to whom Byron allowed the choice, preferred the first.

remark about having read the Bible 'through and through' before he was 'eight years old' is found in his letter to Murray of 9 October 1821 (*L & J*, V, 391).

Our history, for many centuries past, is creditable neither to
our neighbours nor ourselves, and ought not to be read by any
Irishman who wishes either to love England or to feel proud of
Ireland. The loss of independence very early debased our
character. . . . Hence it is that the annals of Ireland, through a
long lapse of six hundred years, exhibit not one of those
themes of national pride, from which poetry borrows her
noblest inspiration; and that history which ought to be the
richest garden of the Muse, yields nothing to her but weeds
and cypress! . . . the only traits of heroism which he [the poet]
can venture at this day to commemorate, with safety to himself
or perhaps with honour to the country, are to be looked for in
those times when the native monarchs of Ireland displayed and
fostered virtues worthy of a better age.
. . . The language of sorrow, however, is, in general, best suited
to our music, and with themes of this nature the poet may be
amply supplied. There is not a page of our annals which cannot
afford him a subject; and while the National Muse of other
countries adorns her temple with trophies of the past, in
Ireland, her altar, like the shrine of Pity at Athens, is to be
known only by the tears that are shed upon it.[12]

The past is idealized as the golden age of freedom and independence.
The present is 'debased'. A regard for safety turned nationalists into
antiquarians. The fall occurred so far back in time that Irish history
affords little material for instilling national pride in the men of the
present. That is the first task of the national melodist. National songs
helped to keep alive the hereditary heroism of a people. (The
English had awarded Charles Dibdin a yearly pension for the songs
that had seemed to inspire English naval heroes.) But the lack of
triumphal themes and a musical tradition congenial to lamentation
turn the Irish melodist into a weeping elegist. This is the meaning
of Moore's 'Oh! blame not the bard'. What else can he do but weep?
Irish melodies meant tears as well as pride, and Byron learned of this
fusion from them. In the Hebrew Melodies he put it to his own use.

William Hazlitt accused Moore of having 'converted the wild
harp of Erin into a musical snuff-box'.[13] Byron did not agree:
'. . . to me, some of Moore's last Erin sparks – "As a beam o'er the
face of the waters" – "When he who adores thee" – "Oh blame not" –

---

[12] *Moore to Power*, pp. 2–3.
[13] *Spirit of the Age*, Howe, XI, 174.

and "Oh breathe not his name" – are worth all the Epics that ever were composed.'[14] Byron's comparison of the *Irish Melodies* with 'Epics' comments on his knowledge of their political content. Posterity may speculate about the critical judgment displayed in this passage, but there can be no speculation about Byron's knowledge of the poems. He heard others sing them, he heard Moore sing them, and he sang them himself. This last fact he communicated to Moore with pride.

> When I was at Aston, on my first visit, I have a habit, in passing my time a good deal alone, of – I won't call it singing, for that I never attempt except to myself – but of uttering, to what I think tunes, your 'Oh breathe not', 'When the last glimpse', and 'When he who adores thee', with others of the same minstrel; – they are my matins and vespers.[15]

The matins Byron refers to in this letter were all published in the First Number of the *Irish Melodies*, and that work exerted much influence on the Hebrew Melodies. Four more numbers appeared before the Hebrew Melodies, but it is not clear that Byron kept up with the later numbers. (Writing in 1813, he refers to poems published in 1808 as 'Moore's last'.)[16] A careful comparison of the Hebrew Melodies with the first editions of Moore's first five numbers illustrates the extent of actual influence.[17] Many of Moore's *Irish Melodies* had no effect on Byron's poems. Some of the poems provided Byron with suggestions for lyrics. A very few of the poems exerted a direct influence, and those that did were the lyrics Byron referred

[14] Journal, 24 November 1813, *L & J*, II, 344.

[15] 8 December 1813, *L & J*, II, 301.

[16] Journal, 24 November 1813, *L & J*, II, 344. In her *Conversations of Byron* the Countess of Blessington records Byron's attitude: 'Moore would go down to posterity by his Melodies, which were all perfect. He said that he had never been so much *affected* as on hearing Moore sing some of them, particularly "When first I met Thee", which he said, made him shed tears: "But", added he, with a look full of archness, "it was after I had drunk a certain portion of very potent white brandy"' (ed. by Ernest J. Lovell, Jun. [Princeton, 1969], p. 9).

[17] The numbers preceding the Hebrew Melodies are: I (1808), II (1808), III (1810), IV (1811), and V (1813). (See Muir.) The arrangement in the collected edition prepared by Moore does not follow the original. Hoover H. Jordan, in 'Byron and Moore', *MLQ*, 1948, IX, 436, and Edgar Dawson, in *Byron und Moore* (Leipzig, 1902), pp. 56–9, make comparisons of their own. Marchand (*Byron's Poetry*, p. 133) echoes Slater (p. 86): 'Some of the harps and minstrels and waters may also have been unconscious imitations of Thomas Moore's *Irish Melodies*.'

to in his correspondence and journal. Looking over his favourite 'Erin sparks', one observes that the tender lament for the *patriot* Robert Emmet, 'Oh! breathe not his name', probably suggested Byron's lines beginning 'I speak not, I trace not, I breathe not thy name'. But Moore's elegy had its greatest effect on Byron's elegiac 'Bright be the place of thy soul', for some of the lines of that lyric echo Moore's (see p. 191, below). Both Byron's 'I Speak Not – I Trace Not' and Moore's 'When he who adores thee' allow the lover to assume the full burden of guilty love. Certainly 'The harp that once, thro' Tara's halls' suggested Byron's 'The harp the monarch minstrel swept'. In those lyrics, as in 'Oh! blame not the bard', both Moore and Byron weep the glories that were. Beutler (p. 91) suggests that Moore's 'Before the Last Battle' sparked the 'Song of Saul Before his Last Battle'. Moore's 'I saw thy form in youthful prime' mourns the passing beauty of his feminine ideal Mary Tighe, in lines that call to mind Byron's 'Oh! snatched away in beauty's bloom':

> I saw thy form in youthful prime,
>> Nor thought that pale decay
> Would steal before the steps of Time,
>> And waste its bloom away, Mary![18]

Nor is there any doubt that 'Tho' the last glimpse of Erin with sorrow I see' (Byron called it 'When the last glimpse') is the source of the Hebrew Melody beginning:

> From the last hill that looks on thy once holy dome
> I beheld thee Oh SION! when rendered to Rome:
> 'Twas thy last sun went down, and the flames of thy fall
> Flashed back on the last glance I gave to thy wall.

Less direct in its influence was Moore's 'As a beam o'er the face of the waters', that Byron drew on for the motto of the *Giaour*:

> One fatal remembrance, one sorrow, that throws
> Its bleak shade alike o'er our joys and our woes,
> To which life nothing darker or brighter can bring,
> For which Joy has no balm, and affliction no sting: –

The mood of these lines is very close to that of Byron's '"All is Vanity, Saith the Preacher"'. It is a mood of grief without a pang, the

---

[18] *Irish Melodies* [1808], I, 49. On Mrs Tighe see Howard Mumford Jones, *The Harp that Once* (New York, 1937), p. 64.

mood of Byron's dirge to his decay of feeling 'There's not a joy the world can give like that it takes away'. Byron sent those lines to Moore and then told him: 'I am very glad you like them, for I flatter myself they will pass as an imitation of your style. If I could imitate it well, I should have no great ambition of originality – I wish I could make you exclaim . . . "That's my thunder, by G–d".'[19] When the Hebrew Melodies were published, Moore did more than exclaim – he cursed. Several of Byron's imitations had surpassed their originals, but, in part, their greatness depended upon Byron's facility in the lyric measures he learned from Moore.

From Moore, Byron learned about nationalism and the national-melodies style. In the Old Testament he found the Jews. Having been Zionists since the destruction of the Temple, they are the Jacobins of that work. Byron joined the national-melodies style he learned from Moore and the Jews he read about in the Bible to write the Jacobin airs of old Zion. Irish, Greeks, and Jews were all equally down-trodden: 'The Greeks . . . have as small a chance of redemption from the Turks, as the Jews have from mankind in general.'[20] Byron was not alone in his comparisons; Moore's 'The Parallel' is an Irish Melody which compares the Irish and the Jews, and finds both their fates miserable.[21] Nor was using the Bible for the purpose of political allegory unheard of in Byron's day or any other day. Byron's espousal of Jewish nationalism was sincere. He 'easily identified himself with an oppressed people reaching for freedom', writes Leslie

[19] To Moore, 8 March 1815, *L & J*, 183–4. The shoe was on the other foot when it came to the later numbers of the *Irish Melodies* and the First Number of Moore's *Sacred Songs*. Moore's 'Sound the Loud Timbrel' appears to have been suggested by 'The Destruction of Semnacherib', and his 'Weep not for those', that opened the *Sacred Songs*, seems an obvious reference to Byron's 'Oh! Weep for Those'.

[20] *Poetry*, II, 192. Byron likened the plight of the Irish to that of the Jews when advocating Catholic emancipation in Parliament, 21 April 1812. *L & J*, II, 438.

[21] This lyric was supposedly written after Moore had read a treatise by a Mr Hamilton, professing to prove that the Irish were originally Jews. Its first stanza might easily have been addressed to Byron:

> Yes, sad one of Sion, if closely resembling,
>> In shame and in sorrow, thy wither'd-up heart –
> If drinking deep, deep, of the same 'cup of trembling'
>> Could make us thy children, our parent thou art.
>
> Like thee doth our nation lie conquer'd and broken. . . .

Thomas Moore, *Poetical Works*, ed. by A. D. Godley (London, 1910), p. 217.

Marchand.[22] Byron's sympathy with the proto-Zionism of his period was not unseconded. The millennium would not arrive until the Restoration of the Jews had been effected. Richard Brothers, who expected to become ruler of the world with its coming, called himself the 'Prince of the Hebrews'. More seriously, when Byron was at Cambridge, Napoleon's convocation of a Grand Sanhedrin of European Jews caused a stir among the clergy. They feared that 'the atheistical democracy of France' was destined to bring about the restoration.[23] In 1814, when it became known that Byron planned a journey to the East, he was urged by a correspondent to seek out

a kingdom of Jews mentioned by Bruce as residing on the mountain of Samen in [Abyssinia]. . . . If providence favours your Lordship's mission to Abyssinia, an intercourse might be established between England and that country, and the English ships . . . might be the principal means of transporting the kingdom of Jews . . . to Egypt, in the way to their own country, Palestine.[24]

Byron journeyed to Greece, not to Egypt. But he did not go to Missolonghi just to wear his Grecian helmet. He endorsed the principles of nationalism, and it is likely that he was familiar with the basic tenets of English proto-Zionism that had been accepted by such men as David Hartley, Richard Hurd, and Joseph Priestley.[25] Like these men, he had read the prophecies of the Old Testament:

then the Lord thy God will turn thy captivity, and have compassion upon thee, and will return and gather thee from all nations whither the Lord thy God hath scattered thee. . . . And the Lord thy God will bring thee into the land which thy fathers possessed, and thou shalt possess it.

Byron did not miss the political burden of these lines from Deuteronomy (30:3–5). He took up the *cause* of Jewish nationalism, and

[22] *Byron's Poetry*, p. 135.

[23] Thomas Witherby, *An Attempt to Remove Prejudices Concerning the Jewish Nation by Way of Dialogue* (London, 1804), pp. 330–1, in Slater, p. 91.

[24] *Works*, II, 232.

[25] Slater's citations (pp. 90–1) illustrate the extent of concern: David Hartley, *Observations on Man* (London, 1834), p. 418; Richard Hurd, *An Introduction to the Study of the Prophecies* (London, 1788), pp. 172–87; Joseph Priestley, *Institutes of Natural and Revealed Religion* (Birmingham, 1782), II, 420; William Hamilton Reid, *Causes and Consequences of the French Emperor's Conduct towards the Jews* (London, 1807); J. Bicheno, *The Restoration of the Jews* (London, 1807), p. 228.

in Ravenna in 1820, he was willing to understand contemporary events in the light of that cause. To Murray, he wrote when the Austrian armies seemed to be about to cross the Italian border:

> Our 'puir hill folk' offered to strike, and raise the first banner, but Bologna paused; and now 'tis autumn and the season half over. 'O Jerusalem! Jerusalem!' The Huns are on the Po; but if they once pass it on their way to Naples, all Italy will be behind them. The Dogs—the Wolves—may they perish like the Host of Sennacherib![26]

Byron the national melodist looked at the politics of the Bible in just this way.

The man of causes, however, was not a man of the proletariat. Commoners had his sympathy as the 'enslaved', but not as the 'mob'. These feelings tempered his sympathies. Byron's split posture is evident in another of his remarks to Kennedy:

> I love the cause of liberty, which is that of the Greek nation, although I despise the present race of Greeks, even while I pity them, I do not believe they are better than the Turks, nay, I believe that in many respects the Turks surpass them . . . I am nearly reconciled to St. Paul, for he says, there is no difference between the Jews and the Greeks, and I am exactly of the same opinion, for the character of both is equally vile.[27]

Byron's differentiation of the 'cause' and the 'Greeks' suggests that his lyrics would ultimately be truest to his uniquely romantic consciousness. The Jews would feature in metaphor serving the higher cause of Promethean liberty. While Byron's espousal was sincere its expression was consistently Byronic. The Hebrew Melodies would be more than an occasion for taking political potshots at the Prince Regent by calling him Herod or Belshazzar.

Byron put together nationalism and Jews to write poems about Jewish nationalism, but in those poems he joined Jewish nationalism

---

[26] 7 September 1820, *L & J*, V, 72.

[27] Quoted in Kennedy, pp. 246–8. Nathan (*FP*, p. 28) found Byron 'entirely free from the prevalent prejudices against that unhappy and oppressed race of men', the Jews. Byron may have been thinking that after Waterloo the Rothschilds had become the bankers of reaction. The Balfour Declaration was a century away.

and a Calvinistically inclined understanding of the Old Testament to create metaphors of man and of man's condition. As Byron had put it, writing to Annabella, the Hebrew Melodies were written 'partly from Job &c. & partly my own imagination'. In the plight of the exiled Jews, Byron found man's plight, and the tears he shed for fallen nationhood were shed for fallen man as well. 'For Byron the homeless Jews wandering in strange lands, whom not even death can reunite, are symbolic of man — just as the modern Greek, enslaved and cowed, is also man,' writes Robert Gleckner.[28] Leslie Marchand concurs in part: 'Two themes that were congenial to Byron's spirit dominate the lyrics derived from Old Testament sources: one is the deep pathos of the loss of Eden, the wail of a wandering and homeless people, and the other the battle cry of Jewish nationalism. The lost Eden was easily identified in Byron's feelings with the general romantic lament for lost innocence and beauty.'[29] Battle cry and wail, the fused sounds of Moore's preface, are merely different sides of the same romantic coin. When Byron gives in to melancholy, life is all darkness and limits. But he remains romantic: condemned to a fallen world, he is not without anger and defiance. Byron was a rebel with a keen awareness of man's limitations. Those limitations made him both rebellious and melancholy. But Byron does not challenge human action by calling it absurd. 'The Son of God,' he wrote, 'the pure, the immaculate, the innocent, is sacrificed for the Guilty. This proved His heroism. . . .'[30] Man must take Christ as an example of individual atonement predicated upon defiant sympathy. In the Hebrew Melodies, Byron builds a myth in which Promethean love, negating self-consciousness, harmonizes real and ideal. His Prometheanism, regardless of its success or failure, turns its back on the fallen state without an exit. The poet must become the Tasso whom Byron describes in 'The Prophecy of Dante'. Then with 'his high harp', he 'shall, by the willow over Jordan's flood, revive a song of Sion', to revivify human hearts.

The Hebrew Melodies are dominated by melancholy and defiance. These feelings define the poles of Byron's response to life at the time of their writing. As we have seen, these responses are perfectly suited to

---

[28] *Byron and the Ruins of Paradise* (Baltimore, 1967), p. 207.

[29] *Byron's Poetry*, p. 134.

[30] To Hodgson, 13 September 1811, *L & J*, II, 35. McGann (p. 129) writes: 'It does not matter whether men triumph over their natural conditions or are defeated by them: they become as gods merely by their heroic gestures.'

the national-melodies style, with its emphasis on elegy and heroism, and to the 'certain wildness and pathos' that had 'become the chief characteristic of the Sacred Songs of the Jews',[31] and they are thoroughly compatible with romantic consciousness fed on nostalgia and Prometheanism. Recognizing this, we can perceive the Byronic symmetry of the universe of the Hebrew Melodies. To Eden soar the generous Promethean heroes; from it fall the selfish tyrants; the fallen lament it, learning sympathy; and the beautiful dwell in it. This symmetry is apparent in Byron's version of the Books of Samuel: 'Saul', 'My Soul is Dark', 'The harp the monarch minstrel swept', and the 'Song of Saul Before His Last Battle'. These poems on Saul and David show us the universe of the Hebrew Melodies in microcosm and reveal the essential unity of Byron's vision. Because of this they become the necessary parameters and referents of a study of the Hebrew Melodies.

In *Don Juan*, we are told that Samuel rose from the grave 'to freeze once more/The blood of monarchs with his prophecies'. In the Hebrew Melodies, he does just that; all the monarchs (except David) of those lyrics 'fall'. That word becomes a commonplace describing their fate. While the peculiarities of individual lots need to be accounted for, it is important to recognize Byron's archetype. Nor can we ignore the emphasis on fall by vision or spiritual agency: Saul sees Samuel, Belshazzar sees the handwriting on the wall, the host of Sennacherib is destroyed by the 'angel of death', Herod is haunted by the ghost of Mariamne, and Eliphaz the Temanite is chilled by the 'Spirit' who passed before him. Men do not overthrow Byron's tyrants; they are destroyed by the spectre of their own radical selfishness. In a world of death, selfish pride (expressed as political tyranny) is a sin, because it is an enemy of the love upon which Byron's heavenly 'high world' rests. Looking back at the past is as dangerous as looking into the future. In the Hebrew Melodies, fall by vision is extended to all men by being equated with fall by memory. Both hope and memory delude man. The 'future cheats' him as its hope declines into the fallen present:

> Nor can we be what we recall,
> Nor dare we think on what we are.

[31] *ASHM* [1815], I, preface.

In 'Saul', Samuel arises to tell Saul just 'what we are'.[32] Byron's description of the prophet makes his point: 'glassy', 'shroud', 'withered', 'dry', 'bony', 'shrunken', 'sinewless', and 'ghastly bare'. Here and elsewhere, he sacrificed alliteration to keep his tone flat and fatal. 'Mist mantled', 'shrinking from his shroud', 'glared all glassy', and 'Bloodless are these bones' were each revised with this principle presumably in mind. 'Death' stands in Samuel's 'fixed eye' because Samuel is the fear of death personified. 'Saul saw, and fell.' Stretched on the ground like a blasted 'oak', he listens to the prophetic lightning: suicide for Saul, and death for Jonathan. This is the 'sternest answer' that 'the buried Prophet' reveals in Manfred (II:ii, 178). 'Son and sire' die together as they so often do in Byron's verse, where the sins of the selfish father are visited upon his hopes. Joining Saul to Samuel, the internal rhyme of 'mine' and 'thine' (ll. 19–20) confirms the prophecy:

> Crownless, breathless, headless fall,
> Son and sire, the house of Saul!

Samuel's prophecy is not very different from Daniel's explanation in the 'Vision of Belshazzar' of the handwriting on the wall:

> Belshazzar's grave is made,
> His kingdom passed away.

Tyrants provide for their own decay ('made'), and the only 'kingdom' they inherit is the 'grave'. So Byron moralized upon the story of Daniel 5, turning it into political allegory. That allegory does not give way to cliché, because it is embodied in a spare form as forceful as the Old Testament narrative.[33] What Byron called in Don Juan 'The words which shook Belshazzar in his hall,/And took his kingdom from him' were the Rights of Man. The handwriting on the wall, the 'short-hand of the Lord' (Don Juan, VIII:134), was probably not much different in import from that scrawled on the walls of the great houses in Byron's London. Daniel is a 'captive' in Byron's poem,

[32] The story of the Witch of Endor and the summoning of Samuel was a favourite with Byron. 'It beats all the ghost scenes I ever read,' he remarked to Kennedy (p. 154). One such 'scene' was surely Thomas Gray's 'The Descent of Odin'. Another was found in Wm Sotheby's Saul (1807), which proved more influential than Smedley's Saul (1814).

[33] Byron employs the double quatrain, rhyming ababcdcd, that he uses (with variation in metre) in 'When coldness wraps this suffering clay', 'I Saw Thee Weep', and '"All is Vanity, Saith the Preacher"'; he seems to have found it appropriate for poems emphasizing transition.

because (as we shall see later in the Hebrew Melodies) it is the willing martyrdom of captives that will terminate selfishness expressed as divine right.[34] The conflict of captive and king follows upon the clash of corruption and purity manifest in Belshazzar's soiling the sacred vessels of the captive Jews (Daniel 5:2–3):

> A thousand cups were shown
> Of gold along the board
> Which till then had held alone
> Salem's offering to the Lord.

Revising this passage, Byron shortened the hypermetric lines, abandoning the weak rhymes and the forced alliteration of the third line. Between the last draft and the printed text, he made further changes:

> A thousand cups of gold
> In Judah deemed divine –
> Jehovah's vessels hold
> The godless Heathen's wine.

The metre of these lines is regular; the echoing consonants of thousand, gold, deemed, Judah, divine, hold, and divine, Jehovah's, vessels terminate abruptly in the closing line. The unity of Judah and Jehovah is appropriate; that of gold and godless, of divine and wine, is not. So ultimately, when 'in the balance weighed', Belshazzar is ironically 'light' and 'worthless' clay.

The selfishness of Saul and Belshazzar is ironic, for ultimately it destroys what it most desires. Thus Herod casts himself down, by his tyrannical destruction of an ideal Mariamne. Because he is the object of his own selfish pity, there is no reference to tears in 'Herod's Lament for Mariamne'. Mariamne 'soars'; though 'sunk' she is paradoxically 'above' in the world of loving peopled by the feminine ideals of the Hebrew Melodies. Herod's craving after her is in vain precisely because it is vain. The precursor of Porphyria's lover, and an allegorical figure of the Regent, he learns that he must dwell in the fallen world created by his jealous tyranny. The irony of this fate is apparent in Herod's banal plea: 'The heart for which thou bled'st is bleeding.' Mariamne's heart bled for Herod, but metaphor became reality, and now Herod's heart selfishly bleeds for Mari-

---

[34] E. H. Coleridge notes (see this edition, p. 179) that Daniel was not a 'youth' when he interpreted the prophecy. This seems to ignore the contrast of youth and age which hints at an aggressive purifying innocence.

amne.[35] Ironically the sword of Damocles that Byron images now hangs over Herod's head; a kind of handwriting on the wall, it suggests the paradox of egomania. We destroy what we love best and what is most devoted to us, making life a 'hell' in which we suffer the 'unconsumed' and 'still consuming' 'tortures' of Herod. Selfhood generates an ironic, frustrating, tyrannous cycle of possession and destruction, unless it is redefined in Promethean terms:

> Revenge is lost in agony,
> And wild remorse to rage succeeding.

Byron's substitution of 'wild' for 'deep' remorse makes the point. Herod's remorse is another kind of rage; agony is not martyrdom. But more than anything, the singsong of self-pity resulting from Byron's choice of a feminine rhyme ending in ing for all of the lyric's even-numbered lines deprives Herod of our compassion.

In '"All is Vanity, Saith the Preacher"', Ecclesiastes makes much the same point in much the same way as Herod the Great. Doing so he joins with Saul and Belshazzar, suggesting that Byron may have literally interpreted Ecclesiastes' declaration (1:12), 'I the Preacher was king over Israel in Jerusalem.' 'Fame, wisdom, love, and power were mine,' declaims Ecclesiastes. To these prizes are added: 'health', 'youth', blushing 'goblets', the caresses of 'lovely forms', and finally 'all earth can give, or mortal prize'. Byron twice crossed 'wealth' from this list, perhaps ironically, and probably to avoid a hackneyed rhyme with 'health'. Paradise was 'mine', Ecclesiastes tells his audience, and the entire world a 'mine of regal splendour' awaiting the ruler's command. (The substitution of 'regal' splendour for 'joy & Splendour' suggests the importance of that adjective.) But this play on 'mine' and the repetition of possessives ('mine' and 'my') reveals the vanity at the core of Ecclesiastes' character. Because of this vanity his many-splendoured world galls while it glitters; ironically he can recall 'no day' of 'pleasure unembittered'. More is at hand here than simple romantic *Weltschmerz*, as Byron's cancellation of a passage voicing that malady indicates:

> And what hath been? – but what shall be –
> The same dull scene renewing –
> And all our fathers were are we
> In erring & undoing –

[35] Gleckner (p. 209n) suggests that we read the poem as 'Jephtha's answer to his daughter's brave speech'.

Instead we learn that a 'serpent' holds Ecclesiastes' selfish heart in a symbolic vice-like grip, portraying the death of the 'heart' about which it 'coils'. 'Wisdom's lore' and 'music's voice' ('spells' and 'charms') cannot free the heart, for they signify a peace and harmony denied to the vain. The redemptive music that David plays to Saul in Byron's 'My Soul is Dark' symbolizes a catharsis vitiated by Ecclesiastes' self-pity. That self-pity redounds in the lyric's virtuosity. When a system of alternating line length and alternating masculine and feminine rhymes is imposed upon the double quatrain, the total effect is bathetic rather than pathetic. Such rhymes as *lure it, endure it*; *charming, harming*; and *unembittered, glittered* do not allow us to confuse sympathy and judgment as we read this dramatic lyric.

In a mutable universe selfishness is doubly ironic and self-defeating. Sennacherib, 'the Assyrian' who 'came down', proves this by destroying himself. 'The Destruction of Semnacherib' suggests that his fall is as determined as that of a 'wolf' leaping into a fold and a 'wave' rolling 'on deep Galilee', and Byron's substitution of 'Destruction' for 'Rout' in the title confirms this.[36] That destruction is recited in, and hastened by, the quatrains he uses most frequently in the Hebrew Melodies. These are built of anapaestic tetrameter lines (trimeter in a single instance) or heroic iambic pentameter lines (usually beginning with a trochee). The swift, firm beat of the anapaestic line and the brevity of the quatrain are ideally suited for Byron's dramatic and heroic fist-shaking. The *aabb* rhyme scheme, with its drumming reiteration, meets the needs of Jephtha's daughter, of Saul at the crucial moment before his last battle, of the defiant lover of 'I Speak Not — I Trace Not', of the heroic captive of 'Were my bosom as false as thou deem'st it to be', and of the nationalist bard of 'The Destruction of Semnacherib'.[37]

[36] John Ramsay of Ochtertyre, in his letters, calls Bonaparte 'Sennacherib' (quoted in 'The Scottish Enlightenment', *TLS*, 26 October 1967, p. 1010); Byron was probably familiar with this typical equation.

[37] Marchand calls the poem 'a tour de force but a brilliant one with perfect blending of mood and meter' (*Byron's Poetry*, p. 135). G. Wilson Knight writes that 'in short space [it] condense[s] almost all the main values of Byron's weightier, tragic and religious, genius' (*Essays in Criticism*, 1959, IX, 88). Martin calls it 'the apex, the crown of Byron's lyrical writing' (p. 15). Samuel C. Chew finds it 'famous but overrated' (*Lord Byron: 'Childe Harold's Pilgrimage' and other Romantic Poems* [New York, 1936], p. 488n); 'I think accurately', says Gleckner (p. 209n) of Chew. Some of the excessive praise may be attributed to those who, wishing to applaud Byron's unrecognized lyric talent, felt free to praise only the very few lyrics traditionally approved. Closer appraisal of the lyric corpus reveals poems of greater beauty and effectiveness.

Concentrating the troops into a single rider, Byron dramatizes the fall of the host. This wolf is found lying dead on the ground with 'rust on his mail'. The wave expires 'as the spray of the rock-beating surf', that echoes in the 'foam' of the steed's last gasp. Sennacherib's destruction stems from the entropic impermanence of human action:

Like the leaves of the forest when Summer is green,
That host with their banners at sunset were seen:
Like the leaves of the forest when Autumn hath blown,
That host on the morrow lay withered and strown.

The initial repetition fosters the cycle that is the eventual victor. The falling leaves and the sunset are natural prophecies of the fall of the selfish. All too soon the 'banners' are 'alone', the 'host' has 'withered', and the shining 'spears' have become rusty 'lances unlifted'. 'The trumphet unblown' serves to introduce by contrast the wailing widows of the poem's concluding stanza. Their music is the only appropriate music. (Byron's revision transported the widows from Babel to Ashur, their proper home. He could not keep the weepers of Psalm 137 out of his mind and in the right poem.) 'The pervasive similes', Michael Cooke correctly insists, 'suggest that nature, or a general will, favors innocence as an ordained state over the contingent state of [tyrannical] terror.'[38]

Eliphaz the Temanite meets with Byron's ultimate vision of 'what we are' as opposed to what we can be. That vision, articulated in 'From Job', reveals the twin ironies of selfishness simultaneously. As in 'Saul', initial emphasis is placed on the appearance of the Spirit. Eliphaz beholds 'the face of Immortality unveiled'. Ironically, that face is 'formless'. Ultimately *nothing* is unveiled in this dark lyric. Sleep veils all eyes but those of Eliphaz. They are emphasized along with 'bones', 'flesh', and 'hair', to contrast Immortal formlessness. Form or self is what keeps us from 'divine' shapelessness. ('Shapeless' was Byron's first choice for the spirit.) Byron deliberately de-emphasized alliteration, rejecting 'stood ... strange' for 'stood ... formless', and 'faithless flesh' for 'creeping flesh' to accentuate the lack of harmony. That dearth is emphasized by the insecurity of Seraphs in the world of Eliphaz. Men are 'creatures of clay' who dwell in vain 'in the dust!'. Because the 'clay' (a familiar metaphor) is not 'pure' (read innocent and selfless), only the 'moth'

---

[38] *The Blind Man Traces the Circle* (Princeton, 1969), p. 32. Knight writes: 'The Assyrian host challenges the stars and sea, man as against the cosmos, its co-equal and rival' (*Byron and Shakespeare* [London, 1966], p. 14).

soars from the dust in 'From Job'. 'Surviving' man, it is a symbol of both human insignificance and the vicious futility of selfish aspiration in a world where men 'wither ere the night' (substituted for 'fall before the Night'), like the withered host of Sennacherib and the Jews in 'The Wild Gazelle' who 'wander witheringly'. Wisdom's light is 'wasted' because men and moths waste it, and because it resembles the light of the 'Sun of the Sleepless!' Such is the 'excellent moral lesson' Byron referred Nathan to in the book of Job.

Eliphaz and his Byronic brethren dwell in a *self*-created fallen world envisioned in three of the Hebrew Melodies. That wasteland is built out of our selfish longing. Embittered by memory, our sympathy atrophies and becomes powerless to mediate real and ideal. In the dim world, Nature incessantly mocks fallen man's un-Promethean display of self-pity. 'The Wild Gazelle' images fallen Judah, and then employs a symbol of vital stability to condemn it. The 'airy steps' and 'tameless eyes' of the Gazelle mimic 'the freedom of [Judah's] living rills'. Those streams flow on to the tune of Byron's $a^4b^3abc^4c^4$ stanza. (The standard sixain shares the rhyme scheme of the final six lines in the *ottava rima*.) 'Judah's hills' survive as the 'holy ground' of a 'lost delight', once embodied in Judah's maids, who, with their 'step as fleet' and 'eye more bright' than the Gazelle's, 'are gone!'. (Perhaps Byron cancelled 'a step as light' to avoid striking a positive note through an internal rhyme with 'bright'.) Meanwhile 'the cedars wave on Lebanon', like the bounding gazelle. But they are rooted as well as waving, anticipating the palms of the lyric's third stanza. The palm is quite the opposite of Byron's gazelle:

> It cannot quit its place of birth,
> It will not live in other earth.

'Taking root', the palm 'remains'. 'Israel's' race is 'scattered'. It 'must wander witheringly', exiled for ever 'in other lands', while at home the wild gazelle's bound in freedom and the palms remain bound to the land that is theirs. The pun suggests that fallen Israel is mocked in one stanza by the gazelle, and in another stanza by the palm. Appropriately, the poem's concluding line installs 'Mockery' on 'Salem's throne'. (Byron rejected the alliteration of 'Darkness dwells' and 'Silence sits'.) Mockery 'sits' (suggesting that the entropic poem falls from action to inaction), for it is the ironic king of the false fallen world man's pride fosters.

The maids of 'The Wild Gazelle' symbolize Byron's feminine ideal, and the memory of that ideal mocks and torments Saul, Herod, and Ecclesiastes. This failing of memory is the subject of the very beautiful 'Sun of the Sleepless!' That simplest of lyrics, which Byron called 'his very best', was composed before his collaboration with Nathan. However, Byron probably realized that its lyric melancholy was quite in keeping with the general tone of the Hebrew Melodies that he numbered it among. Beginning with 'Sun', 'Sun of the Sleepless!' ends with a grim 'cold', and so confirms Byron's decision. Byron's 'sun' was at first the moon, for 'Moonbeam' is the only astronomical reference in the first draft. In his second attempt, Byron added 'Sun' and 'Star' to his solar system. Then he changed 'Moonbeam' to 'nightbeam', belatedly making up his mind, and reserving the moon for his ideal world of love. The star's light is 'melancholy' and 'tearful'. Byron made it weaker by substituting 'glows tremulously' for 'shoots trembling'. Ironically this feeble light 'show'st the darkness' it 'canst not dispel'. It merely defines the limits of 'powerless' memory. Having given us the poem's single image, Byron goes on to complete his inverted simile. The sleepless speaker (reminiscent of Eliphaz) tells us what the star is like: 'joy remembered well!' (Originally the simile began with the line 'What is the past?' Beginning with his answer, Byron allows the light from his feebly glowing star to dominate the lyric.) When the 'past' is remembered it tells of joy, but when the past is 'remembered well', it tells us that the joy has decayed. So the star 'shines, but warms not'. Its light is 'distinct, but distant', and 'clear – but . . . cold', ironically revealing 'what we are' and our inability to correct the alliterative contrast.

The torments of the false memory, which helps to cripple the present, are restated darkly in 'They say that Hope is happiness'. That lyric incorporates Byron's most despairing vision of the dimly lit fallen world of the dead heart. Byron's Ecclesiastes vainly 'saith' that all is vanity, and the 'They' who 'say that Hope is happiness' speak in cliché as trite as the glib internal rhyme. So Byron forces the reader from the paradise of platitude to a state of blank despair. The epigraph, *Felix qui potuit rerum cognoscere causas*, makes an ironic comment on this fall. But Byron relinquished irony in his lyric, to speak in a simple, confessional style that succeeds very well. This may be why Swinburne chose to include only this lyric (of the thirty Hebrew Melodies) in his edition of Byron's poems. The fallacy underlying the prosaic conclusion that 'hope is happiness' is exposed by 'Genuine' in the second line. Hope leads to false paradise; 'memory' holds the real 'prize'. Seemingly the 'thoughts that bless' are the thoughts that 'rose the first'. We turn back, but only to fall twice. What 'mem'ry loves the most' is our earliest hope. 'That hope adored and lost/Hath melted into memory.' Memory was hope; now hope is memory because there is nothing to hope for. Memory becomes a tormenting reminder of what has been 'lost'. The poem ends on a bleak note: 'Alas! it is delusion all —.' Hope and memory delude man, and the 'future cheats' him as its hope declines into the fallen present:[39]

> Nor can we be what we recall,
> Nor dare we think on what we are.

Again Byron's prophetic tone voices the 'sternest answer'. Platitude gives way to platitude; 'delusion' defines the only 'genuine' state, as some years later, Byron explained: 'Why do we live at all? Because Hope recurs to Memory, both false; but—but—but—but — and this but drags on till — What? I do not know, and who does?'[40]

The dimly lit, fallen world of the poems we have been considering may be redeemed. The destruction of Belshazzar and Sennacherib promises this much, and the subsequent history of Saul, made mythic by Byron, transforms promise into accomplishment. 'My Soul is Dark' dramatizes I Samuel 16:14–23, the account of David's easing of Saul's melancholy. Though this biblical episode preceded the raising up of Samuel, it is convenient to think of it as following that event, and to understand Saul's melancholy as stemming from Samuel's prophecy of doom. The heroism proven in the 'Song of Saul Before His Last Battle' will then be seen to stem from the inspiration of 'the harp the monarch minstrel swept'. The evil spirit plaguing Saul is the romantic agony. Because Saul has found out 'what we are', Byron tells us that his 'heart' has been 'doomed to know the worst'. To purge this 'heavy heart' music's 'sound' shall 'charm' forth hope. But only 'if in this heart a hope be dear', as opposed to selfish. (This explains the seeming failure of 'music's voice' in '"All is Vanity, Saith the Preacher"'.) Only then will David's

---

[39] 'Time future and time past fuse in the desert of present ruins', writes Gleckner of the lyric (p. 221).

[40] 'Paper Book of G. G. B., Ld. B.', Ravenna, 1821, *L & J*, V, 439. Prothero gave the title 'Detached Thoughts' to the entries in this combination journal and memoir.

melting strains give rise to the tears that metaphorically quench the melancholic flames which 'burn' Saul's 'brain'. The emphasis falls heavily on the heart, for it is ultimately the heart that must restore the fallen universe which the brain forges. When the heart is wrought to sympathy, self-consciousness is consumed. The success of the catharsis depends on Promethean selflessness attested to by genuine weeping.[41] Music is not so much cause as effect: harmony is a symbol of the mediation suggested by Byron's choice of 'melting' to characterize the process. 'My Soul is Dark' is a Hebrew Melody about the cathartic role of Hebrew melodies, and, as we shall see, the weeping harpers of Byron's sighing versions of Psalm 137 come to learn this truth of their art.

The emphasis on redemptive harmony in 'My Soul is Dark' should evoke more than usual interest in that lyric's versification. Byron does not disappoint those who expect Hebrew Melodies about music to be richly musical. Alliterative phrases (fingers fling, melting murmurs, heart a hope, burn my brain, heavy heart, sleepless silence) and complex patterns of assonance and consonance are set to work in a carefully wrought double-quatrain stanza. But instead of the ababcdcd scheme Byron limits himself to three rhymes, employing the ababbcbc scheme of 'To Belshazzar', 'If that High World', and 'Bright be the place of thy soul'. This is the rhyme scheme of Chaucer's Monk's Tale stanza (Byron preferred terse iambic tetrameter to Chaucer's iambic pentameter), and the rhyme scheme of the Spenserian stanza minus its alexandrine. The facility in forming interlocking quatrains that Byron demonstrates in the Hebrew Melodies probably developed from the Byronic Spenserians of Childe Harold. By limiting himself to three rhymes in eight lines, Byron makes his music richer in texture if less developed in range. But if we compare the stanza rhyming ababbcbc with the simple double-quatrain stanza, a more important gain becomes apparent. The rhyme scheme of the interlocking quatrains suggests the idea of change within the context of permanence, as opposed to the sharp transition of the simple double quatrain. The central couplet within the quatrains marks the cathartic moment. The stanzaic pattern of Byron's sad song about sad songs mediates by articulating change within a seemingly permanent context.

The weeping harpers of Byron's three versions of Psalm 137 resemble Saul more than David. In 'Oh! Weep for Those', Byron twice

[41] Cooke (p. 31) writes that the poem dramatizes 'the self-conscious mind striving to yield away the self'.

commands us to 'weep' in the initial stanza of the lyric. The 'broken' harp of Judah mirrors the state of Judah's heart; it too is a 'desolate' shrine in which 'the Godless dwell'. In the midst of the lamentation, Byron asks a series of questions, When shall the exile symbolized by Israel's 'bleeding feet' come to an end? 'When shall Zion's songs again seem sweet?' The 'bleeding feet' suggest that 'sweet' songs of redemption have their source in willing Christian martyrdom attested to by genuine weeping. Having no 'nest' or 'cave', the outcasts of Zion cannot 'flee away and be at rest', like the 'fox' and the 'wild-dove' of Psalm 55. Israel has no 'country' but 'the grave', but that is the martyr's natural sanctuary.

In a second attempt at Psalm 137, 'By the Rivers of Babylon We Sat Down and Wept',[42] Byron again emphasizes weeping, but he does not leave self-sacrifice to suggestion alone. The unconstrained waters of Babylon 'which rolled on in freedom below' make an ironic comment on the fall of the captive harpers. Reflection on this natural image leads to weeping. But though the river's freedom saddens, the expression of that sadness in wailing complaint is immediately followed by defiance drawing its inspiration from the recognition of natural harmony and vitality. The harp of Judah, no Aeolian harp, is suspended on the willow. 'Its sound should be free,' defiantly exclaims the harpist. (The evolution of courage out of tears is dramatized by the shift from plural to singular.) That music shall never be 'blended with the voice of the spoiler'. His selfish 'slaughters' inhibit harmonious 'soft tones'.[43]

The harpers of 'In the Valley of Waters' (the third version of Psalm 137), refusing to entertain their captors, threaten: 'Our blood they shall spill.' The single rhyme Byron confines himself to in each stanza makes their threat less grandiloquent and more heroic. Willing martyrdom emerges from sympathetic tears, and selfhood is mediated in a catharsis proven by the heart's generosity. Like Manfred, the harpers know that 'it is not so difficult to die'. In a natural world in which the leaves on 'the willow's sad tree' are

---

[42] Cf. 'By the waters of Leman I sat down and wept', T. S. Eliot, *The Waste Land*, l. 182, and 'we have hanged our hearts in her trees; and we list, as she bibs us, by the waters of babalong', James Joyce, *Finnegans Wake*, ch. 4, concl.

[43] Unfortunately Byron's alternation of masculine and feminine rhymes contributes to the lack of harmony, and L. C. Martin writes of the lyric: 'Here is the familiar ambling facility of Byron's anapests, the hit-or-miss *insouciance*, the disturbing flavour of light-hearted indifference' (*Byron's Lyrics*, Byron Foundation Lecture [Nottingham, 1948], p. 16).

'dead' and the 'wind . . . hath died on the hill' (originally 'the wind in the cave of the hill') their gratuitous heroism is not without meaning.

The tearful lyrics we have been examining have much to say about the harp of Judah, and most of what they say is enacted again in 'The harp the monarch minstrel swept'. That poem incorporates the fullest expression of the myth of the Hebrew Melodies. This seems appropriate because David is the best of Byron's psalmists, and because in his lyric he seems to be reciting the very song played to Saul. But Byron's revision has made David a 'monarch' and a 'minstrel' and so very different from his royal counterpart. The harps of the captive minstrels and David's harp are at once similar and dissimilar. 'Its chords are riven', just as the harps of Judah are 'all stringlessly hung'. But at the close of 'The harp the monarch minstrel swept', David's harp has risen and changed its tune. Unselfish heroic aspirations lead to the harp's aspiration or ascent: 'Its sound *aspired* to Heaven and their abode!' (italics added). The riven harp becomes mightier than David's 'throne', and its *harmony* commands tyrants of 'iron mould', who are 'softened' with unselfish 'virtues not their own'. Harmony is again the symbol of mediation.[44] In the natural world, 'vallies ring', 'cedars bow', and 'mountains nod', responding to the melodies of the Hebrew Orpheus and approving (not mocking) his selfless heroism. In the lyric's final stanza, the radical catharsis is elaborated. 'Devotion' and 'love', the minions of the harp now 'heard on earth no more', descend to become the redeemers of Byron's universe. From 'riven' (present) they lead us to 'throne' (idealized past) and then to 'Heaven' (present redeemed). The 'dreams' of love are the heroes of the fallen world. (They are neither the vain 'dreams' of Sorrow in 'Oh! snatched away in beauty's bloom' nor the forsaken 'dream' of the fallen Jews in 'Oh! Weep for Those'.) From the heaven within the heart, they 'bid the bursting spirit soar', commanding it in 'sounds that seem as from above', to free itself from its self and turn real into ideal. This is the music that Saul found irresistible.[45]

[44] Consider the harmonic resonances of 'No ear so dull, no soul so cold'. 'The caesura separates nearly identical phrases, and the dominant consonantal pattern is expanded by the trilling of du*l*l, sou*l*, and co*l*d and the ringing of N*o*, s*o*, n*o*, s*o*ul, s*o*, c*o*ld. These patterns have then been set into an a^4babb^5 stanza.

[45] Cooke (p. 27) writes: 'David's music embodies immortality in music.' Then he adds: 'That immortality, lost in fact, is preserved somehow in memory, which thereby serves as a defense against the experience of mortality.' Byron's Memory is, however, indefensible.

Because 'The harp the monarch minstrel swept' is at the centre of the myth projected in the Hebrew Melodies, it symbolizes Byron's own struggle to pass from negation to affirmation. Cancelled fragments and incomplete stanzas show that he was divided between consolation and continued lament. Before writing the affirmative third stanza of the lyric, Byron cancelled an incomplete stanza beginning darkly: 'His glory bids us mourn the more'. 'But he is dust – and we are sunk', began the present third stanza. Cancelling this line, Byron allowed David to rest on his triumphs in heaven. But he then set down a grim incomplete fourth stanza:

> It there abode – and there it rings
>> But neer on earth its sound shall be –
> The Prophet's race hath passed away –
> And all the hallowed Minstrelsy
From earth that sound & soul are fled
> And shall we never hear again.

No consolation is found here. 'But neer on earth' emphasizes our enslavement. What we 'never hear' cannot bid us soar. *Happily*, this unfinished stanza was cancelled too. Nathan, however, wished to have another 'to help out the melody'. Byron replied: 'Why I have sent you to Heaven – it would be difficult to go further.' In the stanza he finally wrote, as we have seen, Byron made a heaven of earth, and then exclaimed: 'Here, Nathan, I have brought you down again.'[46]

In his martial monologue, the 'Song of Saul Before His Last Battle', Saul 'soars' (another commonplace) from Belshazzar's camp to David's realm. The 'heavy' heart 'doomed to know the worst' has been redeemed by 'devotion' and 'love', transforming selfish tyranny into heroic sympathy and worst into best. Saul becomes another Magdalen for the very reasons set down in Byron's lyric of that title. Byron told Nathan that though 'Saul, who was once gloriously surrounded by strength, power, and the approbation of his God . . . had sunk from this', he could not 'but uphold him originally a brave and estimable man'. The Promethean tones of Saul's monologue confirm that Saul regained Byron's original opinion. Napoleon, Byron's 'little Pagod', failed; Saul did not, and so he remarked to Nathan: '. . . Napoleon would have ranked higher in future history, had he even like your venerable ancestor Saul, on

[46] *FP*, p. 33.

mount Gilboa, or like a second Cato, fallen on his sword, and finished his mortal career at Waterloo.'[47] So Saul, the 'second Cato', tells his troops to pay no 'heed' to his 'corse'; ironically they are to 'bury' their arms in the foe. (Byron's apt heroic measure is smartened by alliteration: 'Corse, though a king's' was preferred to 'carcase that lies', 'buckler and bow' to 'shield and my bow', and 'soldiers of Saul' to 'ranks of your king'.) If the men falter, Saul's armour-bearer is to slay him. 'Mine be the doom which they dared not to meet' threatens the hero on the way to his own doom. The over-tones of martyrdom and self-sacrifice signify regained 'royalty'. Saul's corpse is 'a king's', and his death is 'kingly':

> Bright is the diadem, boundless the sway,
> Or kingly the death, which awaits us to-day!

In death, Byron crowns Saul to signify his redemption through heroism.

Just how far Saul has come may be seen if we contrast Byron's 'To Belshazzar' with the 'Vision of Belshazzar'. While the latter poem is a narrative in which Daniel utters the last stanza, the former is made up entirely of Daniel's defiant monologue. The structure of Byron's myth takes us from fallen king to heroic captive; Saul knows both sides of this romantic coin, having turned from one to the other. The rejected line, 'The prophet dares, before thee glares', suggests the scene. Daniel will be another David. Belshazzar is summoned to the 'banquet', the scene of his ironic last supper. 'The weakest, worst of all', men miscall him 'crowned and anointed from on high', particularly men like Metternich and Castlereagh. But the Prophet is not deluded; he reads the handwriting on the wall, seeing through the man-made myth of divine right to a divine injunction: 'Is it not written, thou must die?' ('A lord as high as thee may fall', Byron first put it.) Just what is 'written' was twice revised by Byron:

> The words of God along the wall –
> The words of God – the graven wall
> The graven words – the glowing wall.

Dividing the line into two repetitive phrases with identical consonant patterns (a favourite device), Byron evolves a spare archaic form.[48]

[47] *FP*, pp. 42–3; *FP*, p. 40.

[48] From the cancelled, incomplete opening stanza, Byron's initial choice of rhyme scheme may be seen:

> The red light *glows*—the wassail *flows*
> Around the royal *hall*

That *graven* suggests grave is no disadvantage in a poem in which every stanza ends on the word 'die'. The repetition culminates with the insult that Belshazzar is 'unfit to . . . die'. This paradox proves the truth of Daniel's heroism and Byron's myth, and is imaged in the concluding stanza:

> Oh! early in the balance weighed,
> And ever light of word and worth.[49]

'Light' in the scales of justice, Belshazzar is a 'mass of earth'.

Byron again affirms heroic redemption and suggests its source in praising the hero[50] of 'Thy Days are Done':

> The generous blood that flowed from thee
> Disdained to sink beneath:

'Generous' is brought to our attention, because to be generous in a selfish world is heroic not otiose. The blood of the hero disdains to sink because it is as selfless as the heart of Byron's 'Prometheus':

> Triumphant where it dares defy,
> And making Death a Victory.
>
> (III : 24–5)

---

[49] Cf. 'He in the balance weighed,/Is light and worthless clay' ('Vision of Belshazzar', 6:2–3). The similarity suggests that Byron intended to choose between the poems on Belshazzar, and that he was unwilling to part with an effective Old Testament image.

[50] Byron does not tell us who the hero of 'Thy Days are Done' is. Nathan, hinting that the poem memorializes Napoleon, writes: 'Lord Byron, in this melody had some reference to a fallen warrior, whose deeds remain a monument to his memory, and though dead to the world, he still leaves a lasting impression on the minds of the living' (*FP*, pp. 39–40). But Byron's cousin Sir Peter Parker is the likely warrior, as correspondence and the circumstances of the poem's composition suggest. He fell fighting a band of Americans, near Baltimore, in August 1814, and Byron's 'Elegiac Stanzas on the Death of Sir Peter Parker' were first published in the *Morning Chronicle* of 7 October. They were reprinted in *Hebrew Melodies*, published at the time of Parker's state funeral.

> And who on *earth* dare mar the *mirth*
> Of that high festi*val*
> Belshazzar *rise*—nor dare de*spise*
> The writing on the *wall*!

The italicized rhymes show that a stanza much like that of Shelley's 'The Cloud' was intended. This stanza yields nine rhymes in six lines; those rhymes and additional alliteration make it too singsong for angry rhetoric. Byron rejected his initial attempt, preferring interlocking quatrains of uniform length rather than the simple quatrains he employed elsewhere in the heroic poems.

The same thoughts are expressed in Byron's 'Ode from the French',
beginning 'We do not curse thee, Waterloo!':

> Though Freedom's blood thy plain bedew;
> There 'twas shed, but is not sunk –
> Rising from each gory trunk,
>
> . . . .
> It soars, and mingles in the air.

Because the death of the 'chosen Son' is a victory: 'To weep would
do thy glory wrong;/Thou shalt not be deplored.' This may be a
studied ambiguity (as Gleckner [p. 208] has noted), and Byron's
addition of 'the slaughters of his sword' to the list of his hero's
deeds is another. The point is that the nationalist bard has confused
fame and glory. So in his national melody the hero's name becomes
the 'battle-word', but in Byron's the 'strains' of the first stanza
become the 'choral song' of 'virgin voices', who echo the 'virgins of
Salem' in 'Jephtha's Daughter'. The hero's glory has begun, for he is
worshipped by the innocent.

Precisely because her death is a 'victory', Jephtha's daughter
prompts us in her very last line: 'And forget not I smiled as I died.'
Calling to mind Saul, Charlotte Corday, and the Maid of Saragoza,
she commands, 'Strike the bosom that's bared for thee now.'[51]
Because the sacrificial element is emphasized Jephtha's daughter
becomes a Hebrew Iphigenia, who willingly gives her life to preserve
her father's vow. Her passionate resolve is voiced in familiar
quatrains, here composed of breathless anapaestic trimeter. Their
music is not simple, and the effect (as in the comic rhyme of *sire* and
expire) serves to make a pathetic poem seem bathetic today. But the
heroics of Jephtha's daughter are not mock heroics.[52] She has come
down from the 'mountains' to the hand that will 'lay me low'. But
'the last thought that soothes [her] below' implies that ascension
must follow sacrifice. Her 'hushed' voice will echo on earth like the
music of David's harp.

Though Palestine is divided and fallen the bard of 'On Jordan's
Banks' is as heroic as Saul or Jephtha's daughter. 'Jordan's banks',
'Sion's hill', and 'Sinai's steep' are the possessions of 'Arabs', 'False
Ones', and 'Baal-adorers'. Their false worship is contrasted with the

---

[51] Jephtha's daughter echoes Zuleika, who remarks in the *Bride of Abydos*, 'Thou
led'st me here perchance to kill . . . my breast is offered – take thy fill!' (ll. 655-7).

[52] Gleckner, however, asks us to read the poem with a 'sense of horror, not
jubilation' (p. 209).

worship of the past that merited Jehovah's favour; now his 'thunders sleep'. But once before God had awakened his glory, 'shrouded in its garb of fire' on Sinai. Now the defiant bard calls on Jehovah to unshroud that image of life-in-death:

> Oh! in the lightning let thy glance appear!
> Sweep from his shivered hand the oppressor's spear:
> How long by tyrants shall thy land be trod?
> How long thy temple worshipless, Oh God?

The tone is both defiant and prophetic. The bard suggests that the harsh fulfilment of the prophecies is reason for renewed faith and ensuing redemption returning the fallen from the waters of Babylon to the banks of the Jordan.

In 'On the Day of the Destruction of Jerusalem by Titus', Byron puts the sentiments of 'On Jordan's Banks' into the mouth of a captive Jew staring down upon the ruins of Jerusalem. 'Oh! in the lightning let thy glance appear,' cries the bard of 'On Jordan's Banks'. 'Oh! would that the lightning had glared in its stead,' echoes Titus' captive of the twilight beam falling on Jerusalem. He looks on the fallen city 'from the last hill', as the 'last sun went down', with his 'last glance', chanting heroic defiance like Saul before his last battle. The dramatic lyric gains its main strength from a central metaphor involving reflected light. As Byron's captive is led away over the hill-tops, he looks back on Jerusalem, 'and the flames of' the city's 'fall flashed back on' his 'glance'. Then the captive remembers the events of pre-Lapsarian days when, 'on many an eve, the high spot whence I gazed/Had reflected the last beam of day as it blazed.' Seen from below, 'the rays from the mountain', shone on the Temple, bathing it in the fading light of the sunset. In this manner, the Temple becomes a symbol of heavenly light on earth, and earth is transformed by the light of ancient faith into paradise. But now, ironically, the captive no longer sees 'the last beam of day as it blazed'; he sees the blazing Temple and the death-fire consuming it. (By changing 'ruin' to 'death-fire' Byron gained more than another alliterative f.) Though the sun is sinking in the west, the captive 'marked not the twilight beam melting away' as he had in the past. The light continues unnaturally, for the heaven of Jerusalem has become a hell, whose flames ironically replace the sun. This is Byron's version of Jeremiah 15:9, 'Her sun is gone down while it was yet day.' Provoked by the destruction he witnesses, the captive carries the metaphor one step further by wishing that the 'lightning had glared' and the thunderbolt 'burst' in the twilight's 'stead'. (Byron first wrote 'burst', changed 'burst' to 'crashed', and then, apparently, changed 'crashed' to 'burst' in the proofs, thinking the alliteration would prevent his anapaestic tetrameter from languishing.) But the 'Gods of the Pagan shall never profane' the 'fane' that is in ashes. That consolation calls to mind another. The harsh fulfilment of the prophecies serves to restore faith in those prophecies yet to be fulfilled:

> And scattered and scorned as thy people may be,
> Our worship, Oh Father! is only for thee.

Byron rewrote the opening couplet of 'On the Day of the Destruction' to incorporate the alliterative phrase 'rendered to Rome'. The biblical echo and other similarities suggest that the captive of that poem becomes the martyred dying exile of 'Were my bosom as false as thou deem'st it to be'. That poem takes its cue from the last lines of the former: 'And scattered and scorned as thy people may be,/Our worship, Oh Father! is only for thee.' So scattered and scorned, the dying exile heroically affirms his faith. His bosom is not false to Jehovah. Had it been so there had been no need to endure the fallen state, no need to 'have wandered from far Galilee'. By proving his bosom faith and belief in the 'creed' that the tyrant terms a 'curse', not by 'abjuring' it, the exile unselfishly turns curse into blessing:

> If the Exile on earth is an Outcast on high,
> Live on in thy faith, but in mine I will die.

It is precisely because the 'Exile', the 'Outcast', and the 'slave' must 'triumph' in the world 'on high', that they live on in their 'faith', regardless of the prohibitions. A bosom's faith is its generosity. The selflessness it attests to is ample reason for 'making Death a Victory'. Because he is a hero in disguise, the exile expires with the calm resignation of the faithful:

> In his hand is my heart and my hope – and in thine
> The land and the life which for him I resign.

The emphasis on the 'heart' and on the 'high world' in 'Were my bosom as false as thou deem'st it to be' reminds us that in a selfish world love too is defiance. So in the secular lyric 'I Speak Not – I Trace Not – I Breathe Not' Byron defends clandestine love as zealously as he defends the Zionist ideal. He does so by articulating what must be contained, but what can no longer be contained: 'I speak not – I breathe not – I write not thy name,' Byron had first written. He changed the order of the original to create a sequence that moves toward the enforced 'silence' of the stanza's close and the dramatic silent 'reply' that concludes the poem. ('Trace' eliminates the obtrusive i in 'write'.) Silence was shattered by the original opening line of the lyric's second stanza: 'We have loved – and Oh still my adored one – we love.' Too bold and too simple, this declaration ignores the struggle in the heart that Byron chose to enact in a series of contrasts: 'Too brief . . . too long', 'our passion . . . our peace', and 'their joy . . . their bitterness'. Reform was attempted, but exiles and lovers may not 'abjure' Promethean love:

> We repent – we abjure – we will break from our chain;
> We must part – we must fly to – unite it again.

Ironically, the lovers reunite by breaking the chain of five phrases beginning with 'we'.[53] (Another cancelled line reads: 'Oh the moment is past that forbids our release.') As love conquers guilt, the speaker tests the sympathy of his defiant heart:

> But the heart which I bear shall expire undebased
> And man shall not break it – whatever thou may'st.

The 'undebased' heart confirms the purity that purges the fallen, restoring their 'high world':

> And our days seem as swift – and our moments more sweet,
> With thee by my side – than the world at our feet.

In the paradise above the world there is no need for defiance, and significantly, the poem ends with the same lack of communication it began with. The lovers have no need of words: 'Thy lip shall reply not to them – but to mine.' Once unspoken love has been articulated (and love appears only once) Augusta's kisses are enough.[54]

*   *   *   *   *

[53] The 'flowing anapests', Marchand writes, 'give a ringing earnestness to the lines and make them seem "passion's essence"' (*Byron's Poetry*, p. 121).

[54] The lyric seems to chronicle the affair Byron described in his letters to Lady Melbourne. Writing to her on 21 February 1814, he voices the conflict between guilt and passionate concern: 'It is the misery of my situation, to see it as you see it, and to *feel* it as I feel it, on *her* account, and that of others' (*LBC*, I, 245). By April, he was promising that, 'She and I will grow good . . .' (*LBC*, I, 251). In May, his resolve seemed to weaken: 'She is in truth a very *lovable* woman and I will try and not love any longer. . . . It is indeed a very *triste* and extraordinary

The world 'on high' to which heroes and defiant lovers 'soar' is built of love that redeems by transforming self-consciousness into sympathy. Its testament and structure are made explicit in 'If that High World'. Recognizing this from Byron's remark that 'to him one of the most convincing reasons for believing in Eternity was that we never could love enough in this state of being – that we could not mingle "soul in soul"', Annabella wrote, 'this is beautifully expressed in the Hebrew Melody'.[55] Death liberates only if the eternity of 'When coldness wraps this suffering clay' is transformed into heaven by 'surviving Love' and 'cherished heart'. If so:

> How sweet this very hour to die!
> To soar from earth and find all fears
> Lost in thy light – Eternity!

'The probable nature of happiness in a future state' is confirmed by love.[56] Death severs being and soul and being from being. Because of our loved ones, we 'cling' ironically to 'Being's' paradoxical 'severing link' while 'striving to o'erleap the gulph' that separates high world and fallen present.[57] But by doing just that, we affirm the love that makes a heaven of eternity. There hearts share 'immortal waters', and 'soul in soul', grow 'deathless'.

In 'When coldness wraps this suffering clay', Byron envisions an eternity without love. That vision recalls the nothingness which followed upon the unveiling of immortality to Eliphaz the Temanite. The contrast with 'If that High World' is instructive. Without love

[55] Statement L, quoted in Elwin, p. 284. Some confusion is owing to the fact that Annabella inscribed the manuscript of 'Oh! snatched away in beauty's bloom': 'Given me at Seaham before my Marriage.' The manuscript of 'If that High World' is not extant; the poem was probably set down at the time of Byron's first visit to Seaham in November 1814. Annabella's reference to the last line of that poem ('soul in soul'), her reference to Eternity, and the fact that what is 'beautifully expressed' is expressed in that poem, show her to have intended 'If that High World'.

[56] *FP*, p. 21.

[57] This conflict is reflected in the contrary attitudes of Anah and Aholibamah as they depart for heaven with their angelic lovers at the close of *Heaven and Earth*. Byron described their journey to Medwin: 'The affectionate tenderness of Adah [*sic*] for those from whom she is parted, and for ever, and her fears contrasting with the loftier spirit of Aholibamah triumphing in the hopes of a new and greater destiny, will make the dialogue' (Medwin, p. 157).

business, and what is to become of us I know not, and I won't think just now' (*LBC*, I, 256). It was at this time that he set down 'I Speak Not – I Trace Not – I Breathe Not'. The lines confirmed that his 'perverse passion' was his 'deepest after all' (*LBC*, I, 218).

the probable nature of happiness in the future state is nil, and high world is void. In his journal, Byron outlined this metaphysic of eternity.

> Of the immortality of the Soul, it appears to me that there can be little doubt, if we attend for a moment to the action of Mind. It is in perpetual activity. . . . It acts also so very independent of body: in dreams for instance incoherently and madly, I grant you; but still it is Mind, and much more Mind than when we are awake. Now, that this should not act *separately*, as well as jointly, who can pronounce? . . .
>
> How far our future life will be individual, or, rather, how far it will at all resemble our *present* existence, is another question; but that the Mind is *eternal*, seems as probable as that the body is not so.[58]

Too often critics have been content with Byron's first remarks, ignoring his second 'question' altogether. But the contrast of 'When coldness wraps' and 'If that High World' proves it an important corollary of immortality. Thus the 'immortal mind' in 'When coldness wraps' becomes finally a 'nameless and eternal thing', its loss of identity severely qualified by the paradox it has become. The 'suffering clay' stays behind. That Byron chose to call it that, rejecting the alliterative 'corroding clay' and 'frail flesh', indicates its heroic worth. Byron's rhymes reflect this qualified transition. Like '"All is Vanity, Saith the Preacher"' and 'Vision of Belshazzar', 'When coldness wraps this suffering clay' is written in stanzas rhyming *ababcdcd*. Only in the first stanza has Byron limited himself to three rhymes; the resulting *ababcaca* scheme suggests the metamorphosis and permanence we are concerned with. The mind finds itself in a difficult spot: 'It cannot die, it cannot stay.' It must go off then, but the implication is that in doing so it becomes something else because divided from its self. So the soul takes flight, and that flight is not much different from the trip that Byron's Cain describes:

> And yet I have approached that sun, and seen
> Worlds which he once shone on, and never more
> Shall light; and worlds he never lit . . .
> I had beheld the immemorial works

---

[58] 'Paper Book', Ravenna, 1821, *L & J*, V, 456–7. Prothero gives the passage again with numerous minor differences in *L & J*, II, 20n.

> Of endless beings; skirred extinguished worlds;
> And, gazing on eternity. . . .
>
> (*Cain*, III, i: 56–65)[59]

Byron sends the soul on a cosmic journey from the birthplace of the 'furthest heaven' to where 'sun is quenched or system breaks' and 'where the future mars or makes'. This voyage demonstrates that mind conquers cosmic matter; it is no longer born, and so it no longer dies. Amid the death and regeneration of cosmic chaos, the spirit remains 'fixed' but alienated in 'its own eternity'. Alone, it becomes a detached observer of material process. Byron calls it 'a thing of eyes', and those eyes 'survey', 'trace', 'behold', 'glance', 'roll', and 'dilate'. The emphasis on 'seeing all' ('all' is used in this connection six times) confirms its own nothingness. Ironically 'passionless and pure', it dwells above man, 'above o'er Love, Hope, Hate, or Fear', in a world where time and space are meaningless. Ages 'fleet like earthly year', years endure as 'moments', and 'without a wing', the soul 'shall fly' – 'o'er all, through all'. The emphasis on *over* indicates that detachment is the price of ironic purity. 'Passionless' is indicted for it divorces love and eternity, making the latter colder than clay. Because it has no name, Byron's 'thing' lives for ever in timeless, limitless chaos. Having seen everything, it has all knowledge, and having all knowledge, it has no knowledge of death. 'Forgetting what it was to die', it *suffers*, – 'eternal, boundless, undecayed', but not 'unfettered', for Byron cancelled that adjective.

The contrasting eternities we have been discussing are the subject of the two Thyrza poems (inspired by Byron's adolescent love for John Edleston) Byron numbered among the Hebrew Melodies. Both 'Oh! snatched away in beauty's bloom' and 'Bright be the place of thy soul' are set at the grave of the beloved, both make much of the particulars ('turf' and 'tomb') of the grave, but the former seemingly endorses the tears which the latter rejects. The general point is that love's high world makes death a victory; true sympathy knows that weeping for what remains is selfish. Going from one poem to the other restates the catharsis of Byron's sighing psalms

---

[59] M. K. Joseph (*Byron the Poet*, p. 120) also compared these space journeys. In his edition of *Cain* (p. 275), T. G. Steffan writes: 'The resemblance between the subject of this lyric and Act II of *Cain* is very slight.' E. W. Marjarum (*Byron as Skeptic and Believer*, p. 51) found that Byron 'frequently testified to the power which the heavens exert upon an imaginative spirit. In an outwardly Christian lyric, "When coldness wraps this suffering clay" . . . he mingles with traditional ideas a peculiar notion of a magnetic attraction exercised by the stars.'

from a secular perspective. That the weeping for Judah is not much different from the weeping for Thyrza should not surprise us. In 'Oh! snatched away in beauty's bloom', Byron writes:

> And oft by yon blue gushing stream
> Shall Sorrow lean her drooping head.

These lines call to mind the opening lines of 'In the Valley of Waters':

> In the valley of waters we wept o'er the day . . .
> And our heads on our bosoms all droopingly lay.

Byron had first written:

> And oft by yon blue gushing stream
> Shall Sorrow on the waters gaze.

These unrevised lines seem to echo 'By the Rivers of Babylon':

> While sadly we gazed on the river
> Which rolled on in freedom below.

The inherent similarity in the central images of these passages suggests that Byron turned personal anguish into metaphor in the Thyrza poems and the Hebrew Melodies, by using it to dramatize self-made myth and Jewish history made mythic.

Roses alone serve as a memorial for the beloved of 'Oh! snatched away in beauty's bloom'. (This suggests the tombstone-less graves of 'And thou art dead, as young and fair', and 'Without a stone to mark the spot', and the 'roses o'er a sepulchre' of 'One struggle more, and I am free'.) Their bloom commemorates fallen 'beauty's bloom'. 'Their leaves, the earliest of the year' are the first to wither, and so the first to be 'snatched away'. The conceits are appropriate but trite, and this sentimentality extends into the second stanza.[60] Sorrow steps 'lightly', ironically to avoid disturbing the dead. But 'death nor hears nor heeds distress', and so our 'tears are vain' and inappropriate. But death's deafness to our own vain tears of self-pity makes no wet-eyed 'mourner weep the less'. That it should do so is the point of the mourner's 'wan', deadly 'looks'. Byron meant them to 'unteach us to complain' selfishly. 'Away – it is delusion all,' he had first written in this lyric (echoing 'They say that Hope is happiness'), deadly delusion that frustrates sympathy and misses the point of the rose-decked grave.

[60] H. W. Garrod described the poem as a 'perfect lyrical whole' (*Byron, 1824–1924* [Oxford, 1924], pp. 18–19). Hunt's publication of the poem in the *Examiner* on 23 April was perhaps intended to commemorate Shakespeare.

'Bright be the place of thy soul' again finds us at Thyrza's grave. That 'place' must mirror the 'orbs of the blessed', where Edleston's 'all but divine' spirit, shall be 'immortally'. (Why Byron substituted 'immortally' for 'eternally' is the point of the contrast between 'If that High World' and 'When coldness wraps'.) The spirit is in a bright place, and harmony demands that the grave be a bright place too.[61] 'Light', echoing bright at the beginning of stanza one confirms this. The 'yew' and the 'cypress' of 'Oh! snatched away' are gone. Instead, Byron decorated his tomb with 'fresh flowers and a far spreading tree'. Then he discarded this alliterative 'verdure', for 'young flowers and an evergreen tree'. The new adjectives suggest beauty, innocence, rebirth, and immortality. They are also the colour of 'emeralds'. This shrubbery is to 'spring' from the grave (Byron had first written 'wave', substituted 'grow', and then decided on 'spring') so 'aught that reminds us' of death will be appropriately inappropriate. Why then 'should we mourn for the blest?' We do mourn in 'Oh! snatched away', but doing so, we confirm our persistent belief in the myth of death that Byron's ironic question castigates. The high world reflected in the bright grave is reason enough for 'sorrow' (the 'Sorrow' personified in 'Oh! snatched away') to 'cease to repine'. Love that believes in love will be 'untaught to complain'.

Byron was more than half serious when he replied to a woman who had asked what would make him happy in his high world: 'The pleasure, Madame, of seeing you there.'[62] Having affirmed his heaven, he made it the abode of the women who embody his vision of ideal beauty – particularly in the lyrics he composed before deciding on the Hebrew Melodies, and before his marriage, but subsequently gave to Isaac Nathan along with the Old Testament lyrics. Their subject is secular love, their place is the 'high world', and their protagonists are women: Francisca, Lady Frances Webster (the 'thee' of 'I Saw Thee Weep'), Mrs Wilmot Horton (the 'she' of 'She Walks in Beauty'), and Augusta (the 'name' of the lines beginning 'I speak not, I trace not, I breathe not thy name'). These Eves, like 'devotion and her daughter love' in 'The harp the monarch minstrel swept', show us that real and ideal may be harmonized.

[61] George Saintsbury speaks of the 'magnificent harmony' of the anapaestic trimeter in 'Bright be the place of thy soul', in *A History of English Prosody* (New York, 1961, reprinted), III, 96.

[62] *FP*, p. 22.

Like David's harmonies, their ideal beauty is a symbol of an Eden restored by the unselfish heart.

The Edenic world of love is delineated in Byron's 'It is the Hour'. A serenade composed of the 'high note' of the nightingale, the 'music' of gentle winds and waters, and the 'whispered' words of lovers' vows heralds the coming of that hour. Byron helps this serenade along with internal rhyme (*hour, boughs, hour, vows*), and alliteration (*when, when, sweet, whispered, words, winds, waters*).[63] The harmony of natural music fosters scenic beauty, and Byron builds a paradise of 'flower', 'stars', 'wave', and 'leaf'; repetition (*And in, And on, And on, And in*) preserves the spell. The key to this paradise is its 'Heaven', that 'clear obscure,/So softly dark, and darkly pure'. Much like the night of cloudless climes in 'She Walks in Beauty', the 'darkly pure' sky reflects the mediating power of the ideal. So the moonlight supplants the twilight of the declining 'day', confirming the continuity of the world of love and assuring the 'lonely ear' that strains to hear the whispered lovers' vows.

Francisca dwells in the garden bower of 'It is the Hour'. Much like the woman who 'walks in beauty, like the night', Francisca 'walks in the shadow of night'. That Christabel-like journey suggests her essential spirituality, and that spirituality is confirmed when, worshipping his angel, Francisca's lover pitches himself down 'at her feet'. To him 'shadow' is 'heavenly light'. Thus the union of the lovers, which Byron takes pains to emphasize ('a moment more – and they shall meet'), completes and harmonizes. It allows Francisca to participate in the natural world that her intense concentration has blinded her to, and joins dark and light, anticipating the important fusion of the two in 'She Walks in Beauty'.

When the heroine of 'I Saw Thee Weep' is melancholy, metaphor transforms her eye into 'a violet dropping dew', recalling 'the eye the same, except in tears' of 'If that High World'. When she smiles, her smile more than matches 'the sapphire's blaze'. (Byron changed 'boast' to 'match' because the innocent do not boast.) The continuity of colour suggests that ideal beauty harmonizes conflicting emotional states. More blue than the sapphire, the heroine is happy. This is made explicit when the sapphire's blaze is softened to the 'deep and

---

[63] Contemporary critics referred to the poem as a 'Sonnet to a Hebrew Melody'. In this experimental Byronic sonnet, however, the octave (a series of octosyllabic couplets ending on a decasyllabic alexandrine) follows the sestet (the tail of a Shakespearean sonnet). Byron's sentiments on the sonnet are well known: 'The most puling, petrifying, stupidly platonic compositions' (*L & J*, II, 379).

mellow dye' of sunset, that the 'shade of coming eve' can scarce 'banish'. Even when the sun has set, the heart continues to draw strength from the 'smiles' of ideal beauty:

> Their sunshine leaves a glow behind
> That lightens o'er the heart.

That 'the moodiest mind' is restored by this sunshine so different from the light of the 'sun of the sleepless' suggests that the catharsis of 'My Soul is Dark' has succeeded again. The oxymoronic *sunset light* composed of the 'pure joy' of the innocent heart exorcizes the demon that threatened, in a cancelled line, to 'overshadow' all below. To Lady Blessington he explained:

I do not talk of mere beauty of feature or complexion, but of expression, that looking out of the soul through the eyes, which, in my opinion, constitutes true beauty. . . . A woman's face ought to be like an April day — susceptible of change and variety; but sunshine should often gleam over it, to replace the clouds and showers that may obscure its lustre, — which, poetical description apart, in sober prose means, that good-humoured smiles ought to be ready to chase away the expression of pensiveness or care that sentiment or earthly ills call forth.[64]

In 'She Walks in Beauty', grace 'softly lightens o'er' Mrs Wilmot Horton's idealized face, recalling the sunshine that 'lightens o'er the heart' in 'I Saw Thee Weep'. Her beauty is dark 'like the night', because beauty is in the beholder's eye, and because Byron is the beholder the night is 'cloudless' and 'starry'. 'All that's best of dark and bright', she is a symbol of mediating harmony, like the *sunset light* of 'I Saw Thee Weep'. 'Mellowed' and 'tender' such light is denied to 'gaudy day'. The perfection of ideal beauty rests on a delicate balance suggestive of the unique quality of the harmony achieved: 'One shade the more, one ray the less,' writes Byron, would destroy the 'grace' of the earthborn angel.[65] The starlight thus becomes a halo accenting 'every raven tress', providing another example of the fusion 'of dark and bright' in Eden.[66] The starlight

[64] *Conversations of Byron*, pp. 69–70. The lyric's 'Elizabethanism' is not, as Gleckner (p. 210) has it, 'awkward Elizabethanism'.

[65] Cf. Byron's remarks to Lady Blessington: 'Where is the actual beauty that can come up to the bright "imaginings" of the poet? Where can one see women that equal the visions, half-mortal, half-angelic that people his fancy?' (*Conversations of Byron*, p. 96).

[66] Consider the complex harmony of the opening lines 'She walks in beauty,

shines to all *below* from within Byron's serene Eve. Its sources are

> A mind at peace with all below,
> A heart whose love is innocent!

Again, in the end, we are returned to the 'heart'. 'Below' tells us where we are, even if we don't believe it, and we do believe, for the 'heart' has set the 'mind' at ease. The contour of Byron's myth has brought us round from self-consciousness to a love 'innocent' and thus selfless.

Byron's vision unites the Hebrew Melodies, and the artistic execution of that vision, it needs to be added, is very much part and parcel of the unity achieved.[67] Generally biblical tales and Jewish history are made to serve as the basis of *dramatic* lyrics. Goethe remarked that Byron should have lived 'to execute his vocation . . . to dramatise the Old Testament'.[68] It was in these dramatic lyrics employing biblical

[67] We can see now just how well the secular lyrics which have nothing to do with the Bible fit in with the Hebrew Melodies. The tonal disparity of defiance and lamentation in the biblical poems need not confuse their thematic unity, and the tonal similarity of the secular poems and their biblical counterparts helps to suggest the essential thematic unity of those poems. Because of this, 'tones' seem preferable to 'two voices', to 'public-private' and 'private-public 'voices, and to 'various speakers' (Marchand, *Byron's Poetry*, p. 117; Gleckner, pp. xvi–xvii; W. H. Marshall, *The Structure of Byron's Major Poems* [Philadelphia, 1962], p. 176). In 'Oh! snatched away in beauty's bloom', sorrow weeps by the banks of a river, just as the tearful harpers of Judah weep by the rivers of Babylon. The beloved of Byron's 'Bright be the place of thy soul' soars to his high world in much the same fashion as the hero of 'Thy Days are Done'. Finally, the Byron of 'I Speak Not – I Trace Not – I Breathe Not' defends his unselfish clandestine love for Augusta as heroically as the exile of 'Were my bosom as false as thou deem'st it to be'. The flux of tones ranging from tearful to scornful is consistently Byronic. Marchand (*Byron's Poetry*, p. 134) excludes 'She Walks in Beauty' from the Hebrew Melodies on the grounds that it 'is really out of tone with the haunting sadness and the sense of desolation which informs the poems voicing a wild lament for the lost Jewish homeland'. Gleckner says Marchand acted 'erroneously, I think' (p. 210n) in excluding 'She Walks in Beauty'. He prefers to keep 'apart' (p. 210) Byron's 'I Saw Thee Weep'. None of these lyrics need to be excluded; each has its place.

[68] Quoted in Henry Crabb Robinson, *On Books and Their Writers*, ed. by Edith J. Morley (London, 1938), I, 372.

like the night/Of cloudless climes and starry skies', built from assonance (like, night, climes, skies), consonance (walks, like, cloudless, climes), and alliterative phrasing (starry skies, cloudless climes). Cooke (p. 28n) writes: 'The fusion of the opposites of dark and bright is matter-of-factly stated, but it is a mysterious thing. Only the "best of dark and bright" comes into play, so that neither term really has its natural meaning: they are idealized terms.'

personae, not in his subsequent dramas, that Byron began to do just that. His peculiar *mobilité* informs the quick-change artistry of the poems, giving rise to his unique mastery of the dramatic lyric. The Hebrew Melodies occupy a significant place in the evolution of romantic lyricism, defined by Karl Kroeber as the 'gradual transformation of simple narrative structure as the basis of lyric organization into a discontinuous, non-narrative structure'.[69] We may overlook this, as Wasserman speaking about romantic lyrics reminds us, because their 'superficial appearance' discourages 'an intensive metaphysical reading', and because we too often think, as Leigh Hunt thought, that Byron is merely impersonating for the sake of it.[70] But when we recognize Byron's genius and consider the Hebrew Melodies as dramatic lyrics articulating a consistent mythos, the importance of their execution is manifest. They are examples of the 'worthy nineteenth-century poem' in which Patricia Ball finds the 'coalescence' of 'storyteller with his material . . . taking place within and becoming part of the poem itself'.[71]

The fusion at the centre of Byron's dramatic lyrics gives rise to the monumentality of the Hebrew Melodies, that is, their ability to enlarge their emotional scope through resonance. Byron makes the lyric form bear the full weight of drama in a single moment. As Francis Jeffrey recognized, the Hebrew Melodies express 'a depth and force of feeling which though indicated only by short sobs and glances, is here as marked and peculiar as in [Byron's] greater pieces'.[72] Roden Noel responded to the same quality of monumentality and amplified Jeffrey's remarks: 'Where Byron is effective in drama, it is by lyrically pouring the quintessence of his characters into the mould of one supreme situation, capable of realizing them with the utmost intensity.'[73] This is just what Byron has done in the dramatic lyrics of the Hebrew Melodies. 'Depth', 'force', and 'intensity' are measures of the monumentality of those poems generated by the resonance of 'intensifying reverberation'[74] that enlarges them. Robert Langbaum has observed in his study of Browning's poetic that 'the speakers of dramatic monologues burst into utterance in the

---

[69] *Romantic Narrative Art* (Madison, 1960, reprinted 1966), p. 51.

[70] Earl R. Wasserman, *The Subtler Language* (Baltimore, 1959), p. 252; cf. 'he does not so much go out of himself to describe others, as furnish others out of himself,' *Examiner*, 2 June 1822, p. 341.

[71] *The Central Self*, p. 184.

[72] Jeffrey to Moore, 11 June 1815, *L & J*, III, 294–5n.

[73] *Essays on Poetry and Poets* (London, 1886), p. 57.

[74] Cooke, p. 157.

same sense that the verb is used in connection with song. Just as in opera the singer only wants occasion to burst into an aria the expressiveness of which can hardly be justified by the dramatic situation; so in the dramatic monologue the dramatic situation is less the adequate motive than the occasion for a total outpouring of soul, the expression of the speaker's whole life until that moment.'[75] ''T is the whole spirit brought to a quintessence', as Byron wrote in *Don Juan* (XIII: 38), and it is just this quintessential compression fundamental to the dramatic lyric which generates the bursting resonance of the Hebrew Melodies, giving rise to their monumentality. Nor has Byron neglected to provide the music of his character's intense song.[76] He has taken pains to weave a musical fabric of alliteration, assonance, and carefully rhymed stanzas. On this fabric, he stamps his stark designs. The contrast of plangent sound and simple structure contributes to the intensity of his monumental lyrics. When the Hebrew Melodies succeed, they resemble 'The Song

[75] *The Poetry of Experience* (New York, 1957, reprinted 1963), p. 183.

[76] I discount Northrop Frye's complaint that, in general, Byron's lyrics contain nothing that "modern" critics look for: no texture, no ambiguities, no intellectual ironies, no intensity, no vividness of phrasing, the words and images being vague to the point of abstraction' ('George Gordon, Lord Byron', *Major British Writers*, enl. ed. [New York, 1959], II, 152). Nor can I agree with Ernest De Selincourt when he writes that Byron has 'no magical power over words, no subtlety in verse music' and 'never succeeded in lyric' ('Byron', *Wordsworthian and Other Studies* [Oxford, 1947], p. 121). Sir Arthur Quiller-Couch calls the Hebrew Melodies 'turgid school-exercise work' ('Byron', W. A. Briscoe, ed., *Byron, the Poet* [London, 1924], p. 10, first published in *Studies in Literature*, 2nd ser. [Cambridge, 1922]). This slur is unacceptable. Three modern critics, Andrew Rutherford (*Byron: A Critical Study*) and M. K. Joseph (*Byron the Poet*), and Jerome McGann are completely silent on the Hebrew Melodies. Gleckner's attitude is sensibly middle-of-the-road (p. 204): 'Byron's lyric poetry is an integral part of his developing vision and must be examined, to do it full justice, in the evolving context of his total canon.' Marchand's enthusiasm (*Byron's Poetry*, p. 133) is notable: 'The Hebrew Melodies constitute a group of Byron's lyrics that are finely executed, rich in tone, and unified in mood, and for the most part have their origins in human sympathies not directly related to the author's own emotional quandaries.' This last remark is an indication of the *dramatic* success of the lyrics. In his Byron Foundation Lecture, L. C. Martin almost anticipates what I call 'monumentality' when he writes that in the Hebrew Melodies Byron 'proves his mettle by producing something which can bear comparison with the bare sublimities or enchanting graces of the Authorized Version' (p. 14). Martin's work is an introductory defence of Byron's lyric talent. Herbert Read narrows the source of Byron's lyric success to what he calls an 'explicit felicity' of expression: 'No image, no word, is far-fetched' (*Byron* [London, 1951], p. 24; *The True Voice of Feeling* [New York, 1953], p. 307).

of Deborah' that Byron so admired. Because of the remarkable tautology of that primitive lyric, Wordsworth observed in a note to *The Thorn*, words act 'not only as symbols of the passion, but as things, active and efficient, which are themselves part of the passion'. Byron refines the lyric to a simple statement uniquely his, and he writes that statement large. In doing so he exchanges the self-conscious for the tragic. In his longer narrative poems, Byron turned autobiography into mythology.[77] By making his biblical lyrics monumental, he did much the same. Byron's Hebrew Melodies have a music of their own.

[77] Harold Bloom, *The Visionary Company* (New York, 1961, reprinted 1963), p. 252 *passim*. In 'Shelley's Mythmaking', Bloom analyses the 'Ode to the West Wind' through a comparison with 'The Song of Deborah'.

III

TEXT OF THE HEBREW MELODIES

The purpose of the present edition is to present a text of Byron's Hebrew Melodies, collated with the extant manuscripts, with the editions of the Hebrew Melodies published in Byron's lifetime, with authoritative later editions, and with other relevant printed sources. All variants and decipherable deletions have been reproduced in the present edition.

MANUSCRIPT SOURCES

The Hebrew Melodies are a collection of thirty poems. These poems have their sources in individual manuscripts, rather than in a single Hebrew Melodies manuscript. To speak of such a manuscript, as one speaks of the *Corsair* manuscript, is misleading. The individual manuscripts have been described in detail in the Calendar of Manuscripts given in Appendix III. The great bulk of the surviving manuscripts are those of poems composed at Halnaby and Seaham after Byron's marriage. The holographs of these poems remained at Seaham to pass eventually into the Lovelace papers. Lady Byron's fair copies of these poems were sent on to London, coming to rest in the Murray archives. Of the poems for which no manuscript is extant, seven were composed in London during the earlier period of composition. The manuscripts of these seven poems may have passed into Isaac Nathan's hands, and Nathan may have sold them to ease his later financial troubles.[1] However, their survival was considerably insured by Byron's reputation, and in the twentieth century several have come to light again. In addition to the holographs and fair copies, four clerk's copies are extant in the Murray archives. These were prepared to facilitate the printing of editions by both Murray and Nathan, but, as we have seen, the copying proved to be unnecessary. Altogether forty-seven manuscripts of twenty-one Hebrew Melodies are extant. Manuscripts of nine poems are lacking.[2] All those manuscripts available to previous editors have been consulted by

[1] Nathan's second wife is thought to have burnt his music following his death. (Mackerras, p. 73.)

[2] Lady Byron's fair copy of *Parisina* is not considered to be the manuscript of 'It is the Hour' and 'Francisca' in these calculations (though it and that poem's first and second proofs [revised by Byron] have been consulted).

the present editor. In addition, several manuscripts not known previously have been studied for the first time.[3] This and the recording in this edition of all decipherable variants and deletions in manuscript makes the present text a considerable advancement.

BYRON AT WORK

An examination of the Hebrew Melodies manuscripts reveals that Byron, in spite of the impression that he helped to create, was a careful, not a casual, author. He never tired of tinkering with his verse and was not above revision. The numerous deletions and re-deletions on the many drafts of the Hebrew Melodies show that few of the many lines written without hesitation escaped revision. The heavily scored holographs made fair copies a necessity. Nor was Byron's handwriting a help. 'My handwriting is so horrible that I must entreat your attention to ye printing – if you print the enclosed,' wrote Byron to James Perry in a letter enclosing 'On the Death of Sir Peter Parker'.[4] But the compositors of Thomas Davison's printing house who set up *Hebrew Melodies* were spared the trouble of Byron's holographs. The newly wed Lady Byron served as her husband's amanuensis. Byron admired her neat mechanical handwriting. Later, having given Murray Lady Byron's fair copy of *Parisina*, he remarked: 'I am very glad that the handwriting was a favorable omen of the *morale* of the piece. . . .'[5] But even to one schooled in the correspondence of a difficult engagement, Byron's handwriting was not without its problems. Byron carefully corrected the fair copies when Annabella had deciphered his scrawling incorrectly, and he sometimes revised as he corrected.

Byron was not content to end his revision and correction with the fair copies. His correspondence indicates that he read proofs of all the metrical tales published before the Hebrew Melodies. He read

[3] E. H. Coleridge was the first and only editor to give variants from the manuscripts of the Hebrew Melodies. He reproduced a small number of selected variants from generally unidentified manuscripts. Thus it is impossible to know what manuscripts actually were available to him, particularly because Coleridge does not always give even a single variant from revised manuscripts he must have examined. I have accounted for the sources of all of Coleridge's variants. Coleridge gives selected variants from manuscripts for fourteen of the thirty Hebrew Melodies. I give all variants for twenty-one poems from the increased number of extant manuscripts.

[4] 7 [6] October 1814. Quoted by permission of the Miriam Lutcher Stark Library, the University of Texas, from Byron's holograph, St 6521.

[5] To Murray, 3 January 1816, *L & J*, III, 251.

proof for *Parisina*, published in 1816. The surviving proof of 'Bright be the place of thy soul' has been both corrected and revised by Byron. But the conclusion that Byron read the proofs of the Hebrew Melodies is only to be supported by inference. No such proofs are extant; nor is mention of them made in the poet's letters. But the discrepancy between Lady Byron's fair copies (which served as printer's copy) and the final text of *Hebrew Melodies* certainly indicates that later revision was made. The cancelled leaves of *Hebrew Melodies* and the accuracy of the letterpress text in *A Selection* No. I (1815) also suggest that Byron corrected these works. By comparison, *A Selection* No. II, published at the time of Byron's departure, abounds in just the kind of printer's errors he found most intolerable.

'I wish the printer was saddled with a vampire,' wrote Byron to his publisher.[6] Misprints that altered the sense of his poems, often making them ridiculous, were the source of his rages directed at the compositor. Returning the *Corsair* proofs to Murray, Byron again vented his spleen:

> I do believe that the Devil never created or perverted such a fiend as the fool of a printer. I am obliged to inclose you, luckily for me, this *second* proof, *corrected*, because there is an ingenuity in his blunders peculiar to himself. Let the press be guided by the present sheet. . . . There is one mistake he made, which, if it had stood, I would most certainly have broken his neck.[7]

Byron's angry concern probably accounts for the cancels in *Hebrew Melodies*. Just why the cancels were made is not known, but misprints are the likely cause.

Sense was what Byron most valued from the compositor, but punctuation, as Byron put it to use, did not seem to affect sense. Concerned with revision and the correction of misprints, he little bothered with pointing and accidentals. To Murray he wrote: 'Do attend to the punctuation: I can't, for I don't know a comma – at least where to place one.'[8] Instead Byron employed the dash as a sort of universal punctuation mark. William Gifford changed these dashes to commas: 'From Mr. G. every comma is an obligation for which thank him in my name and behalf,' wrote the poet to his publisher.[9] Gifford, then editor of Murray's *Quarterly Review*, had

[6] To Murray, 6 December 1813, *L & J*, II, 300.
[7] To Murray, 16 January 1814, *L & J*, III, 14.
[8] 15 November 1813, *L & J*, II, 284.
[9] To Murray, 4 January 1814, *L & J*, III, 3.

gained Byron's respect with his early satires, and that respect deepened with his praise of Byron's *Childe Harold*. Byron often abdicated to Gifford in matters of punctuation, less so in matters of sense.

Finally, it was by the criterion of sense that Byron judged the finished product. No evidence indicates that he later made a careful review of the Hebrew Melodies, but Byron did read the poems following their publication in the fourth volume of his *Collected Works* (1815). On 26 August 1815 he wrote to Murray:

> In reading the 4th vol. of your last Edition of the poems published in my name, I perceive that piece 12, page 55 ['To Thyrza'], is made nonsense of (that is greater nonsense than usual) by dividing it into Stanzas 1, 2, etc., etc. in which form it was not written, – and not printed in the 8vo Editions.

Of the Hebrew Melodies included in the very same volume, Byron had nothing to say. His complaint went unheeded. Murray never completely relinquished control of his press and its ability to check his author's politics and persuasion. But Byron made a revealing comment on the edition when he wrote to John Taylor: 'I ought to tell you that there are many errors of the press in this Edition of Murray's which are disgraceful to him & me!'[10]

EDITIONS

The twelve editions of the Hebrew Melodies which had appeared by 1829 and Murray's collected edition of 1815 have been discussed earlier and have been described in the Calendar of Editions (Appendix IV). The thirteen editions include four American and two English pirated editions, and these editions have no authority. But because the pirated editions reprint the text of the earliest editions, they should not be completely ignored. They may always comment on their sources, by suggesting a previously unidentified state of the edition from which they have been reprinted, and by indicating the nature of material cancelled in later issues of their sources. Five early editions (1819, 1821, 1823, 1831, 1832–3) of Byron's *Collected Works* published by Murray need to be considered as well.

---

[10] *L & J*, III, 215. Pforzheimer MSS. The lines beginning 'Without a stone to mark the spot', were printed incorrectly in subsequent collected editions (including Wright's of 1832) until E. H. Coleridge restored the poem to its proper form in *Poetry*, III, 30.

There is always the possibility of authorial correction in the first three of these editions. 'To Belshazzar', as we have seen, was first published in the collected edition of 1831. Finally, the collected edition of 1832–3, prepared for Murray by John Wright, fixed the form of the *Collected Works* for succeeding generations.

The Victorian editors of Byron's poems, Swinburne, Arnold, and William Michael Rossetti, produced works derived from Wright's edition, but their selections generally excluded the Hebrew Melodies.[11] Swinburne includes in his edition only 'They say that Hope is happiness'; Arnold includes only five Hebrew Melodies: 'She Walks in Beauty', 'Oh! snatched away in beauty's bloom', 'Song of Saul Before His Last Battle', 'Vision of Belshazzar', and 'The Destruction of Semnacherib'. Robert Browning commented on Arnold's choice in a letter to William Hale White: 'Did it not strike you that Matt. Arnold's selection of passages and poems from Byron was a poor one?'[12] But the major limitation of the Victorian editors was their failure to provide new readings, their willingness to select and not to edit. Because of this their editions are of no consideration to the present work.

Only two authoritative modern editions of the Hebrew Melodies have been published, and both of these are part of editions of Byron's *Collected Works*. At the turn of the century, Ernest Hartley Coleridge prepared a seven-volume edition of Byron's *Poetry*, the second part of Murray's thirteen-volume edition of Byron's *Works*. Coleridge based his edition on the collected edition of 1831 and enriched it with selected variants from manuscripts and first editions. Volume III, published in 1900, contains the Hebrew Melodies. That volume was reprinted in 1904 and 1922, and these reprints need to be considered, for slight changes were made in the text and notes of these works. In 1905, Paul Elmer More's scholarly one-volume edition of Byron's *Collected Works* was published. More based his edition on Wright's edition of 1832–3, and his edition is marked by careful attempts to clear away many of the earlier edition's garbled readings and to correct some of Coleridge's errors. (More refrained from giving manuscript variants.) Together with the eighteen early

---

[11] *A Selection from the Works of Lord Byron*, ed. by A. C. Swinburne (London: Moxon, 1866); *Poetry of Byron*, chosen and arranged by Matthew Arnold (London: Macmillan & Co., 1881); *The Poetical Works of Lord Byron*, ed. by Wm. Michael Rossetti (London: Moxon, [1880]).

[12] Quoted in B. R. Jerman, 'Nineteenth-Century Holdings at the Folger', *Victorian Newsletter*, 1962, No. 22, 23.

editions, the editions of More and E. H. Coleridge form the twenty editions upon which the present edition rests.

COPY-TEXT

The copy-text of the present edition is a composite one. The text of twenty-four poems is that of *Hebrew Melodies*. The text of five of the six Hebrew Melodies not included in that edition is that of the respective poems' first publication, while the text of 'Bright be the place of thy soul' is that of *Poems* (1816), which incorporates Byron's final revision. *Hebrew Melodies* is, as we have seen, the first edition of twelve poems (the second) and the second edition of twelve poems (the first). However, a study of the changes from manuscript to printed text indicates that Byron revised the text of *Hebrew Melodies* at press, and that, like other authors, he accepted printing-house normalization of accidentals. Though a text based on the First Number of *A Selection of Hebrew Melodies* and the second twelve poems of *Hebrew Melodies* would represent the 'first edition', in such a text the accidentals would be at great variance. (A text based on the First and Second Numbers of *A Selection* would display similar variance, for the Second Number agrees with *Hebrew Melodies* in its choice of accidentals.) The adopting of the entire text of *Hebrew Melodies* as copy-text thus ensures publishing-house uniformity in twenty-six instances and a resulting uniformity of texture. As the discrepancy between this edition and the First Number yields but a single substantive variant, little is sacrificed. The copy-text of each poem is identified in the textual notes.

COLLATION OF THE COPY-TEXT

Twenty editions have been collated with the copy-text. These include the twelve individual editions described in the Calendar of Editions (Appendix IV), six early collected editions published by John Murray (to 1832), and the collected editions of 1900 and 1905. In addition, twenty-five copies of *Hebrew Melodies* were collated in the preparation of the present edition. When individual poems have been published in authoritative works (e.g. Moore's *Letters and Journals*, the *Examiner*) these too have been collated.

ALTERATION OF THE COPY-TEXT

I have retained the spelling, punctuation, and capitalization of the copy-text, even where the practice is inconsistent, except as indicated below. The copy-text is closer to the manuscripts than any modernized edition could hope to be. In a very few cases of alteration of the copy-text, the reading selected is a matter of editorial judgment. But with the exception of the change in the weak past tense ending, the original reading of the copy-text can always be reconstructed from the variants. Keeping these principles in mind I have altered the copy-text as follows:

1. The Hebrew Melodies have been arranged in the order of their composition, determined from Byron's dating, and from historical, physical, and stylistic evidence.

2. Line numbers have been assigned to the poems to facilitate the transcription of variants.

3. Arabic numerals have been substituted for the Roman numerals used to designate stanzas in the copy-text. Byron's manuscripts show that he regularly employed Arabic numerals.

4. The full form of the weak past tense ending has been substituted for the contracted form employed in the copy-text, and the reading of the copy-text is not recorded. Byron wrote 'mellowed' not 'mellow'd', 'impaired' not 'impair'd'; the contracted form is never found in the manuscripts of the Hebrew Melodies.

5. Printer's errors in the copy-text have been corrected, and the reading of the copy-text recorded in the *apparatus criticus*.

6. The punctuation, capitalization, and spelling have been altered, in a few instances, to clarify meaning or to indicate Byron's practice in manuscript. All such changes are indicated and the reading of the copy-text recorded in the *apparatus criticus*.

TRANSCRIPTION OF VARIANTS

Variants and deletions in manuscripts and variants from authoritative editions (the copy-text and editions published in England before 1816) have been recorded in the *apparatus criticus*. Variants from derivative and later editions have been recorded in the Historical Collations (Appendix I); variation in spelling and punctuation has not been recorded unless the meaning of the text was affected. When a later edition not collated for the *apparatus criticus* provides the copy-text of an individual poem (because it is the first edition of that poem), variants from that edition are recorded in the *apparatus criticus* for the respective poem, but other variants from that edition are recorded in the Historical Collations. A table of Sigla Employed in the *Apparatus Criticus* precedes the text, and a separate table of sigla precedes the Historical Collations. The Contents of Editions Collated are specified in Appendix II, for not every edition contains all thirty Hebrew Melodies. In both the *apparatus criticus* and the Historical Collations, variants have been recorded and their source identified according to the standard system consisting of line number, lemma, right square bracket, variant, and siglum or sigla. The copy-text for each poem is specified directly below the text. When the copy-text is not the first edition, the first edition is also specified. The extant manuscripts are then specified. When no siglum appears following the lemma, it is understood that the reading is that of the copy-text and that the copy-text agrees with all manuscripts and editions collated but not specified. Thus

big] bit M1815W

indicates that the copy-text and all manuscripts and editions collated but not specified read 'big' and that the specified manuscript or edition reads 'bit'. When I have departed from the copy-text, the source of the new reading is given immediately after the lemma, the reading of the copy-text and of those manuscripts and editions that agree with it is recorded, and all collated but not specified manuscripts and editions agree with the reading of the text as given in the lemma. Thus

big] A; bit M1815

indicates that I have altered or corrected the copy-text (M1815) which reads 'bit', preferring the reading of Byron's holograph ('big'), and that all manuscripts and editions collated but not specified agree with the reading of the holograph and not with the reading of the copy-text. *Thus the reading of the text given in the lemma always agrees with the manuscripts and editions collated but not specified*, and the placing of a siglum immediately after the lemma always indicates that the copy-text has been altered and that the reading of the copy-text no longer agrees (as it normally does) with the manuscripts and editions collated but not specified. When Byron has revised a poem by deleting a word and substituting another word for it in the same draft, the change is indicated in this manner:

big] [large] big A

Here the copy-text (as no siglum immediately follows the lemma) and all manuscripts (such as copies made after *A*) and editions collated but not specified agree with the reading of the text given in the lemma ('big'). On occasion, Byron has revised a poem by introducing a new word in a later draft in place of a word used in an earlier draft; the change is indicated in this manner:

big] large *A*, *B*; big *C*

Here the holograph (*A*) and a subsequent draft (*B*) read 'large', and (*C*) a later extant draft (the fair copy) reads 'big'. The copy-text (for again no siglum follows immediately after the lemma) and all manuscripts (such as copies made after *C*) and editions collated but not specified agree with the reading of the text given in the lemma. The reading of the fair copy (*C*), normally inferred, is provided to illustrate clearly Byron's practice when revising from draft to draft. In this last instance, the formula follows the order of Byron's changes and is necessary to avoid confusion with the formula used to indicate alteration or correction of the copy-text (in which the siglum always follows immediately after the lemma). I have economized on this system where clarity permitted and have adjusted my practice as follows:

1. Line numbers corresponding to the appropriate lines in the text have been assigned to the readings. When necessary, successive steps in the composition of a line are lettered *a*, *b*, *c*, etc. and placed beneath one another in the order of their composition.

2. Variants are given in roman type; sigla and editorial comment have been italicized. When a word has been underscored in manuscript that word is underlined by a straight line as follows, _____.

3. When they are present, *all* manuscript titles are given. No manuscript titles remain unspecified.

4. When revision is confined to part of a line, the full line is not normally given.

5. Byron's deletions have been enclosed in square brackets. Words found beneath superimposed revisions have been treated as deletions.

6. Words added above, below, or to the side of a line, or superimposed on others are enclosed in round brackets. This practice enables the reader to distinguish the stages of composition.

7. A word (or words) that could not be deciphered is designated by xxx.

8. Doubtful readings are enclosed in question marks.

9. Alternative words or short phrases have been enclosed in curving brackets as follows, $\left\{ \begin{array}{l} \text{to my Royalty} \\ \text{of my Monarchy} \end{array} \right\}$.

10. Uncompleted lines are labelled fr.

11. *Ante* read as 'preceding' and *post* read as 'following' are used to designate lines not in the copy-text preceding or following specified lines in the copy-text.

12. All revisions and corrections are by Byron even though a particular draft had been copied by someone else. A dagger precedes the scribe's corrections of his own copy.

13. Unless it was desirable to clarify meaning or to illustrate Byron's practice in a particular case, no reading has been given in which Byron's punctuation, spelling, or capitalization differs from the copy-text provided the difference was not substantive.

ANNOTATION

In the explanatory notes, I have attempted to identify Byron's sources and allusions, and to provide a context for the Hebrew Melodies by transcribing pertinent comment from Byron's letters, journals, and other poems. Notes from the editions of Isaac Nathan, John Wright, and Ernest Hartley Coleridge have also been transcribed. As later editors have quoted the notes of those who came before them, I have followed certain procedures to avoid endless duplication. When Nathan's commentary in *Fugitive Pieces* bears on the poem, I quote Nathan and identify my source. When a later editor provides an original note, I quote that note and give the source. If the note is derivative, I have identified the source and have corrected the note from that source when necessary. When a later editor has quoted or summarized the notes of an earlier annotator, the quotation or summary is not given, for in every instance the earlier note has been given in full. Thus when E. H. Coleridge quotes or summarizes Nathan's commentary, I have given Nathan's commentary alone. Sigla used to identify editions in the *apparatus criticus* and the Historical Collations have been used to identify the same editions when they are the source of explanatory notes. Thus annotation in Nathan's *Fugitive Pieces* is identified by N1829. My own additions to the notes of others have been enclosed in square brackets.

SIGLA
Employed in the *Apparatus Criticus*

A	The earliest extant manuscript.
B	The earliest extant draft made after *A*.
E	Engraved Text.
P	Letterpress Text.
PS	Proof.
W	Works.
N1815	*A Selection of Hebrew Melodies*, No. I, London: Nathan, 1815.
M1815	*Hebrew Melodies*, London: Murray, 1815.
M1815W	*The Works of the Right Hon. Lord Byron*, 4 vols, London: Murray, 1815.
Ex1815	*Examiner*, London, 1815.
SS1815	'Bright be the place of thy soul', song sheet, London: Nathan, [1815].
M1816	'Bright be the place of thy soul', in *Poems*, London: Murray, 1816.
Parisina	*The Siege of Corinth. A Poem. Parisina. A Poem*, London: Murray, 1816.
N1816	*A Selection of Hebrew Melodies*, Nos I–II, London: Nathan, 1816.*
N1827–29	*A Selection of Hebrew Melodies*, Revised Edition, Nos I–IV, London, 1827–29.*
M1831W	*The Works of Lord Byron*, 6 vols, London: Murray, 1831.*

* In the *apparatus criticus*, variants are recorded only for the poem or poems for which this edition serves as copy-text; other variants from this edition are given in the Historical Collations (Appendix I) and are identified by the same siglum.

a Selection of

HEBREW MELODIES
ANCIENT and MODERN

---

with appropriate Symphonies & accompaniments

By

I: BRAHAM & I: NATHAN

the Poetry written expressly for the work

By the Right Honble

LORD BYRON

ent^d at Sta^{rs} Hall   1st Number

Published & Sold by I: Nathan N° 7 Poland Street
Oxford Str^t. and to be had at the principal Music
and Booksellers

Price one Guinea

Drawn by Edward Blore.   *Engraved by W. Lowry.*

Substantive Text: N1815

[AUTHOR'S NOTE]

The subsequent poems were written at the request of my friend, the Hon. D. Kinnaird, for a Selection of Hebrew Melodies, and have been published, with the music, arranged, by Mr. Braham and Mr. Nathan.

Text: M1815, not found in any ed. pub. by Nathan
1 of my] *M1815W*; of the author's *M1815*

PREFACE

THE Title under which this Work appears before the PUBLIC, requires that a few words should be said in explanation of what are the pretensions of the Music. "The HEBREW MELODIES" are a Selection from the favourite Airs which are still sung in the religious Ceremonies of the Jews. Some of these have, in 5 common with all their Sacred Airs, been preserved by memory and tradition alone, without the assistance of written characters. Their age and originality, therefore, must be left to conjecture. But the latitude given to the taste and genius of their performers has been the means of engrafting on the original Melodies a 10 certain wildness and pathos, which have at length become the chief characteristic of the Sacred Songs of the Jews.

Of this feature it has been endeavoured to preserve as much as was consistent with the rhythm of written Music, and the adaptation of the Words. 15

Of the Poetry it is necessary to speak, in order thus publicly to acknowledge the kindness with which LORD BYRON has condescended to furnish the most valuable part of the Work. It has been our endeavour to select such Melodies as would best suit the style and sentiment of the Poetry. 20

I. BRAHAM.
I. NATHAN.

LONDON, April, 1815.

Text: N1815, only found in editions pub. by Nathan
PREFACE] rep. N1816, rev. N1824, new pref. N1827–29, rep. N1829
14 rhythm] N1816; rythm N1815

HEBREW MELODIES.

BY LORD BYRON.

LONDON:

PRINTED FOR JOHN MURRAY, ALBEMARLE-STREET.

1815.

Substantive Text: M1815

125

IT IS THE HOUR

IT IS THE HOUR when from the boughs
 The nightingale's high note is heard;
It is the hour when lovers' vows
 Seem sweet in every whispered word;
And gentle winds and waters near   5
Make music to the lonely ear.
Each flower the dews have lightly wet,
And in the sky the stars are met;
And on the wave is deeper blue,
And on the leaf a browner hue;   10
And in the Heaven that clear obscure,
So softly dark, and darkly pure,
That follows the decline of day
As twilight melts beneath the moon away.

Text: M1815; first pub. N1815
13 That] Which *Parisina*

1 Francis Jeffrey, describing *Parisina*, writes: 'The opening verses, though soft
and voluptuous, are tinged with the same shade of sorrow which gives character
and harmony to the whole poem.' (*Edinburgh Review*, 1816, XXVII, 289.)

FRANCISCA

FRANCISCA walks in the shadow of night,
But it is not to gaze on the heavenly light –
But if she sits in her garden bower,
'Tis not for the sake of its blowing flower.
She listens – but not for the nightingale,   5
Though her ear expects as soft a tale.
There winds a step through the foliage thick,
And her cheek grows pale – and her heart beats quick.
There whispers a voice thro' the rustling leaves,
And her blush returns – and her bosom heaves;   10
A moment more – and they shall meet –
'Tis past – her Lover's at her feet.

Text: N1816P

1–4   But it is not to list to the waterfall
     That Parisina leaves her hall,
     And it is not to gaze on the heavenly light
     That the lady walks in the shadow of night;
     And if she sits in Este's bower,
     'Tis not for the sake of its full-blown flower – *Parisina*
7   winds] glides *Parisina*

---

3 Cf. Sir Walter Scott, *The Lay of the Last Minstrel* (1812), I:12; 5–8:

        And now she sits in secret bower
        In old Lord David's western tower,
        And listens to a heavy sound,
        That moans the mossy turrets round.

I SPEAK NOT – I TRACE NOT –
I BREATHE NOT

I.

I SPEAK not – I trace not – I breathe not thy name,
There is grief in the sound – there were guilt in the fame;
But the tear which now burns on my cheek may impart
The deep thought that dwells in that silence of heart.

Text: N1827–29P; MSS: A
Inscription: Stanzas for music May 10 1814 *A, not in Byron's hand*

1 I . . . name,] [I speak not – I breathe not – I write not that name] (I speak not –
   I trace not – I breathe not thy name) *A*
2 grief] [love] (Grief) *A*
   were] is *A*
3 on . . . impart] [on my cheek may impart] (on my cheek [to] (may) impart) *A*
4 thought . . . dwells] thoughts that dwell *A*
   in that] in this *N1827–29E*

Inscription. E. H. Coleridge quotes (M1900W, III, 413) Byron's letter to Thomas
Moore of 4 May 1814: 'Thou hast asked me for a song, and I enclose you an
experiment, which has cost me something more than trouble, and is, therefore,
less likely to be worth taking any in your proposed setting. Now, if it be so, throw
it into the fire without *phrase*.' [Moore was the last to see this letter. He gives
another letter of 4 May as well. The date of the second letter, also from Byron to
Moore, may be confirmed on the basis of content. The first mention of the poem
may have been in the final paragraph of Byron's letter to Lady Melbourne dated
25 April 1814 (*LBC*, I, 252): 'I don't often bore you with rhyme – but as a wrapper
to this note I send you some upon a brunette, which I have shown to no one else.
If you think them not much beneath the common places you may give them to
any of your "album" acquaintances.']

1 E. H. Coleridge writes (M1900W, III, 319): 'There can be little doubt that
both song ['I Speak Not – I Trace Not – I Breathe Not'] and dedication [the
rejected opening lines of *Lara*] were addressed to Lady Frances Wedderburn
Webster. . . .'

Leslie A. Marchand writes: 'E. H. Coleridge thought these stanzas were written
to Lady Frances Webster . . . but he had not seen Byron's letters to Lady Melbourne and did not know how far past that affair was by May 4, 1814, and how
completely absorbed Byron had become in [his sister] Augusta. In the margin of
his copy of Moore (M1830, I, 554), however, Coleridge wrote opposite the first
stanza: "Does this apply to Lady Frances Wedderburn Webster? *does* it?"
Coleridge sensed that the feelings expressed in the poem had their origin in some
more searing passion than that roused by Lady Frances.' (Marchand, I, 449.)

2.

Too brief for our passion, too long for our peace,   5
Were those hours, can their joy or their bitterness cease?
We repent — we abjure — we will break from our chain;
We must part — we must fly to — unite it again.

ante 5 *1.* [We have loved – and Oh still my adored one – we [love] (love)
   2. Oh the moment [when] (is) past [when] [(when that Passion might cease)] (that forbids our release)] *A, two cancelled lines*
6 *a.* [Were the moments – [when] [Remembrance can never release] (how could they)] *fr.*
  b. (Was that hour – [Oh *xxx* for] (can its hope) – can its memory cease?) *A*
7 our] [the] our *A*

3.

Oh! thine be the gladness and mine be the guilt.
Forgive me adored one — forsake if thou wilt;   10
But the heart which I bear shall expire undebased,
And man shall not break it — whatever thou may'st.

4.

And stern to the haughty, but humble to thee,
My soul in its bitterest blackness shall be;
And our days seem as swift — and our moments more sweet, 15
With thee by my side — than the world at our feet.

9 Oh!... guilt.] [The [hope] thought may be madness [the wish may be] (to utter it)] (Oh! thine be the gladness – and mine be the) Guilt – *A*
10 Forgive] [Forsake] (Forgive) *A*

Lovelace writes (*Astarte*, 1905, p. 162): 'Lady Byron wrote (in 1817) of these meetings with Augusta: "She acknowledged that the verses ('I speak not, I trace not, I breathe not thy name') of which I have the original, were addressed to her."'

Nathan writes (N1829, pp. 65–6): 'The foregoing verses were written more than two years previously to his marriage; and to shew how adverse his Lordship was from touching in the most distant manner upon the theme which might be deemed to have a personal allusion, he requested me the morning before he last left London, either to suppress the verses entirely or to be careful in putting the date when they were originally written.... Observing his Lordship's anxiety, and fully appreciating the noble feeling by which that anxiety was augmented, I acquiesced, in signifying my willingness to withhold the melody altogether from the public rather than submit him to any uneasiness. "No, Nathan," ejaculated his Lordship, "I am too great an admirer of your music to suffer a single *phrase* of it to be lost; I insist that you publish the melody, but by attaching to it the date it will answer every purpose, and it will prevent my lying under greater obligations than are absolutely necessary for the liberal *encomiums* of my *friends*."'

5.

One sigh of thy sorrow — one look of thy love,
Shall turn me or fix, shall reward or reprove;
And the heartless may wonder at all we resign,
Thy lip shall reply not to them — but to mine.   20

11 But . . . undebased,] [But I cannot repent what we neer can recall] But the
     heart which is thine [would disdain to recall –] [(is too proud of its vow –)]
     ([still remains] (shall expire) undebased) *A*

12 may'st.] *A*; may'st, *N1827–29P*
     whatever . . . may'st.] [whatever thou] ([though I feel that] (whatever) thou)
     may'st. *A*

13 And . . . haughty,] [Oh proud] (And [high] stern) to the [mighty] (haughty)
     – *A*

14 My] This *A*
     blackness] moment *A*

15 And . . . seem] And [our] [the Years of our] our days [glide] (seem) *A*

16 by my] [the *xxx*] at my *A*
     our] my *A*

ante 17 1. [And thine is that [love] [(heart)] (love) which I will not [resign]
               (forego)]

          2. [Though the price that] [Though [that [love] (heart) may be bought
               by] (the price which I pay be) Eternity's woe]

          3. [But if thine too must suffer – Oh take it again –] *A, three cancelled
               lines*

17 One . . . love,] [And thine is that love which I could not forego] One [tear]
     (sigh) of thy sorrow – one [smile] (look) of thy love *A*

19 wonder . . . resign,] [smile & the rig] (wonder at [all] [what] all I resign) *A*

---

ante 17 Lovelace compares (*Astarte*, 1921, p. 329) *Manfred*, II:iv, 124–6:

               Say that thou loath'st me not – that I do bear
               This punishment for both – that thou wilt be
               One of the blessed – and that I shall die.

with the cancelled lines preceding the fifth stanza.

SHE WALKS IN BEAUTY

I.

SHE WALKS IN BEAUTY, like the night
Of cloudless climes and starry skies;
And all that's best of dark and bright
Meet in her aspect and her eyes:
Thus mellowed to that tender light   5
Which heaven to gaudy day denies.

Text: M1815; first pub. N1815
4 Meet] Meets *M1815W*

---

1 In a manuscript note to a letter of Byron's, dated 11 June 1814 (*L & J*, III, 92n), Wedderburn Webster writes: 'I *did* take him to Lady Sitwell's Party in Seymour road. He there for the first time saw his cousin, the beautiful Mrs. Wilmot. When we returned to his rooms in the Albany, he said little, but desired Fletcher to give him a *tumbler* of *Brandy*, which he drank at once to Mrs. Wilmot's health, then retired to rest, and was, I heard afterwards, in a sad state all night. The next day he wrote those charming lines upon her –

> She walks in Beauty like the Night
> Of cloudless Climes, and starry Skies, etc., etc.'

[Wright (M1832W, X, 75) summarizes Webster's note and adds: 'On this occasion Mrs. W. H. had appeared in mourning, with numerous spangles on her dress.' E. H. Coleridge quotes from Webster's note and adds (M1900W, III, 381): 'Anne Beatrix, daughter and co-heiress of Eusebius Horton, of Catton Hall, Derbyshire, married Byron's second cousin, Robert John Wilmot (1784–1841), son of Sir Robert Wilmot of Osmaston, by Juliana, second daughter of the Hon. John Byron, and widow of the Hon. William Byron. She died 4 February 1871.']

In a note to *Cain* (M1900W, V, 231), E. H. Coleridge compares Adah's speech to Lucifer:

> . . . but thou seem'st
> Like an ethereal night, where long white clouds
> Streak the deep purple, and unnumbered stars
> Spangle the wonderful mysterious vault. . . .

James D. Merritt, in 'Disraeli as a Byronic poet' (*Victorian Poetry*, 1965, III, 138–9), compares the lyric recited by the heroine of Benjamin Disraeli's *Alroy* (1833) beginning:

> He rose in beauty like the morn
> That brightens our Syrian skies;
> Dark passions glittered in his eyes
> And Empire sparkled in his form!

2.

One shade the more, one ray the less,
    Had half impaired the nameless grace
Which waves in every raven tress,
    Or softly lightens o'er her face;   10
Where thoughts serenely sweet express
    How pure, how dear their dwelling place.

3.

And on that cheek, and o'er that brow,
    So soft, so calm, yet eloquent,
The smiles that win, the tints that glow,   15
    But tell of days in goodness spent,
A mind at peace with all below,
    A heart whose love is innocent!

Alroy, the subject of these lines, is a Hebrew prince, and it is likely that Disraeli, who emphasized his Jewish origins in his novels, was attracted by Byron's Hebrew Melodies.

4   In a note to *Childe Harold* (M1900W, II, 273), E. H. Coleridge compares

        Oh Night
And Storm, and Darkness, ye are wondrous strong,
    Yet lovely in your strength, as is the light
    Of a dark eye in Woman!

with 'the well-known song which forms the prelude of the *Hebrew Melodies*'. [Cf. Neuha of Byron's *The Island* (II: ii): 'Dusky like night, but night with all her stars'.]

I SAW THEE WEEP

I.

I SAW THEE WEEP — the big bright tear
Came o'er that eye of blue;
And then methought it did appear
A violet dropping dew:
I saw thee smile — the sapphire's blaze   5
Beside thee ceased to shine;
It could not match the living rays
That filled that glance of thine.

Text: M1815; first pub. N1815; MSS: A

7 match] $\left\{ \dfrac{\text{boast}}{\text{match}} \right\}$ *A, 'match' pencilled in the right margin in another hand,
'boast' underscored in pencil*

8 that glance] $\left\{ \dfrac{\text{those eyes}}{\text{that glance}} \right\}$ *A, as in 7 above; each glance N1815E*

---

2 E. H. Coleridge writes (M1900W, III, 390): 'Compare the first "Sonnet to
Genevra" (addressed to Lady Frances Wedderburn Webster), "Thine eye's blue
tenderness".' [The second 'Sonnet to Genevra' refers to 'thy deep-blue eyes'.]

Moore (M1900W, I, 119) tells us that Lord Strangford's *Translations from the
Portuguese by Luis de Camoëns* (London, 1803) was a favourite with Byron. Byron
refers to the work in his 'Stanzas to a Lady, with the Poems of Camoëns', and
twice in *English Bards and Scotch Reviewers* (ll. 295–308, 921–2). In the latter work
he addresses 'Hibernian Strangford! with thine eyes of blue', and then refers in a
note to the canzonet 'Naõ sei quem assella' (Strangford, p. 56) 'Thou hast an eye
of tender blue', adding 'It is also to be remarked, that the things given to the
public as poems of Camoëns are no more to be found in the original Portuguese,
than in the Song of Solomon.'

Husain Haddawy in 'Oriental Translations and the Romantic Movement' (a
paper presented to the Modern Language Association of America, 28 December
1964) compares a translation from the Arabic of Ibnul Rumi by Joseph Dacre
Carlisle (*Specimens of Arabic Poetry* [Cambridge, 1796], p. 75):

When I beheld thy blue eye shine
Thro' the bright drop that pity drew,
I saw beneath those tears of thine
A blue-eyed violet bath'd in dew.

Haddawy discusses the subject at length in 'English Arabesque: The Oriental
Mode in Eighteenth-Century English Literature' (unpub. Cornell Univ. diss.,
1963).

2.

As clouds from yonder sun receive
A deep and mellow dye,   10
Which scarce the shade of coming eve
Can banish from the sky,
Those smiles unto the moodiest mind
Their own pure joy impart;
Their sunshine leaves a glow behind   15
That lightens o'er the heart.

10   dye] die *M1815W*
10–12 a.   A deep [but parting glow]
            [Ere down the mountain] coming Eve
            [Oershadows all below]
        b.   A deep (and mellow dye)
            (Which scarce the Shade of) coming Eve
            (Can banish from the sky) *A*
15   glow] $\left\{ \begin{matrix} \text{beam} \\ \hline \text{glow} \end{matrix} \right\}$ *A, as in 7 above*

Inscription: Byron's initial 'D' and signature A

SUN OF THE SLEEPLESS!

SUN OF THE SLEEPLESS! melancholy star!
Whose tearful beam glows tremulously far,
That show'st the darkness thou canst not dispel,
How like art thou to joy remembered well!

So gleams the past, the light of other days, 5
Which shines, but warms not with its powerless rays;
A night-beam Sorrow watcheth to behold,
Distinct, but distant – clear – but, oh how cold!

Text: M1815; MSS: A, B, C

1–8   [What is the past? the light of other days?
      That shines but warms not with its [fading] (powerless) rays
      A Moonbeam Sorrow lingers to behold
      Distinct but distant – dazzling – clear – but cold –
      Which shows the darkness it may not dispel
      [To those that [sle] cannot] Unto the [xxx] (sleepless) eyes that ?know?
      it well] *A, cancelled first draft of lines 11–16 of 'Harmodia'*
2   glows . . . far,] shoots trembling from afar – *A*; glows tremulously far – *B*
3   That] [Why] (That) *A*
5   So gleams] Such is *A*; So gleams *B*
6   Which] That *A, B*; Which *C*
7   A night-beam] A Moonbeam *A*; A night-beam *B*
      watcheth] watche[s]th *A*
8   clear . . . cold!] [dazzling – clear] (clear) but ([oh how] deathlike) cold. *A*;
      clear but – Oh how cold! – *B*

---

1   Nathan writes (N1829, p. 81): 'In a conversation with Lord Byron, I mentioned
to him that several admirers of his writings were sceptical in their judgement as to
what his Lordship addressed in this melody – whether the *moon* or the *evening star*,
both receiving their light from the *sun*; to which his Lordship replied, "I see,
Nathan, you have been *star* gazing, and are now in the *clouds*; I shall therefore
leave the *Astronomer Royal* to direct you in that matter".'

6   Cf. 'Newstead Abbey', I: 3–4:

> It shines from afar like the glories of old;
> It gilds, but it warms not – 'tis dazzling but cold.

Cf. also *Giaour*, ll. 101–2:

> Spark of that flame, perchance of heavenly birth,
> Which gleams, but warms no more its cherished earth!

To the Countess of Blessington Byron remarked: 'Memory precludes happiness, whatever [Samuel] Rogers may say to the contrary [in *The Pleasures of Memory*], for it borrows from the past, to imbitter the present, bringing back to us all the grief that has most wounded, or the happiness that has most charmed us; the first leaving its sting, and of the second, – "Nessun maggior dolore,/Che ricordarsi del tempo felice,/Nulla miseria."' *Conversations of Byron*, p. 164.

OH! WEEP FOR THOSE

1.

OH! WEEP FOR THOSE that wept by Babel's stream,
Whose shrines are desolate, whose land a dream;
Weep for the harp of Judah's broken shell;
Mourn – where their God hath dwelt the Godless dwell!

2.

And where shall Israel lave her bleeding feet?   5
And when shall Zion's songs again seem sweet?
And Judah's melody once more rejoice
The hearts that leaped before its heavenly voice?

Text: M1815, first pub. N1815

6 when] where *N1815E*

3.

Tribes of the wandering foot and weary breast,
How shall ye flee away and be at rest?   10
The wild-dove hath her nest, the fox his cave,
Mankind their Country – Israel but the grave!

10 rest?] *N1815*; rest! *M1815, M1815W*

---

10 Cf. Psalms 55:6: 'And I said, Oh that I had wings like a dove! for then would I fly away, and be at rest.' Cf. also *Don Juan*, X:6: 'Oh!' saith the Psalmist, 'that I had a dove's Pinions to flee away, and be at rest!' and 'I would I were a careless child', VII:8:

> Then would I cleave the vault of heaven,
> To flee away, and be at rest.

11 Cf. Matthew 8:20: 'The foxes have holes, and the birds of the air *have* nests.'

THE HARP THE MONARCH
MINSTREL SWEPT

1.

THE HARP THE MONARCH MINSTREL SWEPT,
The King of men, the loved of Heaven,
Which Music hallowed while she wept
O'er tones her heart of hearts had given,
Redoubled be her tears, its chords are riven!   5

Text: M1815; first pub. N1815; MSS: A, B (Hanson's transcript); the formal arrangement of the stanzas is that of the MSS; the copy-text divides the poem into two ten-line stanzas, indents lines 5, and 10, and fails to indent line 2.

ante 1   [Oh then farewell I could have borne
          Without a murmur all [the] save this –
          The false on] *A, cancelled incomplete lines*

1   The . . . swept,] The harp [a] (the) monarch['s fingers] (minstrel) swept *A*;
    The Harp the Minstrel Monarch swept *B*
2   King] [king] (first) *A*; first *B*
3   Which . . . hallowed] [Oer which] (Which) Music cherished *A*; Which
    Music cherished *B*
4   O'er . . . hearts] Oer tones her [highest Soul] (heart of hearts) *A*; On Tunes
    her Heart of Hearts *B*
5   riven!] risen *B*

1   Wright summarizes (M1832W, X, 76) Charles Burney's *A General History of Music* (1782–9, I, 233–4): 'In the reign of King David, music was held in the highest estimation by the Hebrews. The genius of that prince for music, and his attachment to the study and practice of it, as well as the great number of musicians appointed by him for the performance of religious rites and ceremonies, could not fail to extend its influence and augment its perfections: for it was during this period, that music was first honoured by being admitted in the ministry of sacrifice, and worship of the ark; as well as being cultivated by a king.'
1–5   Cf. Thomas Moore's 'The Harp that once, thro' Tara's halls', *Irish Melodies* [1808], I, 22:

> The Harp that once, thro' Tara's halls,
>   The soul of Music shed,
> Now hangs as mute on Tara's walls
>   As if that soul were fled: –
> So sleeps the pride of former days
>   So glory's thrill is o'er;
> And hearts, that once beat high for praise,
>   Now feel that pulse no more!

2.

It softened men of iron mould,
 It gave them virtues not their own;
No ear so dull, no soul so cold,
 That felt not, fired not to the tone,
Till David's Lyre grew mightier than his throne!   10

7   *a.* It [saved] the hearts [that felt its tone]
   b. It [(made) the hearts (that heard its own)]
   c. It (gave them virtues not their own –) *A*
8   no soul] no[r] soul *A*
10   Till . . . grew] [When Jesse's son] (And David's) lyre was *A*; And David's
   lyre was *B*

3.

It told the triumphs of our King,
 It wafted glory to our God;
It made our gladdened vallies ring,
 The cedars bow, the mountains nod;
Its sound aspired to Heaven and there abode!   15

post 10   3
   [His [Glory] [(Memory)]] (Glory) bids us mourn the more
   Ablest of Kings and bards the chief
   [Its strain that] (His name but) tells of [Glories] (triumphs) oer
   For him so hig] *A, cancelled incomplete stanza*

ante 11   3.] [4] 3 *A*

11   It . . . King,] [An] [But he is dust – and we are sunk] It told the triumphs of
   our King *A*

10   Wright summarizes (M1832W, X, 77) Henry Hart Milman's *The History of
the Jews* (1829–30, I, 248–9): 'The hymns of David excel no less in sublimity and
tenderness of expression, than in loftiness and purity of religious sentiment. In
comparison with them, the sacred poetry of all other nations sinks into mediocrity.
They have embodied so exquisitely the universal language of religious emotion,
that (a few fierce and vindictive passages excepted, natural in the warrior-poet of
a sterner age,) they have entered, with unquestionable propriety, into the Christian
ritual. The songs which cheered the solitude of the desert caves of Engedi, or
resounded from the voice of the Hebrew people as they wound along the glens
or hill-sides of Judea, have been repeated for ages in almost every part of the
habitable world, – in the remotest islands of the ocean, among the forests of
America, or the sands of Africa. How many human hearts have they softened,
purified, exalted! – of how many wretched beings have they been the secret
consolation! – on how many communities have they drawn down the blessings
of Divine Providence, by bringing the affections in unison with their deep devo-
tional fervour!'

It] † I[f]t B, *Hanson correcting himself*
12 It . . . God;] [The] (It [*xxx* its] wafted) Glory [from] (to) our God – *A*
13 gladdened] [far] gladdened *A*

post 15   4

[It there abode – [the] and there it rings
      But neer on earth its sound shall be –
The Prophet's race hath passed away –
      And all the hallowed Minstrelsy
From earth [its] that sound & soul are fled
      And shall we never near again
      And shall] *A, cancelled incomplete stanza*

rings] reigns *B*

Note: copied from Manuscript Ch. H. 8 Feb 15 N.B. The last stanza crossed out in original *B, Hanson's note refers to the cancelled incomplete fourth stanza.*

4.

Since then, though heard on earth no more,
      Devotion and her daughter Love
Still bid the bursting spirit soar
      To sounds that seem as from above,
In dreams that day's broad light can not remove.   20

16–20   *This stanza is not found in the extant MSS.*

16   Nathan writes (N1829, p. 33): 'When his Lordship put the copy into my hand, it terminated thus –

Its sound aspired to Heaven, and there abode.

This, however, did not complete the verse, and I wished him to help out the melody. He replied, "Why I have sent you to Heaven – it would be difficult to go further". My attention for a few moments was called to some other person, and his Lordship, whom I had hardly missed exclaimed – "Here, Nathan, I have brought you down again", and immediately presented me the beautiful and sublime lines which conclude the melody.'

17   Cf. *Giaour,* ll. 1135–8:

Devotion wafts the mind above,
But Heaven itself descends in Love;
A feeling from the Godhead caught,
To wean from self each sordid thought.

THY DAYS ARE DONE

1.

THY DAYS ARE DONE, thy fame begun;
  Thy country's strains record
.The triumphs of her chosen Son,
  The slaughters of his sword!
The deeds he did, the fields he won,   5
  The freedom he restored!

Text: M1815; first pub. N1815

2.

Though thou art fall'n, while we are free
  Thou shalt not taste of death!
The generous blood that flowed from thee
  Disdained to sink beneath: 10
Within our veins its currents be,
  Thy spirit on our breath!

3.

Thy name, our charging hosts along,
  Shall be the battle-word!
Thy fall, the theme of choral song   15
  From virgin voices poured!
To weep would do thy glory wrong;
  Thou shalt not be deplored.

---

1 Nathan writes (N1829, pp. 39–40): 'Lord Byron, in this melody had some
reference to a fallen warrior, whose deeds remain a monument to his memory,
and though dead to the world, he still leaves a lasting impression on the minds of
the living.' [Cf. 'On the Death of Sir Peter Parker, Bart.' (M1900W, III, 417).
Though Nathan implies that Napoleon is the poem's subject, these lines may well
be a second elegy for Byron's naval hero cousin, Sir Peter Parker. Byron's lines
on Parker were composed on 6 October 1814, and it is likely that 'Thy Days are
Done' was one of the 'nine or ten' Hebrew Melodies completed by 20 October
1814. (The poem was composed after Napoleon's first abdication and well before
the Hundred Days began.) Parker died fighting Americans near Baltimore on
31 August 1814. His state funeral took place on 15 May 1815 shortly before the
publication of *Hebrew Melodies*, and Byron added 'On the Death of Sir Peter
Parker, Bart.' at the close of that work.]

ON JORDAN'S BANKS

1.

ON JORDAN'S BANKS the Arabs' camels stray,
On Sion's hill the False One's votaries pray,
The Baal-adorer bows on Sinai's steep —
Yet there — even there — Oh God! thy thunders sleep:

2.

There — where thy finger scorched the tablet stone!   5
There — where thy shadow to thy people shone!
Thy glory shrouded in its garb of fire:
Thyself — none living see and not expire!

3.

Oh! in the lightning let thy glance appear!
Sweep from his shivered hand the oppressor's spear: 10
How long by tyrants shall thy land be trod?
How long thy temple worshipless, Oh God?

Text: M1815; first pub. N1815; MSS: A

1 Arabs'] Arab's *N1815E*
post 2 [God! can thy thunders sleep on dark Sinai] *A, cancelled line*
3 Baal . . . bows] [idol] Baal-adorer [walks] (bows) *A*
4 thy . . . sleep:] thy [slee] (thunders sleep –) *A*
5 scorched the tablet] [traced] (scorched) the table[s of](t) *A*
6 thy . . . to] [thyself unto] (thy shadow to) *A*

1 'From Mr. [John] Pierpont's [1785–1866] *Airs of Palestine* [1816, ll. 90–9] after describing the poetic traditions of classic mythology –

> No no a lonelier lovelier path be mine
> Greece and her charms I leave for Palestine
> There purer streams thro' happier valleys flow
> And sweeter flowers on holier mountains blow
> I love to breathe where Gilead sheds her balm
> I love to walk on Jordan's banks of palm
> I love to wet my feet on Hermon's dews
> I love the promptings of Isaiah's muse
> In Carmel's holy grot I court repose
> And deck my midnight couch with Sharon's rose.'

Byron's Commonplace Book, Folger Library, MS. M. a. 5., f. 31.

7   *a.* [There where thy] Glory [like] [sate] [(shadowed] in its) *fr.*
    b. [(Thy)] (Thy) Glory (in its) shrouded in *fr.*
    c. (Thy) Glory (in its) shrouded in (in its [garb] garb of fire –) *A, Byron failed*
       to cancel some phrases completely.

8   Thyself –] [For thee] (Thyself) *A*

9   Oh! in the] [Mask not thy] (Oh in the) *A*

10 And shiver in his grasp the oppressor's spear – *A*

11 trod?] *A*; trod! *M1815, M1815W*

12 worshipless, Oh] [Priestless–Oh my] (worshipless Oh) *A*
    God?] *A, N1815,* God! *M1815, M1815W*

FROM JOB

1.

A SPIRIT passed before me: I beheld
The face of Immortality unveiled —
Deep sleep came down on ev'ry eye save mine —
And there it stood, — all formless — but divine:
Along my bones the creeping flesh did quake;   5
And as my damp hair stiffened, thus it spake:

2.

'Is man more just than God? Is man more pure
Than he who deems even Seraphs insecure?
Creatures of clay — vain dwellers in the dust!
The moth survives you, and are ye more just?   10
Things of a day! you wither ere the night,
Heedless and blind to Wisdom's wasted light!'

Text: M1815; MSS: A, B

MS title: From Job *B*

ante 1 ['Twas a dream — it is nothing — except in my heart
     Where it cannot deceive — yet it will not depart] *A, cancelled lines*
2 face] [shapeless] (face) *A*
3 ev'ry] every *A, B*
4 all . . . divine:] [strange –] (all) formless [&] (but) divine *A*

---

1 Byron has versified Job 4:13-21.

    Nathan writes (N1829, p. 73): 'Being consulted as to his opinion of the authenticity of the book of Job, he made several evasive replies. I however pressed the subject, when he exclaimed, "Nathan, I plainly perceive you are desirous of putting *my* patience to the test:" he at length quaintly observed, "the book contains an excellent moral lesson, we will therefore not attempt to sap its credit, or shake its authenticity;" and to confirm that his ideas were not grounded upon a superficial view of the subject, sat down, and wrote the foregoing sublime lines.'

3 Cf. *Don Juan*, XVI:113:

    Again, through shadows of the night sublime
      When deep sleep fell on men, and the world wore
    The starry darkness round her like a girdle

The source of the expression is Job, 4:13:

    In thoughts from the visions of the night, when deep
    sleep falleth on men.

5 Along] [And on] ([And] (Al)on)(g) *A*
creeping] [faithless] (creeping) *A*
6 my damp] [cold] (my chill) *A*; my damp *B*
9 vain dwellers] [what –] ye dwellers *A*; vain dwellers *B*
11 Things . . . night,] 'The Morning comes – [the Night you shall not see –]
(you fall before the Night –) *A*; Things of a day! you wither ere the night *B*

8 In the *Monthly Review* (1815, LXXVIII, 46), Francis Hodgson writes: 'The
word *insecure* has no more business here than the nettle on the Monk's grave.'

IF THAT HIGH WORLD

1.

IF THAT HIGH WORLD, which lies beyond
  Our own, surviving Love endears;
If there the cherished heart be fond,
  The eye the same, except in tears —
How welcome those untrodden spheres!   5
  How sweet this very hour to die!
To soar from earth and find all fears
  Lost in thy light — Eternity!

Text: M1815; first pub. N1815

2.

It must be so: 'tis not for self
  That we so tremble on the brink;   10
And striving to o'erleap the gulph,
  Yet cling to Being's severing link.
Oh! in that future let us think
  To hold each heart the heart that shares,
With them the immortal waters drink,   15
  And soul in soul grow deathless theirs!

1 Nathan writes (N1829, p. 6): 'In a subsequent conversation, he observed to me, "they accuse me of atheism – an atheist I could never be – no man of reflection, can feel otherwise than doubtful and anxious, when reflecting on futurity. Yet," continued he, rising hastily from his seat, and pacing the room,

> It must be so – 'tis not for self
> That we so tremble on the brink.

"Alas! Nathan, we either know too little, or feel too much on this subject; and if it be criminal to speculate on it (as the gentlemen critics say) I fear I must ever remain an awful offender."'

The Countess of Blessington writes (*Conversations of Byron*, p. 68): 'They who accuse Byron of being an unbeliever are wrong: he is *sceptical*, but not unbelieving . . . his wavering faith . . . may be[come] as firmly fixed as is now his conviction of the immortality of the soul, – a conviction that he declares every fine and noble impulse of his nature renders more decided.'

12   severing] breaking *N1815*

16   Nathan writes (N1829, pp. 21–2): 'At a party where his Lordship was present, a reference to those elegant lines, commencing with "If that High World," had given rise to a speculative argument on the probable nature of happiness in a future state, and occasioned a desire in one of the Ladies, to ascertain his Lordship's opinion on the subject; requesting therefore to know what might constitute, in his idea, the happiness of the next world, he quickly replied, "the pleasure, Madame, of seeing you there".'

OH! SNATCHED AWAY
IN BEAUTY'S BLOOM

1.

OH! SNATCHED AWAY IN BEAUTY'S BLOOM,
On thee shall press no ponderous tomb;
But on thy turf shall roses rear
Their leaves, the earliest of the year;
And the wild cypress wave in tender gloom: 5

Text: M1815; first pub. N1815; MSS: A, B, C

MS title: 'Oh Snatched Away' *Copy in B's writing – Given me at Seaham before my Marriage – C, inscribed by Lady Byron on the cover*

ante 1 [Like the rays on [the] (yon) blue gushing stream] *A, cancelled line*
3 on] [from] (oer) *C*
4 Their leaves] The[ir](ir) [tender] lea[f](ves) *A*; Their Leaf *B*; Their leaves *C*

2.

And oft by yon blue gushing stream
Shall Sorrow lean her drooping head,
And feed deep thought with many a dream,

---

1 Nathan writes (N1829, p. 30): 'In submitting this melody to his Lordship's judgment, I once enquired in what manner they might refer to any scriptural subject: he appeared for a moment affected – at last replied, "Every mind must make its own reference: there is scarcely one of us who could not imagine that the affliction belongs to himself, to me it certainly belongs." His Lordship here, with agitation, exclaimed, "She is no more, and perhaps the only vestige of her existence is the feeling I sometimes fondly indulge."'

E. H. Coleridge notes (M1900W, III, 388): 'It has been surmised that the lines contain a final reminiscence of the mysterious Thyrza.'

4 Cf. Byron's Journal for 27 February 1821: 'The present, at this season reminds one of Gray's stanza omitted from his elegy:

> Here scatter'd oft, the earliest of the year,
>   By hands unseen, are showers of violets found;
> The red-breast loves to build and warble here,
>   And little footsteps lightly print the ground.

As fine a stanza as any in his elegy. I wonder that he could have the heart to omit it.' *L & J*, V, 210. (The stanza originally preceded the 'Epitaph'. Wright compared the Journal entry with *Don Juan*, XIII:77; 5–6.)

> And lingering pause and lightly tread;
> Fond wretch! as if her step disturbed the dead!   10

5 tender] gentle *A, B*; tender *C*
6 And . . . yon] And (oft by) yon *A*
7 lean . . . head,] [on the waters gaze] (lean her drooping head) *A*
8 feed . . . dream,] [lost in deep remembrance dream] (feed [her] (deep) thoughts with many a dream) *A*
  deep thought] (deep) thoughts *A*; dull thoughts *B*; deep thought *C*
9 lingering] [long shall] (lingering) *A*
10 Fond . . . dead!] As if [her steps] [fearful to] (her footsteps could) disturb the dead – *A*; As if her footsteps could disturb the dead *B*; Fond wretch! as if her step disturbed the dead *C*; Fond wretch! as if her steps disturb'd the dead. *Ex1815*

3.

> Away; we know that tears are vain,
> That death nor hears nor heeds distress:
> Will this unteach us to complain?
> Or make one mourner weep the less?
> And thou – who tell'st me to forget,   15
> Thy looks are wan, thine eyes are wet.

ante 11   1. [But] *recto* [But thou for whom the land laments
          2. Was raised [Oh neer wept]] *verso A, cancelled incomplete lines*
11 Away – we know [tis idle all –] (that tears are vain –) *A*; Away – we know that Tears are vain *B*; Away – [it is delusion all] (we know that tears are vain –) *C*
12 That . . . heeds] *A*; That death [is] nor hears nor heeds *A*; That death nor hears nor heeds *B*; The dead nor hear nor heed *C*; That death nor heeds nor hears *M1815, N1815, M1815W, Ex1815*
13 Will] Can *C*
15 And thou] [Even] (And) thou *A*; And <u>thou</u> *C*
16 looks are] cheek is *C*
   thine] thy *Ex1815*

post 16   4
> Nor need I write to tell the tale
>   My pen were doubly weak
> Oh what can idle words avail
>   Unless my heart could speak

        5
> By day or night in weal or woe
>   That heart no longer free

Must bear the love it cannot show
And silent turn †[to] for thee –

copied from Manuscripts 8 Feb. 1815 Ch. H. *B*

*Charles Hanson, copying 'from Manuscripts', mistook the MS of the last two stanzas of
the lines beginning 'The kiss, dear maid! thy lip has left' (M1900W, III, 23) for two
additional stanzas. He may have been making a copy for Nathan, who did set the poem,
first published in 1812, to music. Nathan added the song to the advertisement published in
the first edition of* A Selection of Hebrew Melodies, No. I *while the work was at
press. E. H. Coleridge gives the variants but fails to identify them.*

16   E. H. Coleridge compares (M1900W, III, 389): 'Nay, now, pry'thee weep
no more! you know . . . that 'tis sinful to murmur at . . . Providence.' – 'And
should not that reflection check your own, my Blanche?' – 'Why are your cheeks
so wet? Fie! fie, my child!' M. G. Lewis, *Romantic Tales* (1808), I, 53. (Lewis'
authorship of these tales is discussed by Morchard Bishop in 'A Terrible Tangle',
TLS, 19 October 1967, p. 989.)

JEPHTHA'S DAUGHTER

1.

SINCE our Country, our God – Oh, my Sire!
Demand that thy Daughter expire;
Since thy triumph was bought by thy vow –
Strike the bosom that's bared for thee now!

2.

And the voice of my mourning is o'er,   5
And the mountains behold me no more:
If the hand that I love lay me low,
There cannot be pain in the blow!

Text: M1815; first pub. N1815
4   for] to N1815E

3.

And of this, oh, my Father! be sure –
That the blood of thy child is as pure   10
As the blessing I beg ere it flow,
And the last thought that soothes me below.

---

1   The story of the vow is given in Judges 11:30–40.

Wright summarizes (M1832W, X, 81) Milman's *History of the Jews* (1829–30, I, 201–2): 'Jephtha, a bastard son of Gilead, having been wrongfully expelled from his father's house, had taken refuge in a wild country, and become a noted captain of freebooters. His kindred, groaning under foreign oppression, began to look to their valiant, though lawless compatriot, whose profession, according to their usage, was no more dishonourable than that of a pirate in the elder days of Greece. They sent for him, and made him head of their city. Before he went forth against the Ammonites he made the memorable vow, that, if he returned victorious, he would sacrifice as a burnt-offering whatever first met him on his entrance into his native city. He gained a splendid victory. At the news of it, his only daughter came dancing forth, in the gladness of her heart, and with jocund instruments of music, to salute the deliverer of his people. The miserable father rent his clothes in agony; but the noble-spirited maiden would not hear of the disregard of the vow: she only demanded a short period to bewail upon the mountains, like the Antigone of Sophocles, her dying without hope of becoming a bride or mother, and then submitted to her fate.'

4.

Though the virgins of Salem lament,
Be the judge and the hero unbent!
I have won the great battle for thee,   15
And my Father and Country are free!

5.

When this blood of thy giving hath gushed,
When the voice that thou lovest is hushed,
Let my memory still be thy pride,
And forget not I smiled as I died!   20

---

20 Nathan writes (N1829, pp. 10–12): 'When these beautiful lines were composed by Lord Byron, I was anxious to ascertain his real sentiments on the subject,
hinting my own belief that it might not necessarily mean a positive sacrifice of
the daughter's life, but perhaps referred to a sentence of perpetual seclusion, a state
held by the Jews as dead indeed to society, and the most severe infliction that
could be imposed. With his usual frankness, he observed, "Whatever may be the
absolute state of the case, I am innocent of her blood; she has been killed to my
hands: besides, you know *such an infliction*, as the world goes, would not be a
subject for sentiment or pathos – therefore do not seek to exumate [*sic*] the lady."
On another occasion when Jephtha was the subject of conversation, his lordship
with much good humour suddenly put an end to the argument exclaiming, "Well
my hands are not imbrued in her blood! I shall not by killing her incur censure
from the world, for an attempt to deprive them of the pleasure of thinking a
little more on the subject."'

THE WILD GAZELLE

1.

THE WILD GAZELLE on Judah's hills
    Exulting yet may bound,
And drink from all the living rills
    That gush on holy ground;
Its airy step and glorious eye   5
May glance in tameless transport by: –

Text: M1815; first pub. N1815; MSS: A
1 [Oer Judah's hills the wild Gazelle] (The wild Gazelle [oer] on Judah's hills) A
3 living] [mountain['s]] ([mountain]) (living) A
4 gush] [spring] (gush) A
6 in . . . transport] [untamed [unfrighted] (in gladness)] (in tameless transport) A

2.

A step as fleet, an eye more bright,
    Hath Judah witnessed there;
And o'er her scenes of lost delight
    Inhabitants more fair.   10
The cedars wave on Lebanon,
But Judah's statelier maids are gone!

7 fleet] [light] (fleet) A
8 Hath . . . witnessed] [Did] (Hath) Judah['s singer's] (witnessed) A
9 *a.* And [round] her [forests a fairer sight]
    b. And (oer) her (scenes of lost delight) A
11 wave] [rest] (wave) A

3.

More blest each palm that shades those plains
    Than Israel's scattered race;

5 E. H. Coleridge compares (M1900W, III, 384): 'To Ianthe', IV, 1–3:

> Oh! let that eye, which wild as the Gazelle's,
> Now brightly bold or beautifully shy,
> Wins as it wanders, dazzles where it dwells,

and *Giaour*, ll. 473–4:

> Her eye's dark charm 'twere vain to tell,
> But gaze on that of the Gazelle.

For, taking root, it there remains   15
   In solitary grace:
It cannot quit its place of birth,
It will not live in other earth.

4.

But we must wander witheringly,
   In other lands to die;   20
And where our fathers' ashes be,
   Our own may never lie:
Our temple hath not left a stone,
And Mockery sits on Salem's throne.

13   *a.* Ye Trees – th[an our vanished] *fr.*
      b. [Ye Trees – th(at shade our vanished plains –)]
      c. [How] (More) blest each [Tree] (Palm) that shades th[e](ose) plains *A*
14   [Than] Than [Jud] Israel's [exiled] (scattered) race *A*
16   [Eternal in its place] (In solitary grace) *A*
19   witheringly,] witheringly [on] *A*
23   *a.* [[And] (And) where o]ur [fathers and our throne]
      b. (O)ur (temple hath not left a stone) *A*
24   Mockery sits] [Silence] [Darkness dwells] (Mockery sits) *A*

MY SOUL IS DARK

1.

My soul is dark — Oh! quickly string
    The harp I yet can brook to hear;
And let thy gentle fingers fling
    Its melting murmurs o'er mine ear.
If in this heart a hope be dear,   5
    That sound shall charm it forth again;
If in these eyes there lurk a tear,
    'Twill flow, and cease to burn my brain:

Text: M1815, first pub. N1815

2.

But bid the strain be wild and deep,
    Nor let thy notes of joy be first: 10
I tell thee, minstrel, I must weep,
    Or else this heavy heart will burst;

---

1   Byron has dramatized I Samuel 16:14–23.

Nathan writes (N1829, p. 37): 'It was generally conceived, that Lord Byron's reported singularities, approached on some occasions to derangement, and at one period indeed, it was very currently asserted, that his intellects were actually impaired. The report only served to amuse his Lordship. He referred to the circumstance, and declared, that he would try how a *Madman* could write; seizing the pen with eagerness, he for a moment fixed his eyes in majestic wildness on vacancy; when like a flash of inspiration, without erasing a single word, the above verses were the result, which he put into my possession with this remark: "if I am mad who write, be certain that you are so who compose!"'

Byron copied lines 283–8 of John Pierpont's *Airs of Palestine* (1816) into a commonplace book, noting: 'The [deliverance] description of David's deliverance of Saul by the magic of his lyre from the enchantment of the evil spirit is highly animated –

As the young harper tries each quivering wire,
It leaps & sparkles with prophetic fire,
And, with the kindling song, the kindling rays
Around his fingers tremulously blaze,
Till the whole hall, like those bless'd fields above
Glows with the light of melody and love.'

Folger Library, MS. M. a. 5, f. 31.

For it hath been by sorrow nurst,
  And ached in sleepless silence long;
And now 'tis doomed to know the worst,   15
  And break at once – or yield to song.

E. H. Coleridge compares (M1900W, III, 399): '"My soul is dark". – Ossian, "Oina-Morul," *The Works of Ossian*, 1765, ii. 279.'

8 Haidee's 'dark' soul is similarly relieved in *Don Juan*, IV:65–6.
14 Cf. *Childe Harold's Pilgrimage* (III:33):

And thus the heart will do which not forsakes,
Living in shattered guise; and still, and cold,
And bloodless, with its sleepless sorrow aches . . .

THEY SAY THAT HOPE IS HAPPINESS

'Felix qui potuit rerum cognoscere causas.' – VIRGIL.

1.

THEY say that Hope is happiness –
But genuine Love must prize the past;
And mem'ry wakes the thoughts that bless:
They rose the first – they set the last.

Text: N1827–29P; the formal arrangement of the stanzas follows that given in editions published by Murray, in the copy-text the poem is divided into two stanzas of eight and four lines respectively
Epigraph: only given in editions published for Nathan

2.

And all that mem'ry loves the most   5
Was once our only hope to be:
And all that hope adored and lost
Hath melted into memory.

3.

Alas! it is delusion all –
The future cheats us from afar: 10

Epigraph: 'Happy he is who has been able to gain knowledge of the causes of things.' (*Georgics*, II, 490.)

1 Nathan writes (N1829, p. 71): 'The foregoing lines were officiously taken up by a person who arrogated to himself some self-importance in criticism, and who made an observation upon their demerits, on which his Lordship quaintly observed, "they were written in haste and they shall perish in the same manner," and immediately consigned them to the flames; as my music adapted to them, however, did not share the same fate, and having a contrary opinion of anything that might fall from the pen of Lord Byron, I treasured them up, and on a subsequent interview with his Lordship I accused him of having committed suicide in making so valuable a *burnt offering*; to which his Lordship smilingly replied, "the act seems to *inflame* you: come, Nathan, since you are displeased with the *sacrifice*, I give them to you as a *peace offering*, use them as you may deem proper."'

'What is Hope? nothing but the paint on the face of Existence; the least touch of Truth rubs it off, and then we see what a hollow-cheeked harlot we have got hold of.' Byron to Moore, 28 October 1815, *L & J*, III, 232.

Nor can we be what we recall,
Nor dare we think on what we are.

11 recall] *N1827–29E*; recal *N1827–29P*

---

8 'If it were not for Hope, where would the Future be? – in hell. It is useless to say *where* the Present is, for most of us know; and as for the Past, *what* predominates in memory? – *Hope baffled*. Ergo, in all human affairs, it is Hope – Hope – Hope. I allow sixteen minutes, though I never counted them, to any given or supposed possession. From whatever place we commence, we know where it all must end.' Diary, 1821, *L & J*, V, 190.

HEROD'S LAMENT FOR MARIAMNE

1.

OH, Mariamne! now for thee
    The heart for which thou bled'st is bleeding;
Revenge is lost in agony,
    And wild remorse to rage succeeding.
Oh, Mariamne! where art thou?   5

    Thou canst not hear my bitter pleading:
Ah, could'st thou — thou would'st pardon now,
    Though heaven were to my prayer unheeding.

2.

And is she dead? — and did they dare
    Obey my phrensy's jealous raving?   10
My wrath but doomed my own despair:
    The sword that smote her 's o'er me waving. —

Text: M1815; MSS: A, B, C
MS title: 'Oh Mariamne' – First (& Second) Copy Halnaby. Jan. 1815 *A, cover*;
Herod's lament for Mariamne. – *B, C*
3 [And what was rage is] (Revenge is turned to) agony – *A*; Revenge is lost in
    agony *B*
4 wild] deep *A*; wild *B*
6 [And what am I thy tyrant] (Thou can'st not hear my bitter) pleading *A*

1 Wright (M1832W, X, 93) summarizes Milman's *History of the Jews* (1829–30,
II, 107–8): 'Mariamne, the wife of Herod the Great, falling under the suspicion of
infidelity, was put to death by his order. She was a woman of unrivalled beauty,
and a haughty spirit: unhappy in being the object of passionate attachment, which
bordered on frenzy, to a man who had more or less concern in the murder of her
grandfather, father, brother, and uncle, and who had twice commanded her
death, in case of his own. Ever after, Herod was haunted by the image of the
murdered Mariamne, until disorder of the mind brought on disorder of body,
which led to temporary derangement.'
    'I don't know what Scrope Davies meant by telling you I liked Children, I
abominate the sight of them so much that I have always had the greatest respect
for the character of Herod.' Byron to Augusta, 30 August 1811, *L & J*, II, 11.
    E. H. Coleridge notes (M1900W, III, 400): 'See Voltaire's drama, *Mariamne,
passim.*'

But thou art cold, my murdered love!
And this dark heart is vainly craving
For her who soars alone above,   15
And leaves my soul unworthy saving.

3.

She's gone, who shared my diadem;
She sunk, with her my joys entombing;
I swept that flower from Judah's stem
Whose leaves for me alone were blooming.   20
And mine's the guilt, and mine the hell,
This bosom's desolation dooming;
And I have earned those tortures well,
Which unconsumed are still consuming!

7   Ah . . . now,] [Thou can'st not [*xxx*] ([view] see) my burning brow] Ah
    could'st thou – [would'st thou see me] (thou would'st pardon) now – *A*
    would'st] would('st) *B, added in pencil*

8   Though] [But] Though *A*

9   *a.* [Oh look on me if [?yet? above] ([in] from that heaven)]
    b. [Thy gentle Spirit] *fr.*
    c. Thou art not dead – they [dared not] (could not dare) *A*
    d. And is she dead? and did they dare *B*

10   *a.* [?Obl?] [Fulfil] my Fury's raving –
    b. (Obey) my (jealous) Fury's raving – *A*
    c. Obey my Phrenzy's jealous raving? *B*

12   [They might have saved me] [I *xxx*] The sword that smote thee 's oer me
    waving *A*; The Sword that smote her 's oer me waving *B*

14   And . . . craving] [But yet in death my soul enslaving] And this [?hel?] dark
    heart is vainly craving *A*

15   *a.* For her [its] [I [neer] shall not meet above]
    b. For her (who went alone above) *A*
    c. For her who [went] (soars) alone above *B*

16   leaves] left – *A*; leaves *B*

18   *a.* She's gone – [who made me blest]
    b. She's [gone – (who made my [life] blessing)]
    c. She's (low – with her my hope entombing) *A*
    d. She sunk – with her my joys entombing *B*

20   Whose . . . for] [While yet the leaves] *fr.* (Whose leaves for) *A*

21   guilt] [deed] (guilt) *A*
    and mine] and mine['s] *B*

22   This . . . desolation] [My] (This) bosom's des[t]olation *A*

23   And . . . well,] [That] [I] Oh I have earned [its] (those) tortures well *A*; And
    I have earned those tortures well *B*

Inscription: Jan. 13. 1815 *initial 'D' signature B*

24   Nathan writes (N1829, p. 51): 'At the time his Lordship was writing for me the poetry to these melodies, he felt anxious to facilitate my views in preserving as much as possible the original airs, for which purpose he would frequently consult me regarding the style and metre of his stanzas. I accordingly desired to be favored with so many lines pathetic, some playful, others martial, &c. One evening, when his Lordship was obligingly submitting to my wishes in that respect, I unfortunately (while absorbed for a moment in worldly affairs) requested so many *dull* lines – meaning *plaintive*. His Lordship, observing that I was wrapt up in deep meditation, and understanding my real meaning, instantly caught at the expression, which so much tickled his fancy, that he was convulsed with laughter, and exclaimed, "Well! Nathan! you have at length set me an easy task." This afforded him amusement for the rest of the evening, and observing my confusion whenever his eye met mine, he would occasionally make some witty allusion to the *dull* lines, until I enjoyed the joke equally with himself. The result, however, proved very fortunate for me, for before we parted he presented me these beautifully pathetic lines, saying, "Here, Nathan, I think you will find them *dull* enough."'

BY THE RIVERS OF BABYLON
WE SAT DOWN AND WEPT

1.

WE sate down and wept by the waters
Of Babel, and thought of the day
When our foe, in the hue of his slaughters,
Made Salem's high places his prey;
And ye, oh her desolate daughters!   5
Were scattered all weeping away.

Text: M1815; MSS: A, B, C

MS title: 'We sate down & wept' &c. Fair Copy B̲ B; *see* '*On the Day of the Destruction of Jerusalem by Titus*', *MS B, cover.*
1 *a.* We sate [by] by the waters
   b. We sate (down and wept) by the waters *A*
2 *a.* And wept [oer the day]
   b. And [wept (bitter tears)]
   c. And ([mourned oer] the day)
   d. (Of Babel) [And] (and thought of) the day *A*
3 foe] foe[s] *A*

2.

While sadly we gazed on the river
Which rolled on in freedom below,

---

1 Byron's treatment of Psalms 137:1: 'By the rivers of Babylon, there we sat down, yea, we wept, when we remembered Zion.'

'I am going to the Chapple Royal at St. James. Do you ever go there? It begins at ½ past 5, and lasts till six; it is the most beautiful singing I ever heard; the choristers sing "By the waters of Babylon."' Caroline Lamb to Byron, 1812, *L & J*, II, 448.

3 E. H. Coleridge writes (M1900W, III, 402–3): 'Landor, in his "Dialogue between Southey and Porson" (*Works*, 1846, I, 69), attempted to throw ridicule on the opening lines of this "Melody": "A prey in the hue of his slaughters! This is very pathetic; but not more so than the thought it suggested to me, which is plainer –

> We sat down and wept by the waters
> Of Camus, and thought of the day
> When damsels would show their red garters
> In their hurry to scamper away."'

They demanded the song; but, oh never
   That triumph the stranger shall know!   10
May this right hand be withered for ever
   Ere it string our high harp for the foe!

6   scattered] borne *A*; scattered *B*
ante 7   [Our (mute) harps were hung on the willow
        That grew by the [Conqueror's stream] Stream of our foe
        And in sadness we [look] gazed on each billow
          That rolled on in freedom below –] *A, four cancelled lines*
7   While] [And wh] [And w](W)hile *A*
8   Which] That *A, B, C*
    in freedom] [so freely] (in freedom) *A*
9   They] [The] They *A*
10   That ... know!] [That sound shall] *fr*. [Our harps shall be strung for the
    foe –] (That triumph the stranger shall know) *A*
11   for ever] forever *A, B*; for ever *C*
12   it] [it] it *A*

3.

On the willow that harp is suspended,
   Oh Salem! its sound should be free;
And the hour when thy glories were ended   15
   But left me that token of thee:
And ne'er shall its soft tones be blended
   With the voice of the spoiler by me!

13   On ... suspended,] [Hang mutely my harp] *fr*. On the willow that harp
    [shall hang mutely] (is suspended) *A*
14   should be free;] [was for thee –] (should be free –) *A*
15   hour] day *A*; hour *B*
    glories] Glor[y]ies *A*
18   voice] song *A*; [song] (voice) *B*
Post 18   *4 stanza number inscribed on A*
Inscription: Jan. 15. 1815 Halnaby, *signed* B B
Pencil note on C:

2

Dear Kinnaird –
    Take only one of these marked [sic] *1 & 2* – as both are but different versions
of the same thought – leave the choice to any competent person you like
                              Yours
                              B—

*The two 'different versions' are 'In the Valley of Waters' (1) and 'By the Rivers of
Babylon We Sat Down and Wept' (2).*

18 Nathan writes (N1829, p. 45): 'Lord Byron observed, on my singing this melody, "Why, Nathan, you enter spiritedly into the oriental feeling; recollect, however, that although you *captivate*, you are no *captive*; and with all due submission to the Babylonians, I think their levity was ill-timed in trying to extort mirth from sorrow."'

IN THE VALLEY OF WATERS

1.

IN the valley of waters we wept o'er the day
When the host of the stranger made Salem his prey,
And our heads on our bosoms all droopingly lay,
And our hearts were so full of the land far away

2.

The song they demanded in vain – it lay still   5
In our souls as the wind that hath died on the hill;
They called for the harp – but our blood they shall spill
Ere our right hands shall teach them one tone of their skill.

*Text: N1827–29P; MSS: A, B; the formal arrangement of the stanzas follows
MSS A and B; in the copy-text the poem is not divided into stanzas*
MS title: 'In the Valley of Waters' – B A
1   o'er] o[n]('er) B
6   that . . . the] [in the cave of the] (that hath died on the) A
8   Ere] [Our] (Eer) A
    hands . . . skill.] A; hands shall teach them one tone of [its] (their) skill A;
    hand shall teach them one tone of our skill N1827–29P; hand shall teach them
    one tone of their skill N1827–29E

3.

All stringlessly hung on the willow's sad tree,
As dead as her dead leaf those mute harps must be;   10
Our hands may be fettered – our tears still are free,
For our God and our glory – and, Sion! – Oh, thee.

9   stringlessly hung] stringless(ly) [& mute] (hung) A
10 dead leaf] dead-lea[ves]f A
11 are] (are) A

---

1   Nathan writes (N1829, p. 69): 'When I submitted the MS. composition of
this melody to Lord Byron, he seemed surprized, and observed that the subject
had already been published. I pointed out the difference of style in my arrangement
of them, and likewise how his Lordship had varied the present version. He remarked that in writing two he only wished me to make a selection, "but," added
he, "I must confess I give a preference to the latter, and since your music differs so
widely from the former I see no reason why it should not also make its public
appearance."'

Inscription: Halnaby. 1815 *A*
Note on B:

1

Dear K.ᵈ
Vide note on Number 2 – I think this the best of the two –

Yᵣˢ B

---

9 'By the waters of Cheltenham I sat down and *drank*, when I remembered thee, Oh Georgiana Cottage! As for our *harps*, we hanged them up upon the willows that grew thereby. Then they said, "Sing us a song of Drury Lane," etc.; – but I am dumb and dreary as the Israelites.' Byron to Lord Holland, 10 September 1812, *L & J*, II, 143.
11 Cf. *Don Juan*, II:16:

So Juan wept, as wept the captive Jews
    By Babel's waters, still remembering Sion:
I'd weep, but mine is not a weeping muse. . . .

Byron alludes to Claudius James Rich's *Memoir on the Ruins of Babylon* (1815) in *Don Juan*, V:62.

ON THE DAY OF THE DESTRUCTION
OF JERUSALEM BY TITUS

1.

FROM the last hill that looks on thy once holy dome
I beheld thee, Oh SION! when rendered to Rome:
'Twas thy last sun went down, and the flames of thy fall
Flashed back on the last glance I gave to thy wall.

Text: M1815; MSS: A, B, C
MS title: 'From the last hill that looks' *B.* 1815. *verso:* MS. Compositions of Lord
B's 1815. *A, cover;* 'From the last hill that looks' &c. *B* – 1815. Hebrew Melodies
& 'We sat down & wept' &c. *B, cover;* On the day of the destruction (of Jerusalem) by Titus. – *C, in Byron's hand*
1 the] th[y]e *B*
   on] oer *A, B;* on *C*
   dome] [wall] (dome) *A*
2 when ... Rome:] [the day of thy fall] (when rendered to Rome) – *A*
3 sun] [sun] day *A;* day *B, C*
   and] [?amid?] (and) *A*
4 Flashed] [But] Flashed *A*

2.

I looked for thy temple, I looked for my home,   5
And forgot for a moment my bondage to come;
I beheld but the death-fire that fed on thy fane,
And the fast-fettered hands that made vengeance in vain.

3.

On many an eve, the high spot whence I gazed
Had reflected the last beam of day as it blazed;   10
While I stood on the height, and beheld the decline
Of the rays from the mountain that shone on thy shrine.

4 Cf. *Irish Melodies,* [1808], I, 39:
> Tho' the last glimpse of Erin with sorrow I see,
> Yet wherever thou art shall seem Erin to me;
> In exile thy bosom shall still be my home
> And thine eyes make my climate wherever we roam.

6 for a moment] for a moment *A*; [in their ruin] for a moment *B*
7 death-fire] [ruin] (death fires) *A*; death fire[s] *B*; death fire *C*
8 fast-fettered] [chains] fast fettered *A*
9 On many an eve [?on?] the (high) spot whe[re]nce I gaz[e(d)](ed) *A*
whence] whe[re]nce *A*; whence *B*; whe[re](nce) *C*
11 *a*. While I [looked from thy wall with that quiet] *fr*.
b. While I (stood on it's height and beheld the decline) *A*
on the] on it's *A*, *B*; on [its] (the) *C*
12 on] [oer] on *A*; oer *B*; on *C*

4.

And now on that mountain I stood on that day,
But I marked not the twilight beam melting away;
Oh! would that the lightning had glared in its stead,   15
And the thunderbolt burst on the conqueror's head!

5.

But the Gods of the Pagan shall never profane
The shrine where Jehovah disdained not to reign;
And scattered and scorned as thy people may be,
Our worship, oh Father! is only for thee.   20

13 And] [But] (And) *A*
14 marked] saw *A*; marked *B*
16 thunderbolt .. on] [red bolt] (thunderbolt) burst [oer] on *A*; thunderbolt
[burst] (crashed) on *B*; thunderbolt crashed on *C*
19 thy] [our] (thy) *A*
Inscription: Halnaby Jan. 18 1815 *B*

---

14 Cf. Jeremiah 15:9: Her sun is gone down while it was yet day.'
20 Nathan writes (N1829. p. 61): 'In the composition of the foregoing stanzas,
he professed to me, that he had always considered the fall of Jerusalem, as the
most remarkable event of all history; "for" (in his own words) "who can behold
the entire destruction of that mighty pile; the desolate wanderings of its inhabit-
ants, and compare these positive occurrences with the distant prophecies which
foreran them and be an infidel?"'

WERE MY BOSOM AS FALSE
AS THOU DEEM'ST IT TO BE

1.

WERE MY BOSOM AS FALSE AS THOU DEEM'ST IT TO BE,
I need not have wandered from far Galilee;
It was but abjuring my creed to efface
The curse which, thou say'st, is the crime of my race.

2.

If the bad never triumph, then God is with thee!　　　5
If the slave only sin, thou art spotless and free!
If the Exile on earth is an Outcast on high,
Live on in thy faith, but in mine I will die.

3.

I have lost for that faith more than thou canst bestow,
As the God who permits thee to prosper doth know;　　10
In his hand is my heart and my hope — and in thine
The land and the life which for him I resign.

Text: M1815; MSS: A, B
MS title: 'Were my bosom as false' – &c. Seaham. 1815. B *A, verso*; Seaham *A,*
verso at the upper right
7　Outcast] [o]Outcast B

SAUL

1.

THOU whose spell can raise the dead,
Bid the prophet's form appear.
'Samuel, raise thy buried head!
King, behold the phantom seer!'

Earth yawned; he stood the centre of a cloud: 5
Light changed its hue, retiring from his shroud.
Death stood all glassy in his fixed eye;
His hand was withered, and his veins were dry;
His foot, in bony whiteness, glittered there,
Shrunken and sinewless, and ghastly bare: 10

Text: M1815; MSS: A, B, C; the formal arrangement of the stanzas follows the MSS. The copy-text divides the poem into two stanzas; MS A divides the first of these stanzas into two parts, breaking the poem following 1 : 4. In the space between these parts Byron has written: [2] 1. MSS B and C follow the division of MS A, but give no number after line 4
MS title: Saul A, B, C
1 spell can] [voice] (spell) can[st] A

---

1 Byron has dramatized I Samuel 28:7–20.

    Wright summarizes (M1832W, X, 86) Milman's *History of the Jews* (1829–30, I, 228–9): 'Haunted with that insatiable desire of searching into the secrets of futurity, inseparable from uncivilised man, Saul knew not to what quarter to turn. The priests, outraged by his cruelty, had forsaken him: the prophets stood aloof: no dreams visited his couch; he had persecuted even the unlawful diviners. He hears at last of a female necromancer, a woman with the spirit of Ob; strangely similar to the Obeah women in the West Indies. To the cave-dwelling of this woman, in Endor, the monarch proceeds in disguise. He commands her to raise the spirit of Samuel. At this daring demand, the woman first recognises, or pretends to recognise, her royal visitor. "Whom seest thou?" says the king – "Mighty ones ascending from the earth." – "Of what form?" – "An old man covered with a mantle." Saul, in terror, bows down his head to the earth; and, it should seem, not daring to look up, receives from the voice of the spectre the awful intimation of his defeat and death. On the reality of this apparition we pretend not to decide: the figure, if figure there were, was not seen by Saul; and, excepting the event of the approaching battle, the spirit said nothing which the living prophet had not said before, repeatedly and publicly. But the fact is curious, as showing the popular belief of the Jews in departed spirits to have been the same with that of most other nations.'

From lips that moved not and unbreathing frame,
Like caverned winds, the hollow accents came.
Saul saw, and fell to earth, as falls the oak,
At once, and blasted by the thunder-stroke.

3   head!] [d]head! – *A*
5   *a.* He [ros] stands [amidst an earthly] cloud –
    b. (Earth yawned) He st[ands](ood) (the centre of a) cloud – *A*
6   *a.* [And the Mist mantled oer his floating] shroud
    b. (Light changed its hue [as shrinking] (retiring) from his) shroud *A*
7   Death [glared] (stood) [in] all glassy [oer] (in) his [aged] (fixed) eye *A*
8   was] [was] [(is)] (was) *A*
    were] [are] (were) *A*
9–10 *a.* [H[is]e stood erect & motionless]
    b. [The boney whiteness of his foot was there]
    written parallel with the right margin:
    c. His foot in [boney] boney whiteness glittered there
       Shrunken & sinewless – and ghastly bare *A*
11   From . . . frame,] From [lips that] (lips [that [moved] (stir) not)] (that moved
    not – and unbreathing frame –) *A*
13   fell] [bowed] (fell) *A*
14   At once and scorched beneath the thunder stroke *A, B, C*

---

4   Cf. Manfred, II:ii, 175–82:

> . . . I have one resource
> Still in my science – I can call the dead,
> And ask them what it is we dread to be:
> The sternest answer can but be the Grave,
> And that is nothing: if they answer not –
> The buried Prophet answered to the Hag
> Of Endor . .

Cf. also *Don Juan*, ded., 11:

> Think'st thou, could he – the blind Old Man – arise
> Like Samuel from the grave, to freeze once more
> The blood of monarchs with his prophecies,
> Or be alive again – again all hoar. . . .

Cf. also the *Age of Bronze*, ll. 380–3:

> . . . With the sound arise,
> Like Samuel's shade to Saul's monarchic eyes,
> The prophets of young Freedom, summon'd far
> From climes of Washington and Bolivar . . .

12   Compare the appearance of the spectre of Francesca in the *Siege of Corinth*
(ll. 612–17):

> And her motionless lips lay still as death,
> And her words came forth without her breath,
> And there rose not a heave o'er her bosom's swell,

2.

'Why is my sleep disquieted?   15
Who is he that calls the dead?
Is it thou, Oh King? Behold
Bloodless are these limbs, and cold:
Such are mine: and such shall be
Thine, to-morrow, when with me: 20
Ere the coming day is done,
Such shalt thou be, such thy son.
Fare thee well, but for a day;
Then we mix our mouldering clay.
Thou, thy race, lie pale and low,   25
Pierced by shafts of many a bow;
And the falchion by thy side,
To thy heart, thy hand shall guide:
Crownless, breathless, headless fall,
Son and sire, the house of Saul!'   30

15 'Why is] '[Who is] Why [am] (is) *A*
16 that calls] [dare] that calls *A*
18 these limbs,] [my] (these) bones *A*; these bones *B, C*
21 'Ere . . . done,] 'Ere [hath sunk tomorrow's Sun] [(tomorrows)] (the coming
     day [hath] (is) done –) *A*
23 for a] for [the] a *A*
24 mix] [mingle] (mix) *A*

And there seemed not a pulse in her veins to dwell.
Though her eye shone out, yet the lids were fixed . . .

15 Nathan writes (N1829, pp. 54–5): 'I scarcely need add what delight I felt in
discovering his Lordship's enthusiasm in the repetition of his own writing "Why
is my sleep disquieted, &c." continued after its performance, and he declared that
the passage would haunt him. With perfect good humour he assured me the
next morning, that he had greeted some early intruder with what he could
recollect of that passage. It is hoped I shall be pardoned when I confess that my
vanity was highly gratified at this declaration, but my *curiosity*, to know who the
unwelcome visitor was, predominated: his Lordship, however, anticipating my
desire on that subject, exclaimed "Come, Nathan, do not imagine that I have
been honored by an interview with Lady Endor, or with Samuel's vision – the
intruder that greeted me was no hobgoblin I assure you, it was only Douglas
Kinnaird."'

18 Cf. Shelley's 'Lines Written Among the Euganean Hills' (l.38): 'Bloodless
are these veins and chill.'

25–30   written parallel to the right margin on MS A
26   by] by [the] A
29   headless] [conquered] (headless –) A

Inscription: Seaham Feb. 1815 A

Cancelled fragment written on the verso from bottom to centre:

> [They that go down upon the Deep
> Behold the Almighty's wonders
> When oer the [deep] (deck) the surges sweep
> And Oceans echo thunders –] A

*Byron had made a start on Psalm 107:23–26 but abandoned that work having set down
this fragment. He then turned the leaf over and began 'Saul.' That poem extends on to
the verso, and Byron was forced to write the last six lines in the margin to avoid writing
over the cancelled fragment.*

---

30   Wright summarizes (M1832W, X, 87) James Kennedy's *Conversations on
Religion with Lord Byron* (1830, p. 154): "'Since we have spoken of witches," said
Lord Byron at Cephalonia, in 1823, "what think you of the witch of Endor? I
have always thought this the finest and most finished witch-scene that ever was
written or conceived; and you will be of my opinion, if you consider all the
circumstances and the actors in the case, together with the gravity, simplicity,
and dignity of the language. It beats all the ghost scenes I ever read."' (Byron
reverted to the subject in another conversation; Kennedy, pp. 233–4.)

Cf. Thomas Gray's 'The Descent of Odin' for another 'ghost scene'; Samuel's
prophecy is echoed in Gray's 'The Bard', where Edward I plays Saul.

TO BELSHAZZAR

1.

BELSHAZZAR! from the banquet turn,
    Nor in thy sensual fulness fall;
Behold! while yet before thee burn
    The graven words, the glowing wall.
Many a despot men miscall   5
    Crowned and anointed from on high;
But thou, the weakest, worst of all –
    Is it not written, thou must die?

2.

Go! dash the roses from thy brow –
    Gray hairs but poorly wreathe with them;   10

Text: M1831W; MSS: A, B

MS title: 'Belshazzar' &c – B̲. H.M. *A, cover*

ante 1   *1.* [[Where art thou my God?]]
    2. [*xxx*] *fr.*
    3. The [midnight revel loudly rings] [(wassail)] (red light glows – the wassail flows)
    4.   [Within] (Around) the royal hall
    5. And who on earth [dare] [(*xxx*)] (dare) mar the mirth
    6.   Of that high festival?
    7. [The prophet dares before thee glares] Belshazzar rise – nor dare despise
    8.   The writing on the wall!] *A, cancelled incomplete stanza*

ante 1   1.] [2] *A*

1   the banquet] th[y]e [midnight] [(revels)] (banquet) *A*
2   *a.* [A little shame is left thee still]
    b. A lord [as] high [as] thee may fall
    c. [A lord (more) high (than) thee may] fall
    d. [(Men pray & God *xxx* thy) fall]
    e. Nor [*xxx* dare to] (in thy sensual fullness) fall *A, the final version, 'e', written parallel with the right margin*
3   Behold!] [And read] (Behold –) *A*
4   *a.* The words of God [along the] (– the graven) wall – *A*
    b. The [words of God – the graven] (graven words – the glowing) wall *B*
5   despot] [*xxx* do] [(ruler)] (despot) *A*

Youth's garlands misbecome thee now,
　　More than thy very diadem,
Where thou hast tarnished every gem: –
　　Then throw the worthless bauble by,
Which, worn by thee, ev'n slaves contemn;　　15
　　And learn like better men to die!

6　Crowned] [Anointed of] *fr*. [A thing] [The] Crowned *A*
8　*a*. [Thy *xxx* slave would doom to die –]
　　b. [Behold it written] [(Hast thou forgotten)] (Is it not written) thou must
　　　die – ? *A*
ante 9　[Thy Vice might raise the avenging steel
　　　　Thy Meaness shields thee from the blow –
　　　　And they who loathe thee proudly feel] *A*, *cancelled lines*
9　Go! dash] [G] Go – [*xxx*] dash *A*
10　*a*. [Thy crown scarce misbecomes thee more]
　　b. Grey hairs [ignobly wreath] (but [mildly] (poorly) wreathe) with them *A*
12　*a*. [More than thy sullied] diadem
　　b. [(Scarce less than doth thy)] diadem
　　c. (More than thy very) diadem *A*

3.

Oh! early in the balance weighed,
　　And ever light of word and worth,
Whose soul expired ere youth decayed,
　　And left thee but a mass of earth.　　　　20
To see thee moves the scorner's mirth:
　　But tears in Hope's averted eye
Lament that ever thou hadst birth –
　　Unfit to govern, live, or die.

18　word and worth,] wor[t]d & worth – *A*
19　soul expired] [every] [Virtues lay] (Soul expired) *A*
21–4　written parallel with the right margin on MS A
22　in Hope's] in [baffled] Hope's *A*
23　ever] *A*, *B*; even *M1831W*
Inscription: Feb. 12. 1815 *A*
Note: ((Space for a line or two)) *B*, *written at the top by Byron*

VISION OF BELSHAZZAR

I.

THE King was on his throne,
    The Satraps thronged the hall;
A thousand bright lamps shone
    O'er that high festival.
A thousand cups of gold,   5
    In Judah deemed divine —
Jehovah's vessels hold
    The godless Heathen's wine!

Text: M1815; MSS: A

2 thronged] in A

5–8 *a.* A thousand cups [were shown]
        [Of gold along the board]
        [Which till then had held alone]
        [Salem's offering to the Lord]
    b. A thousand cups (of gold)
        (In Israel deemed divine –)
        (Jehovah's vessels hold)
        (The godless Heathen's wine!) A

2.

In that same hour and hall,
    The fingers of a hand   10
Came forth against the wall,
    And wrote as if on sand:
The fingers of a man; —
    A solitary hand
Along the letters ran,   15
    And traced them like a wand.

3.

The monarch saw, and shook,
    And bade no more rejoice;

---

1 The story of Belshazzar is given in Daniel 5.

All bloodless waxed his look,
  And tremulous his voice.   20
'Let the men of lore appear,
  The wisest of the earth,
And expound the words of fear,
  Which mar our royal mirth.'

21   lore] *Here and in line 30 Byron has traced over the 'r' in Lady Byron's 'lore'. He may have thought the printer likely to read her 'lore' as 'love'.*
24   mar our royal] mar[red a Sovereign's] (our royal) *A*

4.
Chaldea's seers are good,   25
  But here they have no skill;
And the unknown letters stood
  Untold and awful still.
And Babel's men of age
  Are wise and deep in lore;   30
But now they were not sage,
  They saw — but knew no more.

5.
A captive in the land,
  A stranger and a youth,
He heard the king's command,   35
  He saw that writing's truth.
The lamps around were bright,
  The prophecy in view;
He read it on that night, —
  The morrow proved it true.   40

16   E. H. Coleridge compares (M1900W, III, 397): 'To Belshazzar' and *Don Juan*, III:65:

These oriental writings on the wall,
  Quite common in those countries, are a kind
Of monitors adapted to recall,
  Like skulls at Memphian banquets, to the mind
The words which shook Belshazzar in his hall,
  And took his kingdom from him:

[Cf. also *Don Juan*, VIII:134:

'What Daniel read was short-hand of the Lord's. . . .']

33–6   A Stranger and a youth
         A [stripling] (Captive) in the land
         He [knew] (saw) that writing's truth
         He heard the King's command *A*
40   The] And the *A*

6.

    'Belshazzar's grave is made,
      His kingdom passed away,
    He in the balance weighed,
      Is light and worthless clay.
    The shroud, his robe of state,   45
      His canopy, the stone;
    The Mede is at his gate!
    The Persian on his throne!'

41   'Belshazzar's] '[Oh King thy] (Belshazzar's) *A*
42   His kingdom] '[Thy] (His) kingdom['s] *A*
43   He] '[Thou] (He) *A*
44   Is] '[Art] (Is) *A*
45   his] [thy] (his) *A*
46   His] '[Thy] (His) *A*
47   his] [thy] (his) *A*
48   his] [thy] (his) *A*

---

34 E. H. Coleridge writes (M1900W, III, 398): 'It was not in his youth, but in extreme old age, that Daniel interpreted the "writing on the wall".'

42–4 Cf. 'Ode to Napoleon Buonaparte', ll. 109–12:

    Weigh'd in the balance, hero dust
      Is vile as vulgar clay;
    Thy scales, Mortality! are just
      To all that pass away.

THE DESTRUCTION OF SEMNACHERIB

1.

THE Assyrian came down like the wolf on the fold,
And his cohorts were gleaming in purple and gold;
And the sheen of their spears was like stars on the sea,
When the blue wave rolls nightly on deep Galilee.

2.

Like the leaves of the forest when Summer is green,   5
That host with their banners at sunset were seen:
Like the leaves of the forest when Autumn hath blown,
That host on the morrow lay withered and strown.

Text: M1815; MSS: A, B

MS title: 'The Assyrian came down' – B – A, cover; The Rout of Semnacherib B

3   on] on A; [in] (on) B
4   wave rolls] wave[s] [heaves] (rolls) A
6   That . . . with] [Was t] (T)hat host [at] with A
7   Autumn] [?temp?] [(night winds)] (Autumn) A
8   on the morrow] [in] on the [morning] (morrow) A

3.

For the Angel of Death spread his wings on the blast,
And breathed in the face of the foe as he passed;   10
And the eyes of the sleepers waxed deadly and chill,
And their hearts but once heaved, and for ever grew still!

4.

And there lay the steed with his nostril all wide,
But through it there rolled not the breath of his pride:
And the foam of his gasping lay white on the turf,   15
And cold as the spray of the rock-beating surf.

1   The biblical account is given in II Kings 19 and Isaiah 37.

7   E. H. Coleridge compares (M1900W, III, 405) Michael Drayton's *The Barons'
Wars* (II: 57): 'As leaves in autumn, so the bodies fell.'

9 on] [in] on *B*

10 in] [on] in *A*

11   *a.* And their eye[lids grew heavy – their sentinels]

    b. And their eye(s of the sleepers [grew] waxed heavy & chill –) *A, Byron failed to change 'their' to 'the'*

    c. And the eyes of the sleepers waxed [heavy] (deadly) and chill – *B*

12 And ... but] And [that slumber] (their hearts but) *A*

    grew] grew *A*; [were] grew *B*

13 all] [so] (all) *A*

14 rolled] [rushed] (rolled) *A*

15 And the foam [on his [bit] bridle] (of his gasping) lay [cold] (white) on the turf *A*

16 And] [As] And *A*

    rock-beating] cliff-beating *A, B*

5.

And there lay the rider distorted and pale,
With the dew on his brow, and the rust on his mail;
And the tents were all silent, the banners alone,
The lances unlifted, the trumphet unblown.   20

6.

And the widows of Ashur are loud in their wail,
And the idols are broke in the temple of Baal;
And the might of the Gentile, unsmote by the sword,
Hath melted like snow in the glance of the Lord!

17 distorted and pale,] [distorted & pale] (distorted & pale) – *A*

18 With ... mail;] [And stiff as the ?sw?] *fr.* With the crow on his breast – and the rust on his mail – *A*; With the crow on his breast – and the rust on his mail – *B*

19 banners alone,] [banners] (banners alone –) *A*

20 The ... unblown.] [And the trumphet that morning was] *fr.*

    (The lances unlifted – the trumphet unblown.) *A*

    unlifted,] [up](un)lifted *B*

21   *a.* [And God hath prevailed – & his people] *fr.*

    b. And the widows of Babel [*xxx*] (are) loud in their wail *A*

    c. And the widows of [Babel] (Ashur) are loud in their wail *B*

22 And the] And [the] (the) *A*

23   *a.* [And the voices of [S] Israel [*xxx*] (are) joyous & high]

    b. And the might of the Gentile [is smote by the Lord] (unsmote by the sword) *A*

24 in] [to] (in) *A*

Inscription: Seaham. Feb. 19. 1815 *A*

24 '"Oh Jerusalem, Jerusalem!" the Huns are on the Po; but if once they pass it on their march to Naples, all Italy will rise behind them: the Dogs – the Wolves – may they perish like the Host of Sennacherib!' Byron to Murray, 7 September 1820, *L & J*, V, 72.

SONG OF SAUL
BEFORE HIS LAST BATTLE

I.

WARRIORS and Chiefs! should the shaft or the sword
Pierce me in leading the host of the Lord,
Heed not the corse, though a king's, in your path:
Bury your steel in the bosoms of Gath!

2.

Thou who art bearing my buckler and bow,　　　　　5
Should the soldiers of Saul look away from the foe,
Stretch me that moment in blood at thy feet!
Mine be the doom which they dared not to meet.

Text: M1815; MSS: A, B, C, D

MS title: Song of Saul. B. Seaham 1815 *A, cover*; Song of Saul before his last
Battle – *A, B, C, D*

3　corse, though a king's,] $\left\{ \begin{array}{l} \text{carcase that lies} \\ \text{corse – though a King's –} \end{array} \right\}$ *A*

　　[carcase that lies] (corse though a king's –) *B*; corse – though a King's – *C*
5　Thou] Thou! *A, B, C*; Thou[!] *D*

　　buckler and] $\left\{ \begin{array}{l} \text{shield \& my} \\ \text{buckler and} \end{array} \right\}$ *A*; [shield and my] (buckler and) *B*;

　　buckler and *C*
6　soldiers of Saul] ranks of your king *A*; [ranks of your king] (soldiers of Saul)
　　B; soldiers of Saul *C*

7　Nathan writes (N1829, p. 40): '"Nathan," returned his Lordship, "you seem
anxious to support the credit of a great man, but I must repeat, that Napoleon
would have ranked higher in future history, had he even like your venerable
ancestor Saul, on mount Gilboa, or like a second Cato, fallen on his sword, and
finished his mortal career at Waterloo."'
8　W. Morel, in 'Zu Byrons Hebrew Melodies' (*Anglia*, 1955, LXXIII, 215),
compares Lucan, *Pharsalia* (VII, 310–11):

> *fondientem viscera cernet*
> *me mea qui nondum victo respexerit hoste.*

(E. H. Coleridge finds parallels with Lucan in *Childe Harold* [II:86, III:51, and
IV:57].)

3.

Farewell to others, but never we part,
Heir to my royalty, son of my heart! 10
Bright is the diadem, boundless the sway,
Or kingly the death, which awaits us to-day!

10 Heir] *Heir *C*; *Jonathan *C, at the foot*

to my royalty,] $\left\{ \dfrac{\text{to my Royalty}}{\text{of my Monarchy}} \right\}$ *A*; to my Royalty *B*

Note: Turn over   *C, at the foot*;

Note. 1. Samuel – Chapter the last

['Then said Saul unto his armour bearer, Draw out thy sword and thrust me thorow therewith, lest the uncircumcised come and thrust me thorow and marke me: but his armour bearer would not, for he was sore afraid. Therefore Saul tooke a sword and fell upon it.']

'And when the battle went sore against Saul, the archers and bowmen hit him, and he was sore wounded of the archers. Then said Saul unto his armour bearer, Draw out thy sword and thrust me thorow therewith, lest the uncircumcised come and thrust me thorow and marke me: but his armour bearer would not, for he was sore afraid. Therefore Saul tooke a sword and fell upon it.'

Translation of the scriptures – Edition 1608 *C, verso.*

12 Nathan writes (N1829, pp. 42–3): 'The foregoing stanzas cannot be passed unnoticed, as they gave rise to a remark of his Lordship, which is worthy of record: it was in substance as follows: "That man is not to be utterly despised as a coward whom supernatural evils have worn down; nor is it difficult to account for the subsequent weakness of Saul, who was once gloriously surrounded by strength, power, and the approbation of his God, when we perceive that he had sunk from this, to a reliance on his own exertions even for safety. The confidences he possesses; the power he beholds, were all blighted ere he sunk to pusillanimity; in spite of which, I cannot but uphold him originally a brave and estimable man. That he cherished the man fated to destroy him, was more his misfortune than his fault."'

WHEN COLDNESS WRAPS THIS SUFFERING CLAY

I.

WHEN COLDNESS WRAPS THIS SUFFERING CLAY,
  Ah, whither strays the immortal mind?
It cannot die, it cannot stay,
  But leaves its darkened dust behind.
Then, unembodied, doth it trace   5
  By steps each planet's heavenly way?
Or fill at once the realms of space,
  A thing of eyes, that all survey?

Text: M1815; MSS: A, B

MS title: 'When Coldness wraps' &c. B *A, cover*

1 *a.* When [this corroding clay is gone]
   b. When ([c](C)oldness wraps this suffering [?dus?] (clay)) *A*
4 *a.* With that [it [dearly] (sadly)] leaves behind
   b. [With that (frail flesh it) leaves] behind
   c. (But leaves its darkened dust) behind *A*
6 *a.* [The stars in their] eternal way?
   b. (By steps [the stars') eternal] way?
   c. By steps (each planet's heavenly) way? *A*

2.

Eternal, boundless, undecayed,
  A thought unseen, but seeing all,   10

---

6 Edward Sarmiento, in 'A Parallel Between Lord Byron and Fray Luis De
León' (*RES*, 1953, IV, 267–73), compares 'El aire se serena', 'Cuando contemplo
el cielo', and the lines beginning '¿ Cuando será que pueda/Libre de esta prisión
volar al cielo'. He writes: 'Byron's two middle stanzas contain the corresponding
material to the serial consideration of the planets in Leon's various passages. . . .
Each of the three Spanish poems contains a strophe or strophes the content of
which may be, from a certain distance, compared with the fourth verse of
Byron's poem.' [No other evidence corroborates the thesis that Byron was
acquainted with León's works.]
9 Cf. 'Immortal – boundless – undecayed –/ Their souls the very soil pervade';
this couplet appears in the holograph of the *Siege of Corinth*, ff. 1. 417, but was
cancelled in the fair copy (*Poetry*, III, 466).

All, all in earth, or skies displayed,
　　Shall it survey, shall it recall:
Each fainter trace that memory holds
　　So darkly of departed years,
In one broad glance the soul beholds,　　　15
　　And all, that was, at once appears.

10　A thought] A [*xxx*] thought A

post 10　1. *a.* [Which heaven & earth can] *fr.*
　　　　　　b. [A conscious light that can pervade –]
　　　　　　c. [That] [Mingling with aught by Nature made]
　　　　2. [Heaven – earth and *xxx* & all –] A, *cancelled lines*
11　displayed] [surveyed] (displayed) A
12　*a.* [But subject to no future fall –]
　　　b. Shall it [foresee] (survey) – shall it recall – A
　　　recall:] A, B; recal *M1815, M1815W*
13　Each [that Memory] (fainter trace) [that] (that) Memory holds A
14　So darkly] [And] [Uncertain] (So [faintly] darkly) A
15　In] [In] (In) A
16　was, at] (was) [at] at A

3.

Before Creation peopled earth,
　　Its eye shall roll through chaos back;
And where the furthest heaven had birth,
　　The spirit trace its rising track.　　　20
And where the future mars or makes,
　　Its glance dilate o'er all to be,
While sun is quenched or system breaks,
　　Fixed in its own eternity.

17　peopled earth,] [gave the Sun] (peopled earth) A
18　[His] It's eye shall roll [unbounded] (through chaos) back – A
19　[Before] (And where) the furthest [stars] (heaven) had birth A
20　The [Soul shall] (Spirit) trace [their] (it's) rising track A
21　mars or makes,] [makes or mars] (mars or makes) A; mars or [*xxx*] makes B
22　*a.* [Shall follow [on its] (the) eternal path]
　　　b. It's glance dilate [over] (oer) all [that] (to) be A
23　While . . . quenched] Wh[ere earth – or – Sun –] (ile Sun is quenched –) A

19　Cf. 'The Prophecy of Dante', III:9: 'There where the farthest suns and stars
have birth.'
23　Cf. 'Darkness' (ll. 2–3):

　　　The bright sun was extinguished, and the stars
　　　Did wander darkling in the external space. . . .

4.

Above o'er Love, Hope, Hate, or Fear,   25
  It lives all passionless and pure:
An age shall fleet like earthly year;
  Its years as moments shall endure.
Away, away, without a wing,
  O'er all, through all, its thought shall fly;   30
A nameless and eternal thing,
  Forgetting what it was to die.

25 Above o'er] *A*; [Exempt from] ([Ab] Above oer) *A*; Above or *B, M1815,*
    M1815W
26 [All] (It lives all) passionless – [and] [unfettered (*xxx*)] and pure – *A*
27 *a.* [Earth's (Shall)] Ages [seem as] Earthly year
    b. [(It's) An) Age[s] (shall fleet like) Earthly year *A*
28 [Shall] [?m?] (It's) years [but] (as) moments shall endure *A*
29–32 written parallel with the right margin on MS A
29 without] [beyond] without *A*
Inscription: Seaham. Feb. 1815. *A*

26 Cf. *Heaven and Earth,* ll. 714–15: 'Seraphs! . . . Who are, or should be,
passionless and pure . . .'

'ALL IS VANITY, SAITH THE PREACHER'

1.

FAME, wisdom, love, and power were mine,
    And health and youth possessed me;
My goblets blushed from every vine,
    And lovely forms caressed me;
I sunned my heart in beauty's eyes,   5
    And felt my soul grow tender;
All earth can give, or mortal prize,
    Was mine of regal splendour.

Text: M1815; MSS: A, B; the formal arrangement of the stanzas follows MS A; in the copy-text each of the three stanzas is divided into two distinct quatrains but numbered as one stanza

MS title: 'Fame, Wisdom, Love' &c. Seaham 1815. *A, cover;* 'All is Vanity, saith the Preacher' – *B, below a heavily deleted title*

1 power] [health] [wealth] (power) *A*
2 And health] And [wealth] Health *A*
3 blushed] [teemed] [foamed] (blushed) *A*

---

1 'Went out – came home – this, that, and the other – and "all is vanity, saith the preacher," and so say I, as part of his congregation.' Journal, 7 December 1813, *L & J,* II, 370.

Cf. *Don Juan,* VII:6:

> Ecclesiastes said, that all is Vanity –
>   Most modern preachers say the same, or show it
> By their examples of true Christianity;
>   In short, all know, or very soon may know it;
> And in this scene of all-confessed inanity,
>   By saint, by sage, by preacher, and by poet,
> Must I restrain me, through the fear of strife,
> From holding up the Nothingness of life?

Cf. also *Don Juan,* I:15, and the Countess of Blessington's *Conversations of Byron,* p.146

3 Cf. *Childe Harold,* I:11: 'His goblets brimmed with every costly wine.'
5 Cf. Sir Walter Scott, *The Lady of the Lake* (1810), XXIV:18–19:

> No more at dawning morn I rise,
> And sun myself in Ellen's eyes.

6 And] [Until] (And) *A*
7 All ... give,] All [that] Earth (can) give[s] – *A*
   mortal] Mortals *A*; Mortal *B*
8 of regal] [of joy &] (regal) *A, Byron did not restore the cancelled 'of'*; of regal *B*

2.

I strive to number o'er what days
    Remembrance can discover,   10
Which all that life or earth displays
    Would lure me to live over.
There rose no day, there rolled no hour
    Of pleasure unembittered;
And not a trapping decked my power   15
    That galled not while it glittered.

ante 9 [I try to number oer the days
      Which [were my [spring] (*xxx*) beginning] (cured *xxx*)
      xxx Spring of Life had [such] so bright a past] *A, cancelled incomplete lines*

9   what] [the] (what) *A*
10 [So dear to Memory's bosom] (Remembrance can discover) *A*
11 life ... displays] [Heaven & Earth] [(Life's last ray)] [(Love)] (Life on earth)
    display(s) *A*; Life or Earth displays *B*
12 lure] [bribe] (lure) *A*
13 *a.* There[s not a] day – theres [not an] hour
    b. There (rose no) day – theres ([passed] rolled no) hour *A, Byron did not*
    change 'theres' to 'there'
    c. There rose no day – there rolled no hour *B*
14 Of ... unembittered;] [That Sun or Moon] [Without *xxx*] [Nor moment]
    (Of pleasure) [*xxx*] unembittered *A*
15 And ... power] [Theres] (And) not a trapping [flung] (decked) my Power –*A*

3.

The serpent of the field, by art
    And spells, is won from harming;

---

14 E. H. Coleridge compares (M1900W, III, 395) *Childe Harold*, I:82:

      Full from the fount of Joy's delicious springs
      Some bitter o'er the flowers its bubbling venom flings.

(In a note to those lines [M1900W, II, 93], Byron compares Lucan's

        Medio de fonte leporum
        Surgit amari aliquid quod in ipsis floribus angat.)

But that which coils around the heart,
Oh! who hath power of charming?　　　　　20
It will not list to wisdom's lore,
Nor music's voice can lure it;
But there it stings for evermore
The soul that must endure it.

post 16 [And what hath been? – but what shall be –
The same dull scene renewing –
And all are our father's [are] (were) are we
In erring & undoing –
The Growth of wisdom *xxx* woe] *A, cancelled incomplete stanza*

ante 17 [My father was the Shepherds son –
Ah were my lot as lowly –
My earthly course had [slo] softly run] *A, cancelled lines*

17　The . . . art] [There is no magic] The serpent [of the field] (of the field)
[spells] (art) *A*
18　And . . . harming;] [Is charmed from *xxx*] [(And charms] And spells) is
[lured] (won) from harming *A*
21　It . . . list] [Nor] (It) will not [bend] (list) *A*

Written crosswise beneath the third stanza:

　　　　　　　1234567890
　　　[Could
　　　　　The *xxx* in the *xxx*
　　　In youth
　　　Amidst the] *A*

---

19 In her *Conversations of Lord Byron* (pp. 178–9), the Countess of Blessington
records Byron's remarks on memory: 'I have often . . . wished for insanity –
anything – to quell memory, the never-dying worm that feeds on the heart,
and only calls up the *past* to make the *present* more insupportable'.

BRIGHT BE THE PLACE OF THY SOUL

I.

BRIGHT be the place of thy soul!
　No lovelier spirit than thine
E'er burst from its mortal control,
　In the orbs of the blessed to shine.
On earth thou wert all but divine,　　　　　　　　　5
　As thy soul shall immortally be;
And our sorrow may cease to repine,
　When we know that thy God is with thee.

2.

Light be the turf of thy tomb!
　May its verdure like emeralds be:　　　　　　　　10
There should not be shadow of gloom,
　In aught that reminds us of thee.

Text: M1816; first pub. Examiner, 11 June 1815; MSS: A (1–8), B (9–16), C (9–16), D

MS title: 'Bright be the place of thy Soul' First & Second Copies Ld. B. D, *verso*

3　E'er] Ere *D, Ex1815*
　　control] controul *A, D, Ex1815, SS1815*
6　immortally] [eternally] immortally *A*; immortal[it](l)y *PS*
7　sorrow] sorrows *SS1815*
post 8　Inscription: June 9, 1815 *A*
9　*a.* [[Bright] (Soft) be thy pillows of [rest] (sleep)]
　　b. (Green be the turf of thy tomb) *B*
　　c. Green be the turf of thy tomb! *C*
　　d. [Green] (Light) be the turf of thy tomb! *D*
　　　tomb!] tomb *B*; tomb! *C, D*; tomb[;](!) *PS*
　　　of thy] on thy *SS1815*

9　E. H. Coleridge compares (M1900W, III, 426): '"O lay me, ye that see the light, near some rock of my hills: let the thick hazels be around, let the rustling oaks be near. Green be the place of my rest." ("The War of Inis-Thona," *Works of Ossian*, 1765, I, 156).' [Cf. also the commonplace Latin expression, *sit tibi terra levis* (light lie the earth upon thee), and 'Light be the earth on Billy's breast,/And green the sod that wraps his grave' (Henry Mackenzie, *The Man of Feeling* [1771], p. 22).]
10　Cf. 'Oh! Breathe Not His Name', *Irish Melodies*, [1808], I, 16:

Young flowers and an evergreen tree
May spring from the spot of thy rest;
But nor cypress nor yew let us see;   15
For why should we mourn for the blest?

10   *a.* Though its verdure [is nothing to thee]
     b. [Though its verdure ([the] is nothing to thee)]
     c. [(Though its verdure)] *fr.*
     d. (May its verdure be [b] sweetest to see) *B*
     e. May its verdure be sweetest to see *C*
     f. May its verdure be [sweetest] (freshest) to see *D*
     g. May its verdure [be (freshest) to see] (like emeralds be) *D*
11   not . . . shadow] *B, C, D, Ex1815, PS*; (not) be shadow *B*; not be the shadow
     M1816, SS1815
13   Young . . . tree] Fresh flowers and a far spreading tree *B, C*; [Fresh] (Young)
     flowers – and [a far spreading] (an evergreen) tree *D*
14   May . . . from] May wave oer *B, C*; May [wave] (grow) o'er *D*; May grow
     o'er *Ex1815, SS1815*; May [grow [on] (oer)] (spring from) *PS*
15   But nor] *B, C, D, PS, Ex1815, SS1815*; But not *M1816*
     let us see;] let [them] it be – *B*; let it be *C*; let [it be] (us see) *D*
16   mourn] grieve *B*; mourn *C*

But the night-dew that falls, tho' in silence it weeps,
Shall brighten with verdure the grave where he sleeps;
And the tear that we shed, tho' in secret it rolls,
Shall long keep his memory green in our souls.

APPENDICES

SIGLA

Employed in the Historical Collations

E	Engraved Text.
P	Letterpress Text.
W	Works.
+	Agreement of the specified edition with all subsequent editions collated containing this poem.
Ph1815	*Hebrew Melodies*, Philadelphia: Parke, 1815.
B1815	*Hebrew Melodies*, Boston: Eliot, 1815.
N–Y1815	*Hebrew Melodies*, New York: Swords, 1815.
2N–Y1815	*Hebrew Melodies*, New York: Longworth, 1815.
N1816	*A Selection of Hebrew Melodies*, Nos I–II, London: Nathan, 1816.
M1819W	*The Works of Lord Byron*, 3 vols, London: Murray, 1819.
M1821W	*The Works of Lord Byron*, 5 vols, London: Murray, 1821.
D1823	*Hebrew Melodies*, London: Dugdale, 1823.
M1823W	*The Works of Lord Byron*, 4 vols, London: Murray, 1823.
N1824	*A Selection of Hebrew Melodies*, Revised Edition, Nos I–II, London, 1824.
D1825	*Hebrew Melodies*, London: Dugdale, 1825.
N1827–29	*A Selection of Hebrew Melodies*, Revised Edition, Nos I–IV, London, 1827–29.
N1829	*Fugitive Pieces and Reminiscences of Lord Byron*, London: Whittaker, Treacher & Co., 1829.
M1830	*Letters and Journals of Lord Byron*, London: Murray, 1830.
M1831W	*The Works of Lord Byron*, 6 vols, London: Murray, 1831.
M1832W	*The Works of Lord Byron*, 17 vols, London: Murray, 1832–33 (vol. X pub. 1832).
Sh1835	*Poetical Remains of the Late Henry Savile Shepherd*, Devonport, 1835.
M1900W	*The Works of Lord Byron*, Poetry, 7 vols, London: Murray, 1898–1904 (vol. III pub. 1900).
M1904W	*The Works of Lord Byron*, Poetry, 7 vols, London: Murray, 1898–1904, reprinted April, 1904.

H1905W *The Complete Poetical Works of Lord Byron*, Boston: Houghton Mifflin Co., 1905.

M1922W *The Works of Lord Byron, Poetry*, 7 vols, London: Murray, 1898–1904, reprinted September, 1922.

APPENDIX I

HISTORICAL COLLATIONS

[AUTHOR'S NOTE]
   1 of my] of the author's *Ph1815, B1815, N–Y1815, 2N–Y1815*
   post 3 January, 1815 *M1832W*

It is the Hour
   8 sky] skies *N1824E, N1827–29E*
  13 That follows] Which follows *N1824*

I Speak Not – I Trace Not – I Breathe Not
   2 were] is *M1830+*
   4 thought . . . dwells] thoughts that dwell *M1830+*
   8 We . . . fly] We will part, – we will fly *M1830+*
  11 I bear] is thine *M1830+*
  14 My] This *M1830+*
  16 the world] with worlds *M1830+*
  19 we] I *M1830+*

I Saw Thee Weep
   8 that] each *N1816E, N1824E, N1827–29*
  10 dye] die *M1819W, M1821W, D1823, M1823W, D1825*

Sun of the Sleepless!
   6 its powerless] his powerless *N1829*

Oh! Weep for Those
   6 when] where *N1816E, N1824E, N1827–29E*
  10 rest?] rest! *Ph1815, B1815, N–Y1815, 2N–Y1815, M1819W, M1821W, D1823, M1823W, D1825, M1831W+*

Thy Days are Done
   5 he won] the won *D1823*
   9 flowed from] flowed for *2N–Y1815*
  13 hosts] host *N1824, N1827–29E in the harmony only*

On Jordan's Banks
   1 Arabs'] Arab's *N1816E, D1825, M1832W, H1905W*; Arabs *N1824E, N1827–29E*

From Job
   4 but] yet *Sh1835*
   7 Is man more pure] more pure *Sh1835*
  11 You wither ere the night] ye wither ere 'tis night *Sh1835*
  12 Heedless . . . light!] Impure, unwise, and helpless in his sight! *Sh1835*

If that High World

   1 IF THAT HIGH WORLD,] IF THAT WORLD *B1815*
   3 be fond] be found *N1824E, N1827–29E given correctly in the harmony*
 10 brink;] brink; *M1900W*; brink;[i] *M1904W, M1922W*
 12 severing] breaking *N1816, N1824, N1827–29, N1829*
 12 link.] link.[i] *M1900W*; link. *M1904W, M1922W*

Oh! snatched away in beauty's bloom

 12 That . . . heeds] That death nor heeds nor hears *Ph1815+*

Jephtha's Daughter

   4 for] to *N1816E, N1824E, N1827–29, N1829*
 14 judge and] Jude and *N1824E, N1827–29E*; judge of *N1827–29P*

They say that Hope is happiness

Epigraph *rerum*] *ferum N1829*

Herod's Lament for Mariamne

 12 smote her 's] smote her's *Ph1815, B1815, 2N–Y1815, N1816, D1825, N1827–29P, N1829, M1832W, H1905W*; smote her is *N1827–29E*
 15 For her] For he *M1900W, M1904W, M1922W*
 18 She sunk] She's sunk *N1827–29E*
 21 mine] mines *N1816E*
Inscription Jan. 13. 1815] *Jan.* 15. 1815 *M1900W+*

By the Rivers of Babylon We Sat Down and Wept

   3 in the hue] from the hue *N1816E*
 18 With the voice] by the voice *N1816 some lines in the recitative*
Inscription Jan. 15. 1815] *Jan.* 15, 1813 *M1900W+*

In the Valley of Waters

title In the Valley of Waters] 'By the Waters of Babylon' *M1900W, M1904W, M1922W*
   1 wept o'er] wept on *M1900W, M1904W, M1922W*
   8 hands . . . skill] hand shall teach them one tone of their skill *N1829*, hands shall teach them one tone of our skill *H1905W*
   9 hung on] hung in *M1900W, M1904W, M1922W*

On the Day of the Destruction of Jerusalem by Titus

   5 thy temple] my temple *N1816E, N1827–29E*
 16 the thunderbolt] her thunderbolt *D1823, D1825*

Were my bosom as false as thou deem'st it to be

   8 mine I will] mine will I *B1815*
 12 resign] design *D1825*

Saul

   7 his fixed] the fixed *N1816P corrected by an erratum, N1827–29P, N1829*
   9 glittered] glissend *N1827–29E*
 14 the thunder-stroke] a thunder-stroke *N1816E, N1827–29E*

To Belshazzar

23 ever] even *M1832W+*

Vision of Belshazzar

1   his throne] the throne *N1816E, N1827–29E*
19 look] looks *N1816E*
40 The morrow] Tomorrow *N1816E*

The Destruction of Semnacherib

4   wave rolls] waves roll *N1816P, N1827–29P, N1829*
6   with their banners at sunset] at sunset with their banners *2N–Y1815*
13 nostril] nostrill *N1816E*; nostrils *D1825*
16 spray of] spray on *D1823, D1825*
21 widows] windows *N1816P corrected by hand in some copies*
Inscription <u>Feb. 19. 1815</u>] *Feb. 17. 1815 M1900W+*

Song of Saul Before His Last Battle

1   Chiefs] chief *2N–Y1815*
4   steel] steels *2N–Y1815*
11 Bright is] Bright as *N1816E, N1827–29E*

When coldness wraps this suffering clay

1   WRAPS THIS] WRAPS THE *2N–Y1815*
4   its] it *D1823*
11 in earth] on earth *N1827–29E*
18 eye] eyes *D1825, N1827–29P, N1829, no E text*
19 furthest] farthest *M1900W, M1904W, M1922W*
25 Above o'er] Above or *Ph1815+*
28 years] year *D1825*
30 thought] thoughts *N1816P, N1827–29P, N1829, no E text*

'All is Vanity, Saith the Preacher'

5   in beauty's] from beauty's *N1827–29E given correctly in the recitative*

Bright be the place of thy soul

3   control] controul *N1829*
9   of thy] on thy *N1829*
11 not be shadow] not be the shadow *M1819W+*
12 aught] ought *SS1815, N1829*
14 May . . . from] May grow o'er *N1829*

APPENDIX II

CONTENTS OF EDITIONS COLLATED

N1815   twelve Hebrew Melodies: 'She Walks in Beauty', 'The harp the monarch minstrel swept', 'If that High World', 'The Wild Gazelle', 'Oh! Weep for Those', 'On Jordan's Banks', 'Jephtha's Daughter', 'Oh! snatched away in beauty's bloom', 'My Soul is Dark', 'I Saw Thee Weep', 'Thy Days are Done', 'It is the Hour'.

M1815   twenty-four Hebrew Melodies: the contents of N1815, and 'Song of Saul Before His Last Battle', 'Saul', '"All is Vanity, Saith the Preacher"', 'When coldness wraps this suffering clay', 'Vision of Belshazzar', 'Sun of the Sleepless!', 'Were my bosom as false as thou deem'st it to be', 'Herod's Lament for Mariamne', 'On the Day of the Destruction of Jerusalem by Titus', 'By the Rivers of Babylon We Sat Down and Wept', 'The Destruction of Semnacherib', 'From Job'.

M1815W   twenty-four Hebrew Melodies: the contents of M1815.

Ex1815   two Hebrew Melodies: 'Oh! snatched away in beauty's bloom', and 'Bright be the place of thy soul'.

SS1815   one Hebrew Melody: 'Bright be the place of thy soul'.

M1816   one Hebrew Melody: 'Bright be the place of thy soul'.

Ph1815   twenty-four Hebrew Melodies: the contents of M1815.

B1815   twenty-four Hebrew Melodies: the contents of M1815.

N–Y1815   twenty-four Hebrew Melodies: the contents of M1815.

2N–Y1815   twenty-four Hebrew Melodies: the contents of M1815.

N1816   twenty-four Hebrew Melodies: 'Francisca', and the contents of M1815 excluding 'From Job'.

M1819W   twenty-four Hebrew Melodies: 'Bright be the place of thy soul', and the contents of M1815 excluding 'It is the Hour'.

M1821W   twenty-four Hebrew Melodies: the contents of M1819W.

D1823   twenty-three Hebrew Melodies: the contents of M1815 excluding 'It is the Hour'.

M1823W	twenty-four Hebrew Melodies: the contents of M1819W.
N1824	twelve Hebrew Melodies: the contents of N1815.
D1825	twenty-three Hebrew Melodies: the contents of D1823.
N1827–29	twenty-eight Hebrew Melodies: 'I Speak Not – I Trace Not – I Breathe Not', 'In the Valley of Waters', 'They say that Hope is happiness', 'From Job', and the contents of N1816.
N1829	twenty-nine Hebrew Melodies: the contents of N1827–29 and 'Bright be the place of thy soul'.
M1830	one Hebrew Melody: 'I Speak Not – I Trace Not – I Breathe Not'.
M1831W	twenty-six Hebrew Melodies: 'To Belshazzar', 'I Speak Not – I Trace Not – I Breathe Not', and the contents of M1819W.
M1832W	twenty-seven Hebrew Melodies: 'They say that Hope is happiness', and the contents of M1831W.
Sh1835	one Hebrew Melody: 'From Job'.
M1900W	twenty-eight Hebrew Melodies: 'In the Valley of Waters', and the contents of M1832W.
M1904W	twenty-eight Hebrew Melodies: the contents of M1900W.
H1905W	twenty-eight Hebrew Melodies: the contents of M1900W.
M1922W	twenty-eight Hebrew Melodies: the contents of M1900W.

APPENDIX III

CALENDAR OF MANUSCRIPTS

In the preparation of the Calendar the following conventions have been adhered to. Extant manuscripts have been grouped under the titles of the respective poems. (Thus no title is listed when no manuscript is extant.) The order of the titles is alphabetical. Under each title individual drafts have been listed in the order of their composition; the earliest draft extant is always listed as MS. A. Each entry is organized as follows:

Title

MS. A. Author or scribe; no. of leaves; size; paper; watermark; housing; location; reference; additional particulars.

MS. B. . . . .

Standard terminology has been employed in the descriptions. An unfolded sheet makes two pages of manuscript; a folded sheet makes two leaves or four pages. Blank pages and pages containing non-pertinent matter are counted and noted. Measurements are of leaves and have been given in centimetres. Measurements are sometimes approximate, owing to uneven edges on a given leaf.

'All is Vanity, Saith the Preacher'

MS. A. Byron's holograph; cover: 1 lf., blank verso; 18·9 × 10·8 cm.; laid stock; no watermark; text: 1 lf.; 22·1 × 18·1 cm.; wove stock; no watermark; London; Lovelace Papers.

MS. B. Lady Byron's fair copy; 2 lvs., f. 2 blank; 22·8 × 18·6 cm.; wove stock; watermark: GATER 1811; London; Murray Archives.

Bright be the place of thy soul

MS. A. Byron's fair copy, lines 1–8; 2 pp.; 9·2 × 6·1 cm.; pasteboard; no watermark; printed [gothic type] visiting card of 'Lady Louisa Katherine Forester';[1] London; Lovelace Papers.

---

[1] Lady Louisa Katherine Barbara Vane (d. 1821), daughter of William Henry Vane, 3rd Earl of Cleveland and Earl of Darlington, and Lady Katherine Powlett. The Milbankes were long acquainted with Darlington and his family. (Augusta Leigh's husband was a horse-racing associate of the Earl's.) Lady Louisa Katherine

MS. B.   Byron's holograph, lines 9–16; 1 lf., blank verso;
18 × 11 cm.; wove stock; no watermark; London;
Lovelace Papers; in pencil.

MS. C.   Byron's fair copy, lines 9–16; 1 lf., blank verso; 18 ×
11 cm.; wove stock; no watermark; London; Lovelace
Papers; in pencil.

MS. D.   Lady Byron's copy with Byron's holograph revision;
1 lf.; 22·7 × 18·2 cm.; wove stock; no watermark;
Austin; Miriam Lutcher Stark Library, University of
Texas; St. 6533.

Proof.   Proof with Byron's holograph revision; 2 sheets folded
in eights but printed on one side only; 17 × 10·3 cm.;
wove stock; watermark: FELLOWS 1812; London;
Murray Archives; one stanza printed on one page of each
sheet ('When we two parted' completes the first sheet,
'Must thou go, my glorious Chief' the second).

By the Rivers of Babylon We Sat Down and Wept

MS. A.   Byron's holograph; 1 lf.; 22·2 × 18·4 cm.; wove stock;
watermark: WARD & MIDDLETON 1812; London;
Lovelace Papers.

MS. B.   Byron's fair copy; 1 lf.; 22·2 × 18·5 cm.; wove stock;
no watermark; London; Lovelace Papers.

MS. C.   Lady Byron's fair copy; 1 lf.; 22·6 × 18·6 cm.; wove
stock; no watermark; London; Murray Archives; Byron
has pencilled a note to Douglas Kinnaird on f. 1^r.

From Job

MS. A.   Byron's holograph; 1 lf., the recto is 'On Jordan's Banks'
MS. A; 23 × 18·5 cm.; wove stock; watermark: T
STAINS 1803; bound in a volume, brown cloth binding,
spine title: 'Poems by Lord Byron, Lady Byron, Mrs.
Leigh, and Others'; London; British Museum; Add. MS.
31, 038, f. 1.

MS. B.   Lady Byron's fair copy; 1 lf., blank verso; 22·5 × 18·3
cm.; wove stock; no watermark; London; Murray
Archives.

married Major Francis Forester, of the old Shropshire family, in 1813. See
Thomas L. Ashton, 'Naming Byron's Aurora Raby', *English Language Notes*,
1969, VII, 114–20.

Herod's Lament for Mariamne

MS. A. Byron's holograph; cover: 1 lf., blank verso; 19 ×
11·4 cm.; laid stock; no watermark; text: 1 lf.; 22·5 ×
18·2 cm.; wove stock; no watermark; London;
Lovelace Papers.

MS. B. Byron's fair copy; 1 lf.; 22·5 × 18·2 cm.; wove stock;
no watermark; London; Lovelace Papers.

MS. C. Lady Byron's fair copy; 2 lvs., f. 2 blank; 22·6 × 18·3
cm.; wove stock; watermark: WARD & MIDDLETON
1812; London; Murray Archives.

In the Valley of Waters

MS. A. Byron's holograph; 1 lf., title only on recto; 22·7 ×
18·8 cm.; wove stock; watermark: Prince of Wales'
feathers [above] M & J 1813; London; Lovelace Papers.

MS. B. Lady Byron's fair copy; 1 lf., blank verso; 17·6 ×
21·7 cm.; wove stock; no watermark; pasted on brown
paper backing; Cambridge, Mass.; Houghton Library,
Harvard University; bMS Am 1631 (52); Byron has
written a note to Kinnaird at the top of the MS.

I Saw Thee Weep

MS. A. Byron's holograph; 1 lf.; 22·2 × 17 cm.; wove stock;
watermark: J GREEN 1814; preserved in a sunk mount
bound in blue calf; Austin; Miriam Lutcher Stark
Library, University of Texas; St. 6543.

I Speak Not — I Trace Not — I Breathe Not

MS. A. Byron's holograph; 2 lvs., disjunct, f. 2ᵛ blank; 22·8 ×
19 cm. and 6·8 × 19 cm.; wove stock; no watermark;
London; Lovelace Papers; the MS. is reproduced in
Astarte (1905).

Oh! snatched away in beauty's bloom

MS. A. Byron's holograph; 1 lf.; 22·7 × 18·5 cm.; wove stock;
no watermark; London; Murray Archives.

MS. B. Charles Hanson's transcript of MS. A; 1 lf., verso blank
except for initials in the lower right corner: E[rnest]
H[artley] C[oleridge]; 22·8 × 19 cm.; laid stock;
watermark: 1811; London; Murray Archives; inscribed:
'copied from Manuscripts 8 Feb. 1815 Ch. H.'

MS. C. Byron's fair copy; cover: 1 lf., recto inscribed by Lady
Byron, blank verso; 18·5 × 11·5 cm.; laid stock;
watermark: fragment of Prince of Wales' feathers [above]
& JOHNSTON; text: 1 lf.; 23·3 × 18·2 cm.; wove stock;
no watermark; London; Lovelace Papers.

On Jordan's Banks

MS. A. Byron's holograph; 1 lf., the verso is 'From Job' MS. A;
23 × 18·5 cm.; wove stock; watermark: T. STAINS
1803; bound in a volume, brown cloth binding, spine
title: 'Poems by Lord Byron, Lady Byron, Mrs. Leigh,
and Others'; London; British Museum; Add. MS. 31,
038, f. 1.

On the Day of the Destruction of Jerusalem by Titus

MS. A. Byron's holograph; cover: 1 lf., verso inscribed (upside
down) in another hand 'MS. Compositions of Lord B's
1815'; 16·5 × 11·2 cm.; laid stock; watermark: [M &]
J [18]13; text: 1 lf.; 22·4 × 18·7 cm.; wove stock; no
watermark; London; Lovelace Papers.

MS. B. Byron's copy; cover: 1 lf., blank verso; 18·1 × 11·1
cm.; wove stock; no watermark; text: 1 lf.; 22·2 ×
18·4 cm.; wove stock; watermark: WARD & MIDDLETON
1812; London; Lovelace Papers.

MS. C. Lady Byron's copy with Byron's holograph revision;
1 lf.; 22·6 × 18·5 cm.; wove stock; no watermark;
London; Murray Archives.

Saul

MS. A. Byron's holograph; 1 lf.; 22·1 × 18·2 cm.; wove stock;
watermark: WARD & MIDDLETON 1812; London;
Lovelace Papers.

MS. B. Lady Byron's fair copy; 2 lvs., f. 2 blank; 22·7 × 18·6
cm.; wove stock; no watermark; London; Murray
Archives.

MS. C. Clerk's copy; 1 lf.; 22·8 × 19 cm.; laid stock;
watermark: TJ; London; Murray Archives; the handwriting is that of 'Song of Saul Before His Last Battle'
MS. D.

Song of Saul Before His Last Battle

MS. A. Byron's holograph; 1 lf., title only on recto; 23 × 18·9

MS. B.   cm.; laid stock; watermark: lower half of escutcheon and slung horn [above] E; London; Lovelace Papers.

MS. B.   Lady Byron's copy with Byron's holograph revision; 1 lf., blank verso; 22·6 × 18·9 cm.; wove stock; watermark: E & S 1810; London; Murray Archives.

MS. C.   Lady Byron's fair copy; 1 lf.; 22·6 × 18·9 cm.; wove stock; watermark: E & S 1810; London; Murray Archives.

MS. D.   Clerk's copy; 1 lf., blank verso; 22·8 × 19 cm.; laid stock; watermark: a crown device; London; Murray Archives; the handwriting is that of 'Saul' MS. C.

Sun of the Sleepless

MS. A.   Byron's holograph; cover: 1 lf., blank verso; 18 × 11 cm.; wove stock; no watermark; text: 2 lvs., f. 2ᵛ blank; 22·7 × 18·5 cm.; wove stock; no watermark; London; Lovelace Papers; cover inscribed 'Harmodia – a Fragment'; lines 11–16 (f. 1ᵛ) cancelled and rewritten are 'Sun of the Sleepless'; the MS. is reproduced in *Astarte* (1905).

MS. B.   Byron's fair copy; 1 lf., blank verso; 23·3 × 18·3 cm.; wove stock; no watermark; London; Lovelace Papers.

MS. C.   Byron's fair copy; 2 lvs., f. 1 and f. 2ʳ are 'Vision of Belshazzar' MS. A; 22·3 × 18·6 cm.; wove stock; watermark: J Budgen 1814; London; Murray Archives.

The Destruction of Semnacherib

MS. A.   Byron's holograph; cover: 1 lf., blank verso; 19 × 11·4 cm.; laid stock; watermark: part of coronet, escutcheon, and horn; text: 1 lf.; 22·6 × 19 cm.; wove stock; watermark: Prince of Wales' feathers [above] M & J 1813; London; Lovelace Papers.

MS. B.   Lady Byron's copy with Byron's holograph revision; 2 lvs., f. 1ʳ, f. 2ᵛ blank; 20·3 × 14·5 cm.; wove stock; watermark: 1810; London; Murray Archives.

The harp the monarch minstrel swept

MS. A.   Byron's holograph; 2 lvs., f. 2ᵛ blank; 22·9 × 18·3 cm.; wove stock; watermark: J Green 1814; preserved in a sunk mount bound in a copy of *Hebrew Melodies*, Ashley blue calf binding, T. J. Wise bookplate; London;

British Museum; Ashley 4728; f. 1 was reproduced by Wise in *A Byron Library* (1928).[2]

MS. B.   Charles Hanson's transcript of MS. A; 1 lf.; 22·8 × 19 cm.; laid stock; watermark: a crown device; London; Murray Archives; inscribed (f. 1ᵛ): 'copied from Manuscript Ch. H. 8 Feb 1815. . . .'; initialled in the lower right corner (f. 1ᵛ): 'E[rnest] H[artley] C[oleridge].'

The Wild Gazelle

MS. A.   Byron's holograph; 1 lf.; 22·8 × 18·5 cm.; wove stock; no watermark; London; Murray Archives; inscribed in pencil by Eliz. Wesley Dennis at the foot (f. 1ᵛ): 'Lord Byron's manuscript poem given by [the] Hon. Mrs. Leigh (Byron's sister) to Grandfather Wesley (Sebastian Wesley).'[3]

To Belshazzar

MS. A.   Byron's holograph; cover: 1 lf., blank verso; 19 × 11·7 cm.; laid stock; watermark: part of coronet and escutcheon; text: 1 lf.; 23 × 18·7 cm.; laid stock; watermark: top of escutcheon and coronet; London; Lovelace Papers.

MS. B.   Lady Byron's copy with Byron's holograph revision; 1 lf.; 22·7 × 18·8 cm.; wove stock; watermark: E & S 1810; London; Murray Archives.

Vision of Belshazzar

MS. A.   Lady Byron's copy with Byron's holograph revision; 2 lvs., f. 2ᵛ is 'Sun of the Sleepless' MS. C; 22·3 × 18·6 cm.; wove stock; watermark: J BUDGEN 1814; the worn impression of a seal not Byron's is found in the upper left corner of f. 1ʳ; London; Murray Archives.

[2] Preserved with the MS. is a letter from John Murray to Canon Shorter dated 23 December 1920:

I do not know whether you have seen any specimen of Byron's handwriting. If not I think you ought to do so, as you have been a consistent good friend of his literary reputation. I would therefore ask your acceptance of the enclosed in lieu of a Xmas card. With all good wishes. . . . Encl: The harp the Monarch Minstrel Swept.

[3] The composer, Samuel Sebastian Wesley, set 'When we two parted' and 'By the Rivers of Babylon We Sat Down and Wept' to music. Murray acquired the MS. in 1952.

Were my bosom as false as thou deem'st it to be

MS. A. Byron's fair copy; 1 lf., title (upside down) only on recto; 32·5 × 20·1 cm.; laid stock; watermark: ALLEE 1813; London; Lovelace Papers.

MS. B. Lady Byron's fair copy; 1 lf., blank verso; 22·7 × 18·6 cm.; wove stock; watermark: E & S 1810; London; Murray Archives.

When coldness wraps this suffering clay

MS. A. Byron's holograph; cover: 1 lf., blank verso; 10·6 × 7·3 cm.; laid stock; watermark: part of escutcheon and slung horn; spot of black shellac on verso; text: 1 lf.; 22·1 × 18 cm.; wove stock; no watermark; London; Lovelace Papers.

MS. B. Lady Byron's fair copy; 2 lvs., f. 2 blank; 22·8 × 18·4 cm.; wove stock; watermark: IPING 1813; London; Murray Archives.

APPENDIX IV

CALENDAR OF EDITIONS

The Calendar is a chronological listing with bibliographical descriptions of editions of the Hebrew Melodies published before 1830 exclusive of those editions published after 1815 as part of editions of Byron's *Collected Works*. A bibliographical description of R. Harding Evans' *Essay on the Music of the Hebrews* is also included. In each case a representative copy is described. When no copies are truly representative, details from copies other than that described are included as indicated. The census is intended to serve as a guide to the location of existing copies. Editions bound into other works are counted (but no mention of their being so bound is made); when two editions have been bound in one volume they are counted as two volumes. Abbreviations employed in the census are those of the *Union List of Serials* and the *British Union Catalogue of Periodicals*; a table identifying the abbreviations is given immediately before the Calendar.

Summary of the Calendar

I.	*A Selection of Hebrew Melodies*, No. I, 1815.
II.	*Hebrew Melodies*, 1815.
IIA.	*The Works of the Right Hon. Lord Byron*, 2 vols, 1815.
III.	*The Works of the Right Hon. Lord Byron*, 4 vols, 1815.
IV.	*Hebrew Melodies*, Philadelphia, 1815.
V.	*Hebrew Melodies*, Boston, 1815.
VI.	*Hebrew Melodies*, New York: Swords, 1815.
VII.	*Hebrew Melodies*, New York: Longworth, 1815.
VIII.	*A Selection of Hebrew Melodies*, No. I, No. II, 1816.
IX.	*Hebrew Melodies*, London: Dugdale, 1823.
IXA.	*Hebrew Melodies*, London: Dugdale, 1825.
X.	*A Selection of Hebrew Melodies*, No. I, No. II, 1824.
XI.	*A Selection of Hebrew Melodies*, Nos I–IV, 1827–9.
XII.	*Fugitive Pieces and Reminiscences of Lord Byron*, 1829.
XIII.	*An Essay on the Music of the Hebrews*, London, 1816.

ABBREVIATIONS EMPLOYED IN THE CENSUS

BrP	Bristol Public Library, Bristol, England
CSmH	Huntington Library
CT	Trinity College Library, Cambridge, England.
CtHT	Trinity College Library, Hartford, Conn.

CtY	Yale University Library
DLC	Library of Congress
IaU	University of Iowa Library
ICN	Newberry Library
L	British Museum
LdU	Brotherton Library
LU	London University Library
MB	Boston Public Library
MBAt	Library of the Boston Athenaeum
MH	Harvard University Library
MR	John Rylands Library
MSaE	Essex Institute, Salem, Mass.
MSciH	Scituate Historical Society, Scituate, Mass.
MWA	American Antiquarian Society
O	Bodleian Library
NcD	Duke University Library
NJP	Princetown University Library
NN	New York Public Library
NNC	Columbia University Library
NNJ	Jewish Theological Seminary, New York, N.Y.
NNPM	Pierpont Morgan Library
NNUT	Union Theological Seminary, New York, N.Y.
NP	Nottingham Public Library
NRB	Newstead Abbey
NSWML	Mitchell Library, Sydney, Australia
PPL	Philadelphia Public Library
PPLT	Lutheran Theological Seminary, Philadelphia, Pa.
TxU	University of Texas Library

I. a Selection of / Hebrew Melodies / Ancient and Modern / with appropriate Symphonies & accompaniments / By / I: Braham & I: Nathan / the Poetry written expressly for the work / By the Right Honble / Lord Byron / ent^d at Sta^{rs} Hall [ornament: angel crown in hand, 1·4 × 4·8 cm.] 1st Number / Published & Sold by I: Nathan N° 7 Poland Street Oxford Str^t / and to be had at the principal Music and Booksellers / Price one Guinea / [engraved within an ornamental border] / *Drawn by Edward Blore. Engraved by W. Lowry.* / [signed by hand] John Braham I Nathan.

Imprint: [beneath a rule at the foot of the advertisement and at the foot of the printed front and back covers] C. Richards, Printer, 18, Warwick Street, Golden Square, London.

Format: Crown folio; original light-blue printed board covers (identical front and back), blue paper back strip; pages trimmed to 36 × 24·1 cm.; wove stock; watermark: "1814"; stabbed and sewn through the back; bound in light-green contemporary cloth with No. II 1816; Houghton Library, Harvard University.

Collation: []³⁷ (disjunct); 37 leaves, pp. [8] 1–64 [2]: engraved title page with blank verso (i–ii), engraved dedication (protected by tissue) 'To Her Royal Highness The Princess Charlotte. . . .' with blank verso (iii–iv), preface with blank verso (v–vi), index with blank verso (vii–viii), text of twelve Hebrew Melodies and their engraved accompaniments (pp. 1–64), advertisement 'Just Published the Following Songs, Composed by I. Nathan the Poetry By the Right Honourable Lord Byron' with blank verso ([]37).

Census: 4: CtY; 1: DLC, ICN, L, MH, O, NN, NNJ, NP, TxU.

Note: On the title pages of the copies examined, the handwritten signatures of Braham and Nathan are both found or neither signature is found. Braham varies his signature, signing some copies, 'J. Braham'. Why the title page gives 'I: Braham' for J. Braham is not clear, but the cause may have been a desire to create an 'archaic' effect. (Until early in the seventeenth century there was only one uppercase letter 'I' in Roman for the letters represented by I and J.) On p. 3 the Roman numeral indicating stanza 'I' has fallen out in some copies. The last line of each of the three stanzas of 'She Walks in Beauty' (p. 3) was corrected by indenting the line to the right so that in each case it is no longer parallel with the preceding line. The inverted commas preceding the title of 'Jephtha's Daughter' (p. 36) print in only one copy examined. On p. 40 the third stanza of 'Oh! snatched away in beauty's bloom' is misnumbered 'II'. The corrected leaf is found with the final period in the title changed to an exclamation as well (i.e., in the NN copy). The last line of 'It is the Hour' slipped to the left (p. 62), and in some copies, the line is not parallel with the preceding line. The advertisement on []37ʳ lists five songs; a sixth song, 'The kiss, dear maid! thy lip has left', was added to the list after some sheets had been run off. The altered leaf is found in the ICN copy. The statement: 'And of H. FALCONER, Opera Music Warehouse, 3, Old Bond Street' was then added to the foot of the revised list (CtY copy), again after some sheets had been run off; thus the advertisement is found in three states: with five songs listed, with six songs listed, and with six songs and Falconer's name.

II.   HEBREW MELODIES. / [double rule] / BY LORD BYRON. / [double rule] / LONDON: / PRINTED FOR JOHN MURRAY, ALBE-MARLE-STREET. / [rule] / 1815.

Imprint: [beneath a rule at the foot of E4ᵛ and repeated at the foot of the half-title]   T. DAVISON, Lombard-street, / Whitefriars, London.

Format: Demy octavo; original drab brown paper covers; pages untrimmed 22·3 × 14·1 cm.; wove stock; watermark: 'II SMITH 1814' and some sheets 'II SMITH 1815' (the year appears twice in each sheet);[1] T. J. Wise bookplate; British Museum, Ashley 2672.

Collation: [A]⁴, B–D⁸, E⁴, [χ]⁴ (disjunct); 36 leaves, pp. [10] 3–53 [1] [10]: half-title with blank verso (i–ii), title page with blank verso (iii–iv), announcement with blank verso (v–vi), contents (vii–viii), fly-title with blank verso (ix–x), text consisting of twenty-four Hebrew Melodies and 'On the Death of Sir Peter Parker' (pp. 3–53), E3ᵛ blank, advertisements (E4), half-titles and title pages for 'The Works of the Right Honorable Lord Byron' in two volumes, 1815 ([χ]1–4). A fold of 2 leaves of advertisements dated 'June, 1815' is inserted following [χ4].

Census: 7: L, NN; 6: TXU; 4: MH, CtY; 3: CT, O; 2: CSmH, ICN, LU, MB, NcD; 1: BrP, DLC, LdU, MBAt, MR, NJP, NNC, NNPM, NRB, NSWML.

Note: D2, giving stanzas four, five, and six of the 'Vision of Belshazzar', is a cancel in two copies; B2, 'She Walks in Beauty', is a cancel in one copy. In the title of 'On the Death of Sir Peter Parker' (E2ʳ), 'of' has dropped out in many copies. In the advertisement occupying E4, l. 20, 'Plates to illustrate Lord Byron's Works: Thirteen' w.s corrected to 'Twelve'. On the verso, the advertisement for Samuel Rogers' *Jacqueline* was removed and the advertisement for Thomas Campbell's *The Selected Beauties of British Poetry* altered by the removal of 'In the press' (ll. 14–15) and enlarged by the addition of a four-line paragraph: 'In the Biographies, the Editor has exerted the main part of his strength on the *Merits* and *Writings* of *each Poet* as an Author, with an intent to form A COMPLETE BODY OF ENGLISH POETICAL CRITICISM.'

The titles and half-titles for the *Collected Works*, 2 vols, 1815, have been printed on the same stock as the text. After some sheets were

---

[1] H. M. Jones and R. H. Griffith in their *Catalogue: Byron Memorial Exhibition* (Austin: University of Texas Press, 1924) transcribe the watermark incorrectly as 'H S Hɪᴛᴛ' and assert that A 1–4 and E 1–4 are A 1–8 'bent back' (*Catalogue*, p. 39). A survey of the watermarks proves this impossible.

printed, they were altered by the removal of 'THE' (l. 1) from each title page. The page was then re-imposed to provide space following what had been l. 6 (now l. 5) for new matter specifying the exact contents of each volume: [Vol. I] CHILDE HAROLD, / AND / MIS-CELLANEOUS POEMS; [Vol. II] [to the left of a vertical rule] GIAOUR. / BRIDE OF ABYDOS. / CORSAIR. [to the right] LARA. / ODE TO NAPOLEON. / MELODIES. (In one instance the binder confused the Works title leaves with the four-leaf E gathering and bound the titles after D8.)

The imprint: 'Printed by J. F. Dove, St. John's Square, London.' is found at the foot of the verso of the second leaf of the inserted fold of advertisements. These advertisements are not printed on stock identical with that of the text. The earliest fold is entitled: 'The Following Interesting Works are in the course of Publication', and is printed on stock watermarked 'B 1813'. This fold was prepared before the publication of Hebrew Melodies, and only the remaining copies were inserted. 'Books Published During the Present Year', dated 'June, 1815' is the later fold and is found in the majority of copies. It exists in two states: in one the authors' names are given in italics in the inner forme and in small capitals in the outer forme; in the other state this procedure was reversed.

The Murray Ledger (vol. B, f. 127) details the production costs of Hebrew Melodies:

Byron's Hebrew Melodies demy 8°

1815						1815	
June 9	To 1 copy B. Museum	115*	–	–	–	Apr.	By 6000
	„ Entering at St Hall	„		2			Copies 1st
Augt 22	„ 10 Copies for Libraries	118	–	–	–		Edition in
							4/ 1152
1817							
April 26	To Davison Printing	26	70	5	–		
	„ Paper 66 Rms	187	125	8	–		
	„ Stitching 6000 copies	„	72	–	–		
	„ Advertising etc.	„	48	–	–		
			315	15	–		
	Balance being profit		836	5	–		
			1152	–	–		

* Page references to receipts books.

IIA. THE / WORKS / OF THE / RIGHT HON. LORD BYRON. / [rule] / IN TWO VOLUMES. / [rule] / VOL. I. [VOL. II.] / [double rule] / LONDON: / PRINTED FOR JOHN MURRAY, ALBEMARLE-STREET. / 1815.

Imprint: [beneath a rule at the foot of the half-title] T. DAVISON, Lombard-street, / Whitefriars, London.

Format: Demy octavo; separately published works bound up in 2 vols; mauve slip cases, bound in crinkled calf; Byron's bookplate; embossed leather labels glued to fixed endpapers: AUGUSTA / A NEW YEARS GIFT / 1ˢᵗ JANʸ 1816; pages trimmed to 21 × 13 cm.; paper and watermarks vary, but the title pages and half-titles for the Works and the text of the Hebrew Melodies have been printed on wove stock watermarked 'II SMITH 1815'; Stark Library 6771.

Collation: In vol. I the title page and half-title are followed by Childe Harold's Pilgrimage, 10th ed. (1815) including Poems and Appendix (xii, 1–302); the last poem is 'On the Death of Sir Peter Parker'. Vol. II: Giaour, 14th ed. (1815); Bride of Abydos, 10th ed. (1814); Corsair, 7th ed. (1814); Lara, 4th ed. (1814); Ode to Napoleon, 11th ed. (1815); Hebrew Melodies, to E3.

Note: The binder determined the order of the contents in this instance, but the contents of each volume are specified in the later state of the title page. The contents of Vol. II of the British Museum Copy (11604 f. 25), including the Monody on Sheridan and the Lament of Tasso, suggest that the title pages and half-titles were available for some time, see Poetry, VII, 92.

Census: 1 : L, TxU.

III. THE / WORKS / OF / THE RIGHT HONORABLE / LORD BYRON. / [double rule] / IN FOUR VOLUMES. / [double rule] / VOL. IV. [VOL. I, etc.] / ODE TO NAPOLEON BUONAPARTE – POEMS – / HEBREW MELODIES. / [swelled rule] / LONDON: / PRINTED FOR JOHN MURRAY, / ALBEMARLE-STREET. / 1815.

Imprint: [beneath a rule at the foot of the verso of the Works title page] T. DAVISON, Lombard-street, / Whitefriars, London.

Format: Foolscap octavo; marble boards, brown calf backs; pages trimmed to 15·5 × 10 cm.; wove stock; watermark: 'FELLOWS 1812'; Harvard Univ. 17491. 815. Originally bound in light-blue boards, with back label (4 × 2·3 cm.): LORD / BYRON'S / WORKS / [rule] / 28s. / (Without Plates) / [rule] / 4 VOLS. / [rule] / VOL. I.

Collation: Volume IV: [A]⁴, B–K⁸, *K², L–O⁸; 110 leaves, pp. [8] 1–144 [4] [2] 145–203 [3]: general half-title (wanting in this copy)

with blank verso (i–ii), title page (iii–iv), contents (v–viii), text:
Ode to Napoleon (pp. 1–16), Miscellaneous Poems (pp. 17–142),
Notes fly-title ([143–144]), Notes to the Poems (*K² unpaged),
Hebrew Melodies fly-title (unpaged), Hebrew Melodies (pp. 145–
203), O7ᵛ and O8ʳ blank, colophon O8ᵛ. An engraved plate is
inserted, ff. p. 39 and ff. p. 61.

Census: 1 : L, MH, TxU.

Note: Coleridge gives the contents of the first three volumes in
Poetry, VII, 91. One leaf signed *b has been added in Vol. I to the
Table of Contents of the four volumes, giving the contents of the
Hebrew Melodies. Twelve engraved plates have been inserted
throughout; each is imprinted: 'Published by John Murray,
Albemarle Street, Dec. 1, 1814.' These are the plates advertised in
Hebrew Melodies (E4r).

IV.   HEBREW MELODIES. / [ornamental rule] / BY LORD BYRON. /
[ornamental rule] / PHILADELPHIA: / PUBLISHED BY JAMES P.
PARKE, / NO. 74, SOUTH SECOND STREET. / Wm. Fry, Printer. /
1815.

Format: Duodecimo; original light-brown printed boards; pages
untrimmed 14·5 × 8 cm.; wove stock; no watermark; free end-
paper inscribed in pencil: 'Gift of Dr. A. S. W. Rosenbach Nov. 13.
34'; American Antiquarian Society.

Collation: []¹, [A]¹², B¹² (A5 and B5 signed A2 and B2); 25 leaves,
pp. [12] [11] 12–47 [1]: blank lf. ([]¹), fly-title with blank verso
(i–ii), title page with blank verso (iii–iv), announcement with
blank verso (v–vi), contents with blank verso (vii–viii), half-title
with blank verso (ix–x), text (pp. [11]–47), B12ᵛ blank.

Census: MWA.

Note: The contents are those of *Hebrew Melodies*. The back cover
advertises 'Dunlap's Brown', The Life of the Late Charles Brockden
Brown by William Dunlap 'in the press'.

V.   HEBREW MELODIES. / [double rule] / BY LORD BYRON. /
[double rule] / BOSTON: / PUBLISHED BY JOHN ELIOT. / 1815.

Format: Duodecimo; original tan printed paper covers; pages
untrimmed 13·9 × 7·5 cm.; wove stock; no watermark (the
original endpapers are watermarked: 'H Cox [dove device]'); New
York Public Library, *KL.

Collation: [1]¹², 2¹²; 24 leaves, pp. [4] [5] 6–43 [5]: title page with blank verso (i–ii), announcement with blank verso (iii–iv), text (pp. [5]–43), 2.10ᵛ blank, index 2.11, 2.12 blank.

Census: 1 : L, MB, MH, MSaE, MSciH, MWA, NN, NNUT.

Note: The contents are those of *Hebrew Melodies*. The front cover gives the publisher as Thomas Wells. The back cover announces that: 'John Eliot, No. 5, Court Street, And Thomas Wells, 3 Hanover Street, Have Just Published. . .'

VI.   HEBREW MELODIES. / [double rule] / BY LORD BYRON. / [double rule] / THE FIRST NEW-YORK EDITION. / [double rule] / NEW-YORK: / Printed and sold by T. & J. Swords, / No. 160 Pearl-street. / [swelled rule] / 1815.

Format: Duodecimo; original rose printed boards; pages un-trimmed 15·2 × 9·2 cm.; wove stock; no watermark; title page inscribed: 'J. A. Hillhouse'; The Beinecke Library, Yale University, In B996 815b.

Collation: [A]⁶, B–C⁶, D² (A3, B3, C3 signed a2, b2, c2); 20 leaves, pp. [6] 6–39: title page with blank verso (i–ii), announce-ment with blank verso (iii–iv), contents (v–vi), text (pp. 6–39).

Census: 1 : CtY, MH, MWA.

Note: The contents are those of *Hebrew Melodies*. The back cover advertises 'Books Published By. . .'. Thirteen titles are listed.

VII.   HEBREW / MELODIES. / [swelled rule] / BY LORD BYRON. / [swelled rule] / THE SECOND NEW-YORK EDITION / [rule] / [double rule] / NEW-YORK: / PUBLISHED BY D. LONGWORTH, / *At the Dramatic Repository, Shakspeare [sic] Gallery.* / [double rule] / 1815.

Format: Duodecimo; marble boards, white paper back strip; pages untrimmed 14 × 7·4 cm.; wove stock; no watermark; title page inscribed: 'C. R. Demme'; Krauth Memorial Library, Lutheran Theological Seminary, 821 B993.

Collation: [A]⁴, B–F⁴; 24 leaves, pp. [5] 6–45 [3]: title page with blank verso (i–ii), announcement with blank verso (iii–iv), contents (v–6), text (pp. 7–45), F3ᵛ blank, F4 blank.

Census: 1 : CtHT, PPL, PPLT.

Note: The contents are those of *Hebrew Melodies*.

VIII.   [No. I: the title page of the First Number is identical with that of *ASHM* (1815) having been printed from the same engraved plate. No. II:]

A SELECTION OF / Hebrew Melodies / ANCIENT & MODERN /

With *appropriate Symphonies and Accompaniments*, / BY / I. Braham and I. Nathan; / THE POETRY / *Written expressly for the work* BY The Right Honorable / LORD BYRON. / [vignette: King David at the Harp inspired by an angel] H. Moses Sculp. / *'The harp the Monarch Minstrel swept* / *The King of men − the lov'd of Heav'n,* / *Which Music hallowed while she wept* / *O'er tones her heart of hearts had giv'n − /Redoubled be her tears − its chords are riv'n!'* / *See Page 4, Lord Byron.* / 2ⁿᵈ Number. Price 1. Guinea. Entᵈ at Stationers Hall. / Published & Sold by I. NATHAN № 7, *Poland Street Oxford Street; and to be had of all the principal Music & Booksellers.* / *Pickett scrip. et sculp.* / [signed by hand at the foot] I. Nathan

Imprint: [at the foot of the printed covers front and back] C. RICHARDS, Printer, 18, Warwick Street, Golden Square.

Format: Crown folio; two Nos., bound in a collection of Nathan's songs, marble boards, mor. back; pages trimmed to 34·2 × 24·5 cm.; wove stock; watermark: 'W B & Cᵒ 1815'. (Originally issued as two separate Numbers identical in format with *ASHM* [1815].) The Beinecke Library, Yale University, In B996+G815 copy 1.

Collation: First Number: Identical with *A Selection*, 1815; Second Number: []³⁸ (disjunct); 38 leaves, pp. [6] 65–133 [1]: title page with blank verso (i–ii), dedication with blank verso (iii–iv), index with blank verso (v–vi), text of twelve Hebrew Melodies (pp. 65–133), [] 38ᵛ blank.

Census: I & II; 1 : CtY, NN, private; II; 2 : DLC; 1 : CtY, L, MH, NNJ, NP, NSWML, O, TxU. The combination I (1815)+II (1816) is often found.

Note: All the engraved plates of the First Number of 1815, comprising the title page, dedication, and music text, have been used to produce this edition. I (1816) may be distinguished from I (1815) by: the watermark, the use of a swelled rule in the letterpress text for the double rule, 'Harmonized' for 'Harmonised' in the Index l. 16, the note on p. 3 that reads: '. . . observe, this Melody' for '. . . observe, that this Melody', and minor differences in punctuation and capitalization. In all the copies of the Second Number examined an 'Erratum' is given at the foot of the Index: 'In page 105 − first verse, seventh line − for "the fixed eye," read "his fixed eye".' The copy described lacks the covers, the title page of the First Number, and the tissue preceding the dedication.

IX. HEBREW MELODIES. / [rule] / BY THE RIGHT HONOUR-ABLE / LORD BYRON. / [rule] / LONDON: / PRINTED AND PUB-LISHED BY W. DUGDALE, / Green Street, Leicester Square. / [rule] / 1823.

Imprint: [beneath a rule at the foot of p. 36] Printed by W. Dugdale, Green Street, Leicester Square.

Format: Duodecimo; bound in a volume of others of Byron's poems published by Dugdale; dark blue cloth binding; pages trimmed to 13·8 × 8·5 cm.; wove stock; watermark: '1822'; Columbia University Library 825 B99 I8.

Collation: B⁶, (second alphabet) B–C⁶; 18 leaves, pp. [2] 3–36: title page with announcement on verso (i–ii), text of twenty-three Hebrew Melodies (pp. 3–36).

Census: 1 : L, MH, NNC, NP.

Note: The following publications by Dugdale are bound in: Marino Faliero, 1826; Manfred, 1824; Mazeppa, 1824; The Prisoner of Chillon, 1824; Beppo (by H. Dugdale).

IXA. HEBREW MELODIES. / BY LORD BYRON. / LONDON: / PRINTED AND PUBLISHED BY W. DUGDALE, / 23 Russell Court, Drury Lane. / [rule] / 1825.

Imprint: [beneath a rule at the foot of p. 22] Printed by W. Dugdale, 23, Russell Court, Drury Lane.

Format: Duodecimo; orange cloth binding; original yellow printed paper covers; pages trimmed to 15 × 9 cm.; wove stock; watermark: '1824' and some sheets '1825'; Jewish Theological Seminary Library, R*.

Collation: [π]², B⁶, C⁴; 12 leaves, pp. [2] 3–22 [2]: title page with announcement on verso (i–ii), text of twenty-three Hebrew Melodies (pp. 3–22), C4 blank.

Census: 2 : L; 1 : NcD, NNJ.

Note: Some copies were issued with drab printed paper covers.

X. a Selection of / Hebrew Melodies / Ancient and Modern / Newly arranged Harmonized corrected and Revised / with appropriate Symphonies & accompaniments / By / I: Nathan / the Poetry written expressly for the work / By / Lord Byron / entᵈ at Staʳˢ hall [ornament: angel crown in hand, 1·5 × 5·7 cm. (copied from No. I, 1815)] Price fifteen Shillˢ / Published for the Proprietor and to be had / at all the principal Music and Booksellers / 1ˢᵗ Number. [within a border of type ornaments]

A / SELECTION / OF / HEBREW MELODIES, / Ancient and Modern. / NEWLY ARRANGED, HARMONIZED, CORRECTED, AND REVISED, WITH / APPROPRIATE SYMPHONIES AND ACCOMPANIMENTS / BY / LORD BYRON. / [vignette: King David at the harp (copied from the Second Number of 1816)] / [quotation from 'The harp the monarch minstrel swept', ll. 1–5] / Lord Byron. See page 97. / Entered at Stationer's Hall. PUBLISHED FOR THE PROPRIETOR, Price Fifteen Shillings. / AND TO BE HAD OF ALL THE PRINCIPAL MUSIC AND BOOKSELLERS. / 2nd Number.

Imprint: [at the foot of the half-title] LONDON: / PRINTED BY THOMAS DAVISON, WHITEFRIARS. [on the verso of the half-title] Published by / J. FENTUM, 98, STRAND.

Format: Crown fol.; two Numbers; original printed boards, black cloth back strip; pages untrimmed 35·5 × 25·5 cm.; wove stock; watermark: '1823' (the letterpress is printed on light-weight stock having no watermark); No. I: Beinecke Library, Yale University, In B996 + G815d, No. II: Bodleian Library, Mus. 5^{N}. C. 98 (2).

Collation: No. I: [ ]^{39} in twos ([ ] 1–4, 11, 18, 31, 32, 37 disjunct; [ ] 1–4, 11, 19.20, 32, 38.39 light stock); 39 leaves, pp. [8] 1–66 [4]: half-title (i–ii), title page with blank verso (iii–iv), preface (v–vi), index with blank verso (vii–viii), text and music of six Hebrew Melodies (pp. 1–66), advertisements for the History and Theory of Music (1823) and a Catalogue of Nathan's songs ([ ] 37–38). No. II: i–vi, pp. 67–124.

Census: Nos. I, II: O; No. I: CtY, DLC, L.

Note: In No. I of the copy described, pp. 37–38 follow pp. 39–40 the sheet having been folded incorrectly. No. II is bound up with No. I (1824) and No. IV (1827–29); it lacks half-titles and covers. Every page in the text is signed, in No. I, 'Hebrew Melodies N°. 1. (102) Nathan.' and in No. II, 'Hebrew Melodies N°. 2. (103) Nathan.'

These two Numbers were the first to contain Nathan's notes to the Hebrew Melodies, given in the letterpress at the foot of each poem. In No. I the note to 'She Walks in Beauty' consists of a single paragraph of twelve lines of type; in No. II the note to 'On Jordan's Banks' consists of a single paragraph of eleven lines of type.

Song sheets were printed from the plates of these Numbers.

XI. a Selection of / Hebrew Melodies / Ancient and Modern / Newly arranged Harmonized corrected and Revised / with appropriate Symphonies & accompaniments / By / I: Nathan / the Poetry written expressly for the work / By / Lord Byron / ent^{d} at Sta^{rs} hall [ornament: angel crown in hand 1·5 × 5·7 cm. (copied from the First Number of 1815)] Price fifteen Shill^{s} / Published for the

Proprietor and to be had / at all the principal Music and Book-sellers / 1ˢᵗ Number. [within a border of type ornaments]

A / SELECTION / OF / HEBREW MELODIES, / Ancient and Mod-ern. / NEWLY ARRANGED, HARMONIZED, CORRECTED, AND REVISED, WITH / APPROPRIATE SYMPHONIES AND ACCOMPANI-MENTS, / BY / I. NATHAN / The Poetry written expressly for the Composer / BY / LORD BYRON. / [vignette: King David at the harp (copied from the Second Number of 1816)] / [quotation from 'The harp the monarch minstrel swept', ll. 1–5] / Lord Byron. See page 97. / Entered at Stationers' Hall. PUBLISHED FOR THE PROPRIETOR; Price Fifteen Shillings. / AND TO BE HAD OF ALL THE PRINCIPAL MUSIC AND BOOKSELLERS. / Number II.

A Selection of / HEBREW MELODIES / ANCIENT AND MODERN / NEWLY ARRANGED, HARMONIZED, CORRECTED, AND REVISED / WITH APPROPRIATE SYMPHONIES AND ACCOMPANIMENTS / BY / I: Nathan / the Poetry written expressly for the work / By / Lord Byron / Entered at Stationers' Hall. [ornament: a cherub at the harp 5·3 × 4·1 cm.] Price Fifteen Shillings. / PUBLISHED FOR THE PROPRIETOR BY M. A. FENTUM, 78, STRAND; / AND TO BE HAD OF ALL THE PRINCIPAL MUSIC AND BOOKSELLERS. / 3ʳᵈ Number. [within a border of type ornaments]

A SELECTION OF / HEBREW MELODIES, / Ancient and Modern, / NEWLY ARRANGED, HARMONIZED, CORRECTED AND REVISED, / WITH / Appropriate Symphonies and Accompaniments, / BY / I. NATHAN; / THE POETRY WRITTEN EXPRESSLY FOR THE WORK, / BY / LORD BYRON. / ENTERED AT STATIONERS' HALL. [double rule] PRICE FIFTEEN SHILLINGS. / LONDON: / Published for the Proprietor by Faulkner, 3, Old Bond Street, / AND TO BE HAD OF ALL THE PRINCIPAL MUSIC AND BOOKSELLERS. / [rule] / Fourth Number.

Imprint: [at the foot on the verso of the half-title and at the foot of the printed back cover, in Nos. I and II only] J. AND C. ADLARD, PRINTERS, BARTHOLOMEW CLOSE. [on the verso of the half-title in Nos. I and II only] LONDON: / PUBLISHED BY J. FENTUM, 78, STRAND.

Format: Folio; four vols; original printed boards; black cloth back strip; pages trimmed 34·5 × 26 cm.; wove stock; (the letter-press has been printed on light-weight stock having no watermark); watermark: '1828'; Beinecke Library, Yale University, In B996 + G815c 1–4.

Collation: No. I: [ ]³⁹ in twos ([ ] 1–6, 13, 34, disjunct; [ ] 1–6, 13,

21.22, 34 light stock; [] 21.22 inserted ff. [] 20, [] 38 inserted ff. [] 37); 39 leaves, pp. [12] 1–66: half-title (i–ii), title page with blank verso (iii–iv), preface (v–vi), advertisement (vii–x), index with blank verso (xi–xii), text of six Hebrew Melodies (pp. 1–66), No. II: i–iv, pp. 67–124; No. III: i–iv, pp. 125–186; No. IV: i–iv, pp. 187–249.

Census: Nos. I–IV: NSWML (2), CtY; Nos. I–II: MH; No. III: DLC; No. IV: O.

Note: The copy described is a later issue in which the inscription 'Ent. Sta. Hall London, Faulkner, 3, Old Bond Street' and a price were added to each song. Leaves []4 and []5 advertising *Fugitive Pieces* were added to this issue. The letterpress is signed variously '6' and '1'. With the exception of the preliminaries, every page is signed: 'Hebrew Melodies N⁰ 1. (102) Nathan.' The numeral in parentheses changes successively: 'N⁰ 2. (103)', 'N⁰ 3. (104)', 'N⁰ 4. (105)'. The First Number was published jointly with the Second Number, and contains the index to both numbers. The Third Number indexes three numbers, the Fourth Number four numbers. The Third and Fourth Numbers were not issued with half-titles. The plates of the First Number of 1824 were used to print the First Number of 1827. In Nos. I and II Nathan has added to the notes accompanying the poems (which first appeared in Nos. I and II [1824]) so that, for example, in No. I the note to 'She Walks in Beauty' (p. 13) consists of four paragraphs comprising twenty lines of type, and in No. II the note to 'On Jordan's Banks' (p. 77) consists of five paragraphs comprising twenty-two lines of type. These enlarged notes are the most convenient means of distinguishing Nos. I and II (1827) from Nos. I and II (1824).

XII. FUGITIVE PIECES / AND / Reminiscences / OF / LORD BYRON: / CONTAINING AN ENTIRE NEW EDITION OF / THE HEBREW MELODIES, / WITH THE ADDITION OF / SEVERAL NEVER BEFORE PUBLISHED; / THE WHOLE ILLUSTRATED WITH / CRITI-CAL, HISTORICAL, THEATRICAL, POLITICAL, AND THEOLOGICAL / REMARKS, NOTES, ANECDOTES, INTERESTING CONVERSATIONS, / AND OBSERVATIONS, MADE BY THAT ILLUSTRIOUS POET: / TOGETHER WITH HIS LORDSHIP'S AUTOGRAPH; / ALSO SOME / ORIGINAL POETRY, LETTERS AND RECOLLECTIONS / OF / LADY CAROLINE LAMB / [swelled rule] / BY I. NATHAN, / AUTHOR OF AN ESSAY ON THE HISTORY AND THEORY OF MUSIC, / THE HEBREW MELODIES, &c. &c. / [rule] / PASCITUR IN VIVIS LIVOR,

POST FATA QUIESCIT: / TUNE [sic] SUUS, EX MERITO, QUEMQUE
TUETUR HONOS. – OVID. / [rule] / LONDON: / PRINTED FOR
WHITTAKER, TREACHER, AND CO. / AVE MARIA LANE, / [rule] /
1829.

Imprint: [at the foot of p. 196] Plummer and Brewis, Printers,
Love Lane, Eastcheap. [on the verso of the title page] LONDON: /
PRINTED BY PLUMMER AND BREWIS, LOVE-LANE, EASTCHEAP.

Format: Crown octavo; original drab grey boards, green cloth
back strip, white printed paper label on spine 4·6 × 2·3 cm.:
NATHAN'S / FUGITIVE / Pieces / AND / REMINISCENCES / OF /
LORD BYRON / &c. &c. / [rule] / Price 8s. 6d. / [within a printed
border]; pages untrimmed 19·5 × 11·9 cm.; wove stock; no
watermark; Columbia Univ. Library, Special Collections, B825 B99
Q5 1829 copy 2.

Collation: [A]², [B]⁸, C⁸, (second alphabet) B–O⁸ (2B3, 2C7, D2,
I4 cancels); 122 leaves, pp. [i–v] vi–xxxvi 1–196 [12]: half-title
with blank verso (i–ii), title page imprint on verso (iii–iv), preface
advertisements and contents (v–xx), contents and contents to the
poetry (xxi–xxxvi), text (pp. 1–196) including 7 facsimiles, advertisements for Nathan's *History and Theory of Music* (O3–O7ʳ), Catalogue
of Nathan's Music (O7ᵛ–O8ʳ), Advertisements for Lady Gresley's
Memoirs 'to be published', and The Life, Character, low Tricks, and
Dirty *Actions* of Adonis 'in the press' (O8ᵛ).

Census: 3: NNC; 1: CT, CtY, CSmH, IaU, O, NP.

Note: Some copies were issued with a red cloth back strip. The
contents are those of *ASHM*, rev. ed., I–IV plus 'Bright be the place of
thy soul'.

XIII. An Essay / On / The Music of the Hebrews, / Originally
Intended As / A Preliminary Discourse, / To / The Hebrew Melodies,
/ Published by Messrs. Braham and Nathan / [double rule] / By
Robert Harding Evans. / [double rule] / Let us praise famous men –
Such as found out musical tunes and recited / verses in writing. All these
were honoured in their generations, and were the / glory of their
times. *Ecclesiasticus*, c. lxiv. ver. 1–7. / [rule] / London: / Printed for
John Booth, Duke Street, / Portland Place. / [rule] / 1816.

Imprint: [beneath a rule at the foot of p. 48 and repeated at the
foot on the verso of the half-title] Howlett, Printer, 10, Frith Street, /
Soho.

Format: Octavo; dark blue contemporary cloth binding; pages

trimmed to 20·7 × 12·5 cm.; wove stock; watermark: '1814'; Jewish Theological Seminary Library, *Ef.

Collation: [B]⁸, C–D⁸; 24 leaves, pp. [6] 7–48: half-title (i–ii), title page with blank verso (iii–iv), advertisement dated 'Jan. 1, 1816' (v–vi), text (pp. 7–48).

Census: 1 : private, NNJ.

SELECTIVE BIBLIOGRAPHY
&
INDEX OF TITLES AND FIRST LINES

SELECTIVE BIBLIOGRAPHY

'A bibliography of Byron.' Unsigned review of Vol. I of T. J. Wise's *Bibliography. Times Literary Supplement*, 15 September 1932, p. 642.

ABRAHAMS, Israel. *By-paths in Hebraic Bookland*. Philadelphia, 1920.

ANDERSON, J. P. 'Bibliography.' Roden Noel. *Life and Writings of Lord Byron*. London: Walter Scott Pub. Co., 1890.

ASHTON, Thomas L. 'Peter Parker in Perry's Paper: Two unpublished Byron letters.' *Keats-Shelley Journal*, 1969, XVIII, 49–59.

—— 'Hogg to Byron to Davenport: An unpublished Byron letter.' *Bulletin of the New York Public Library*, 1967, LXXI, 39–46.

—— 'Naming Byron's Aurora Raby.' *English Language Notes*, 1969, VII, 114–20.

BALL, Patricia M. *The Central Self*. London, 1968.

BERTIE, C. H. *Isaac Nathan, Australia's First Composer*. Sydney, 1922.

BEUTLER, Karl A. *Über Lord Byrons 'Hebrew Melodies'*. Inaugural Dissertation. Leipzig, 1912.

BLESSINGTON, Countess of (Margaret Power). *Conversations of Lord Byron*. Ed. by Ernest J. Lovell Jun. Princeton, 1969.

BLOOM, Harold. *The Visionary Company*. New York, 1961, reprinted 1963.

BORROW, K. T., and Dorothy Hewlett. 'Byron: A link with Australia.' *Keats Shelley Memorial Bulletin*, 1963, XIV, 17–20.

BRISCOE, W. A., ed. *Byron, the Poet*. London, 1924.

BROUGHTON, Lord [John Cam Hobhouse]. *Recollections of a Long Life*. Ed. by Lady C. Dorchester. 6 vols. London, 1909–11.

BYRON, George Gordon, 6th Bar. *The Works of Lord Byron*. Ed. by John Wright. 17 vols. London: Murray, 1832–3.

—— *A Selection from the Works of Lord Byron*. Ed. by A. C. Swinburne. London: Moxon, 1866.

—— *The Poetical Works of Lord Byron*. Ed. by Wm. Michael Rossetti. London: Moxon, 1880.

—— *Poetry of Byron*. Ed. by Matthew Arnold. London: Macmillan and Co., 1881.

—— *The Works of Lord Byron. Poetry*. Ed. by Ernest Hartley Coleridge. 7 vols. London: Murray, 1898–1904, reprinted 1904.

—— *The Complete Poetical Works of Lord Byron*. Ed. by Paul Elmer More. Boston, 1905.

────── 'Childe Harold's Pilgrimage' and Other Romantic Poems. Ed. by Samuel C. Chew. New York, 1936.

────── Lord Byron's Cain. Twelve Essays and a Text with Variants and Annotations. Ed. by Truman G. Steffan. Austin, 1968.

────── Byron's Don Juan. A Variorum Edition. Ed. by Truman G. Steffan, and Willis W. Pratt. 4 vols. Austin, 1957.

────── The Works of Lord Byron. Letters and Journals. Ed. by Rowland E. Prothero. 6 vols. London: Murray, 1898–1901.

────── Lord Byron's Correspondence. Ed. by John Murray. 2 vols. New York, 1922.

────── Byron: A Self-Portrait, Letters and Diaries, 1798 to 1824. Ed. by Peter Quennell. 2 vols. London, 1950.

CARTER, John. 'Notes on the bibliography of Byron.' Times Literary Supplement, 27 April 1933, p. 300, and 4 May 1933, p. 316.

CHEW, Samuel C. Byron in England. London, 1924.

CHORLEY, H. F. Thirty Years' Musical Recollections. 2 vols. London: Hurst & Blackett, 1862.

COHEN, Francis L. 'Hebrew melody in the concert room.' Transactions of the Jewish Historical Society of England. 1896, II.

────── 'Isaac Nathan.' Jewish Encyclopedia.

COLLINGWOOD, Francis. 'John Braham.' Musical Times, 1956, XCVII, 73–5.

COOK, Davidson. 'Byron's "Fare Thee Well" unrecorded editions.' Times Literary Supplement, 18 September 1937, p. 677.

COOKE, Michael G. The Blind Man Traces the Circle: On the Patterns and Philosophy of Byron's Poetry. Princeton, 1969.

COXE, Rev. William. Musical Recollections of the Last Half-Century. 2 vols. London: Tinsley Bros., 1872.

DALLAS, Robert C. Recollections of the Life of Lord Byron, from the Year 1808 to the End of 1814. Philadelphia: Small, Carey & Lea, 1825.

DAWSON, Edgar. Byron und Moore. Leipzig, 1902.

DE SELINCOURT, Ernest. Wordsworthian and Other Studies. Oxford, 1947.

DIBDIN, Charles I. M. Professional and Literary Memoirs. Ed. by George Speaight. London, 1956.

DIBDIN, Edward R. 'Isaac Nathan.' Music and Letters, 1941, XXII, 75–80.

ELLEDGE, W. Paul. Byron and the Dynamics of Metaphor. Nashville, 1968.

ELWIN, Malcolm. Lord Byron's Wife. London, 1962.

ENKVIST, Nils E. 'British and American literary letters in Scandinavian public collections.' Acta Academiae Aboensis, Humaniora, 1964, XXVII. iii.

EVANS, Robert H. An Essay on the Music of the Hebrews. London: John Booth, 1816.

First Editions Club. *Bibliographical Catalogue of First Editions, Proof Copies, and Manuscripts of Books by Lord Byron*. London, 1925.

FRYE, Northrop. 'George Gordon, Lord Byron.' *Major British Writers*. Gen. ed. G. B. Harrison. Enl. ed., 2 vols. New York, 1959.

FULLER-MAITLAND, J. A. 'Domenico Corri.' *Grove's Dictionary of Music and Musicians*. 5th ed. London, 1954.

GARROD, H. W. *The Profession of Poetry and Other Lectures*. Oxford, 1929.

GLECKNER, Robert F. *Byron and the Ruins of Paradise*. Baltimore, 1967.

GREENE, Herbert E. 'Browning's knowledge of music.' *PMLA*, 1947, LXII, 1098.

HADDAWY, Husain. 'English arabesque: The Oriental mode in eighteenth-century English literature.' Unpub. Cornell University dissertation, 1963.

HADDEN, J. Cuthbert. *George Thomson, The Friend of Burns*. London: Nimmo, 1898.

HAZLITT, William. *Complete Works*. Ed. by P. P. Howe. 20 vols. London, 1930–4.

HEYWOOD, Joseph. 'Recollections and some of his thoughts about music.' *Cornhill*, 1865, XII, 692–3.

HODGSON, James T. *Memoir of the Rev. Francis Hodgson*. 2 vols. London: Macmillan, 1878.

HOPKINSON, Cecil, and C. B. Oldman. 'Thomson's collections of national song.' *Edinburgh Bibliographical Society Transactions*, 1940, II. i, 1–64; 1954, III. ii.

HUMPHRIES, Charles, and William Smith. *Music Publishing in the British Isles*. London, 1954.

HUNT, Leigh. *Autobiography*. Ed. by Roger Ingpen. 2 vols. London, 1903.

—— *Lord Byron and Some of His Contemporaries*. 2 vols. London: Henry Colburn, 1828.

HUSK, W. H. 'Isaac Nathan.' *Grove's Dictionary of Music and Musicians*. 5th ed. London, 1954.

JERDAN, William. *Autobiography*. 4 vols. London: Arthur Hall, Virtue, & Co., 1852–3.

JERMAN, B. R. 'Nineteenth-century holdings at the Folger.' *Victorian Newsletter*, 1962, No. 22, 23.

JONES, Howard Mumford. *The Harp that Once*. New York, 1937.

—— and R. H. Griffith. *Catalogue: Byron Memorial Exhibition*. Austin, 1924.

JORDAN, Hoover H. 'Byron and Moore.' *Modern Language Quarterly*, 1948, IX, 429–39.

JOSEPH, Michael K. *Byron the Poet*. London, 1964.

KELLEY, Michael. *Reminiscences*. 2nd ed. 2 vols. London: Henry Colburn, 1826.

KENNEDY, James. *Conversations on Religion with Lord Byron*. London: Murray, 1830.

KNIGHT, G. Wilson. *Lord Byron: Christian Virtues*. London, 1952.

—— Review of *Byron as Poet* by W. W. Robson. *Essays in Criticism*, 1959, IX, 87–93.

KROEBER, Karl. *Romantic Narrative Art*. Madison, 1960, reprinted 1966.

LAMB, Charles. *Works*. Ed. by E. V. Lucas. 7 vols. London, 1905.

LANGBAUM, Robert. *The Poetry of Experience*. New York, 1957, reprinted 1963.

LEGGE, R. H. 'Isaac Nathan.' *Dictionary of National Biography*.

LEVIEN, John M. *The Singing of John Braham*. London, 1945.

LOVELACE, Ralph Earl of. *Astarte*. London, 1905.

—— *Astarte*. Ed. by Mary Countess of Lovelace. London, 1921.

MCGANN, Jerome. *Fiery Dust: Byron's Poetic Development*. Chicago, 1968.

MACKERRAS, Catherine. *The Hebrew Melodist, A Life of Isaac Nathan*. Sydney, 1963.

MARCHAND, Leslie A. *Byron: A Biography*. 3 vols. New York, 1957.

—— *Byron's Poetry*. New York, 1965.

MARJARUM, Edward W. *Byron as Skeptic and Believer*. 1938, reprinted New York, 1962.

MARSHALL, William H. *The Structure of Byron's Major Poems*. Philadelphia, 1962.

MARTIN, L. C. *Byron's Lyrics*. Byron Foundation Lecture. Nottingham, 1948.

MATHEWS, Elkin. *Byron & Byroniana: A Catalogue of Books*. London, 1930.

MAYNE, Ethel C. *The Life and Letters of Anne Isabella Lady Noel Byron*. London, 1929.

MEDWIN, Thomas. *Conversations of Lord Byron*. Ed. by Ernest J. Lovell Jun. Princeton, 1966.

MERRITT, James D. 'Disraeli as a Byronic poet.' *Victorian Poetry*, 1965, III, 138–9.

MILMAN, Henry Hart. *The History of the Jews*. 3 vols. London: Murray, 1829–30.

MOORE, Thomas. *Poetical Works*. Ed. by A. D. Godley. London, 1910.

—— *Letters and Journals of Lord Byron: with Notices of His Life*. 2 vols. London: Murray, 1830.

—— *Letters*. Ed. by Wilfred S. Dowden. 2 vols. Oxford, 1964.

—— *Notes from the Letters of Thomas Moore to His Music Publisher, James Power*. Ed. by Thomas Crofton Croker. New York: J. S. Redfield, 1853.

MOREL, W. 'Zu Byrons Hebrew Melodies.' *Anglia*, 1955, LXXIII, 215.

MOUNT EDGCUMBE, Earl of. *Musical Reminiscences.* 4th ed. London: John Andrews, 1834.

'Mr Braham.' Unsigned article. *Quarterly Musical Magazine and Review,* 1818, I, 86–95.

MUIR, Percy H. 'Thomas Moore's Irish Melodies, 1808–1834.' *Colophon,* 1933, XV.

MURRAY, John. *A Reference Catalogue of British and Foreign Autographs and Manuscripts.* Part VII. *Lord Byron.* London, 1898.

NATHAN, Mrs [Elizabeth R.]. *Elvington.* London: Stockdale, 1819.

—— *Langreath.* London: Whittaker, 1822.

NATHAN, Isaac. *An Essay on the History and Theory of Music.* London: Whittaker, 1823.

—— *Memoirs of Madame Malibran de Beriot.* London: Joseph Thomas, 1826.

—— *Fugitive Pieces and Reminiscences of Lord Byron.* London: Whittaker, Treacher & Co., 1829.

—— *Musurgia Vocalis.* London: Fentum, 1836.

—— *The Southern Euphrosyne.* London: Whittaker, 1849.

NICKLES, Eduard. *Lord Byrons Hebräische Gesänge.* Karlsruhe, 1863.

NOEL, Roden. *Essays on Poetry and Poets.* London: Kegan Paul, Trench & Co., 1886.

Nottingham Public Libraries. *The Roe-Byron Collection Newstead Abbey.* Nottingham, 1937.

PHILLIPS, Olga S. *Isaac Nathan, Friend of Byron.* London: Minerva, 1940.

POLLARD, Graham. 'Pirated collections of Byron.' *Times Literary Supplement,* 16 October 1937, p. 764.

PRATT, Willis W. *Lord Byron and His Circle. A Calendar of Manuscripts in the University of Texas Library.* Austin, 1947.

—— 'Lord Byron and his circle: Recent manuscript acquisitions.' *Library Chronicle of the University of Texas,* 1956, V, 16–25.

QUENNELL, Peter, and George Paston [E. M. Symonds], eds. *To Lord Byron.* London, 1939.

QUINTANA, Ricardo. *Byron 1788–1938. An Exhibition at the Huntington Library.* San Marino, Cal., 1938.

READ, Herbert. *Byron.* London, 1951.

RIDENOUR, George M. *The Style of Don Juan.* New Haven, 1960.

RIMBAULT, Edward F. 'John Braham.' *Grove's Dictionary of Music and Musicians.* 5th ed. London, 1954.

ROBINSON, Henry Crabb. *Henry Crabb Robinson on Books and Their Writers.* Ed. by Edith J. Morley. 3 vols. London, 1938.

ROBSON, W. W. *Critical Essays.* London, 1966.

RUTHERFORD, Andrew. *Byron: A Critical Study.* Palo Alto, Cal., 1961.

SARMIENTO, Edward. 'A parallel between Lord Byron and Fray Luis De León.' *Review of English Studies*, 1953, IV, 267–73.

SLATER, Joseph. 'Byron's Hebrew Melodies.' *Studies in Philology*, 1952, XLIX, 75–94.

SMILES, Samuel. *A Publisher and His Friends, Memoir and Correspondence of the late John Murray.* 2 vols. London, 1891.

SQUIRE, W. Barclay. 'John Braham.' *Dictionary of National Biography.*

STEFFAN, Truman G. 'Some 1813 Byron letters.' *Keats-Shelley Journal*, 1967, XVI, 9–21.

WASSERMAN, Earl R. *The Subtler Language.* Baltimore, 1959.

WEST, Paul. *Byron and the Spoiler's Art.* New York, 1960.

WISE, Thomas J. *The Ashley Library.* 11 vols. London, 1922–36.

—— *A Byron Library.* London, 1928.

—— *Bibliography of the Writings in Verse and Prose of George Gordon Noel, Baron Byron.* 2 vols. London, 1932–3, reprinted, 1963.

YOUNG, Ione E. *A Concordance to the Poetry of Byron.* 4 vols. Austin, 1965.

INDEX OF TITLES AND FIRST LINES

(Titles are in italics: where title and first line are identical, the title only is indexed)

'All is Vanity, saith the preacher' 188
A spirit passed before me: I beheld 145

Belshazzar! from the banquet turn, 175
Bright be the place of thy soul 191
By the Rivers of Babylon We Sat Down and Wept 163

Destruction of Semnacherib, The 180

Fame, wisdom, love, and power were mine, 188
Francisca 128
Francisca walks in the shadow of night, 128
From Job 145
From the last hill that looks on thy once holy dome 168

Harp the monarch minstrel swept, The 139
Herod's Lament for Mariamne 160

If that High World 147
If that high world, which lies beyond 147
In the Valley of Waters 166
In the valley of waters we wept o'er the day 166
I Saw Thee Weep 134
I saw thee weep – the big bright tear 134
I Speak Not – I Trace Not – I Breathe Not 129
I speak not – I trace not – I breathe not thy name, 129
It is the Hour 127
It is the hour when from the boughs 127

Jephtha's Daughter 152

My Soul is Dark 156
My soul is dark – Oh! quickly string 156

Oh, Mariamne! now for thee 160
Oh! snatched away in beauty's bloom 149
Oh! Weep for Those 138
Oh! weep for those that wept by Babel's stream, 138
On Jordan's Banks 143
On Jordan's banks the Arabs' camels stray, 143
On the day of the Destruction of Jerusalem by Titus 168

Saul 171
She Walks in Beauty 132
She walks in beauty, like the night 132
Since our Country, our God – Oh, my Sire! 152
Song of Saul Before His Last Battle 183
Sun of the sleepless! 136
Sun of the sleepless! melancholy star! 136

The Assyrian came down like the wolf on the fold, 180
The harp the monarch minstrel swept, 139
The King was on his throne, 177
The wild gazelle on Judah's hills 154
They say that Hope is happiness 158
Thou whose spell can raise the dead, 171
Thy Days are Done 142
Thy days are done, they fame begun; 142
To Belshazzar 175

Vision of Belshazzar 177

Warriors and chiefs! should the shaft or the sword 183

Were my bosom as false as thou deem'st it to be 170

We sate down and wept by the waters 163

When coldness wraps this suffering clay 185

Wild gazelle, The 154